PRINCIPLES OF

Exercise Prescription

second edition

Warren D. Franke

Iowa State University

Kendall Hunt

publishing compan

Cover image © Shutterstock, Inc.

Kendall Hunt
publishing company

www.kendallhunt.com
Send all inquiries to:
4050 Westmark Drive
Dubuque, IA 52004-1840

CONTENTS

CHAPTER 1

Let's Begin at the Beginning: What's the Purpose of This Course?

© kentoh/Shutterstock.com

If you are pursuing a degree in Kinesiology and that degree is designed to prepare you for employment in a health/fitness facility, you will most likely enroll in a course focused on developing exercise prescriptions, or exercise programs, for clients. This textbook is designed to help you learn how to do so. Since you're currently reading this textbook, you're probably currently enrolled in this kind of course. So, you may be asking yourself, "Why do I have to take this course? What's the point of it?" Given how expensive a college education has become, these questions are both valid and understandable. So, here are three reasons why this course is important.

One reason for this course is that it will likely tie together some of the coursework you have already taken. For example, in an exercise physiology course, you learned how the human body responds to exercise. In an exercise psychology course, you likely learned theories explaining why people do or do not exercise. And in a biomechanics course, you learned about the physics associated with human movement. Each course covered basic, foundational information that every Kinesiology student should know. Unfortunately, the content of each course may have seemed isolated from the other courses so it was difficult to understand how they may have been interrelated. Because the present course is focused on the *application* of Kinesiology-related skills, it will help you see the big picture of how your other coursework is actually quite integrated.

A second reason for this course is that it will help prepare you to pass a professional certification examination. Doing so is important because a professional certification helps to validate your professional preparation and expertise. For example, the Board of Directors of the International Health, Racquet & Sportsclub Association (IHRSA), a trade association serving the health/fitness industry, recommends that all its member clubs hire personal trainers with at least one certification. A challenge here is determining which certification to pursue. Hundreds, if not thousands, of personal training-oriented certification websites can be found online and they vary markedly in quality. Because of this, IHRSA suggests that these certifications be from an organization that has "third-party accreditation of its certification procedures and protocols from an independent, experienced, and nationally recognized accrediting body." (For full details, do an online search using the terms "IHRSA personal trainer accreditation"; currently at https://www.ihrsa.org/industry-issues/personal-trainer-accreditation/).

Table 1.1 lists certifying organizations that have been accredited by the National Commission for Certifying Agencies. Virtually all the "personal trainer" certifications offered by these organizations should be viewed as basic, entry-level certifications. This is illustrated by the modest prerequisites needed to be eligible to take the examination. They are typically some combination of being at least eighteen years of age, having a high school diploma, and CPR certification. On the other hand, more advanced professional certifications usually require at least a college degree in a relevant field. Two examples that are relevant to the content of this book are the "Certified Exercise Physiologist," offered by the American College of Sports Medicine, and the "Certified Strength and Conditioning Specialist" offered by the National Strength and Conditioning Association. Both require a Bachelor's degree and CPR certification. Depending on your undergraduate coursework, practical experiences and other professional-preparation activities, either or both of these certifications are appropriate goals for you after completing a Kinesiology degree. While this textbook is not written specifically to prepare you for the Certified Exercise Physiologist examination, much of the information provided here is consistent with the knowledge, skills, and abilities assessed in the examination. This is also true, but to a much lesser extent, for the Certified Strength and Conditioning Specialist examination.

Finally, and most importantly, a third reason why this course is critical to your professional development is that the skills you learn will enable you to help clients live healthier lives. Many people join a health/fitness facility to become fitter; however, *many more* people begin exercising to become healthier. A very frequent goal for doing so is to reduce their risk factors for common chronic diseases. Examples of these diseases include cardiovascular diseases, hypertension, diabetes, and obesity. These diseases fall into the category of non-communicable diseases (NCDs). Unlike infectious diseases, NCDs cannot be transmitted between people. NCDs are a major health concern since they cause almost three-fourths of all deaths worldwide (World Health Organization, 2018). The range of NCDs is quite broad and quite diverse. Besides the aforementioned examples, other NCDs are injuries, mental health illnesses, and alcohol abuse. The four chronic diseases of cardiovascular disease, cancer, chronic respiratory disease, and diabetes account for the majority of the deaths attributed to NCDs worldwide (World Health Organization 2018). They also have a marked influence on disability and quality of life; two out of three years of healthy life

TABLE 1.1
Certifying Organizations That Have Been Accredited by the
National Commission for Certifying Agencies

Organization Name	Website
ACTION Certification	http://www.actioncertification.org/
American College of Sports Medicine	http://www.acsm.org/
American Council on Exercise	http://www.acefitness.org/
Collegiate Strength and Conditioning Coaches Association	http://cscca.org/
International Fitness Professionals Association	http://www.ifpa-fitness.com/
National Academy of Sports Medicine	http://www.nasm.org/
National Council for Certified Personal Trainers	http://www.nccpt.com/
National Council on Strength and Fitness	http://www.ncsf.org/
National Exercise and Sports Trainers Association	http://www.nestacertified.com/
National Exercise Trainers Association	http://www.netafit.org/
National Federation of Professional Trainers	http://www.nfpt.com/
National Strength and Conditioning Association	http://www.nsca.com/
Pilates Method Alliance	http://www.pilatesmethodalliance.org/
PTA Global, Inc.	http://www.ptaglobal.com/
The Cooper Institute	http://www.cooperinstitute.org/
World Instructor Training Schools	https://www.witseducation.com/fit/

lost are due to NCDs (Lopez et al. 2014). In the United States, perhaps the most worrisome NCD is one of the cardiovascular diseases (CVD), ischemic heart disease. While the number of premature deaths due to this disease has plummeted in the last twenty-five years, ischemic heart disease remains the leading cause of death in the United States (US Burden of Disease Collaborators 2018). It has been the leading cause of death every year since 1900, except for 1918 (Mozaffarian et al. 2015) when the United States was heavily involved in World War I and the Spanish Flu was rampant.

Numerous risk factors affect the development of CVD, in general, and ischemic heart disease in particular. Some cannot be changed, such as a family history of CVD or increasing age. Fortunately, many CVD risk factors are modifiable and, of relevance to your professional career, physical activity and exercise can play a major role in reducing most of these modifiable risk factors. Moreover, depending on the clientele you work with, the odds are quite high that many of your clients will have at least one of these risk factors—and will therefore benefit from becoming more active. For example, about a third of adults either do not engage in any substantive physical activity, are obese, or have high cholesterol levels (Mozaffarian et al. 2018). Almost half of adults in the United States either have an elevated blood pressure (Whelton et al. 2018) or elevated blood glucose levels (Mozaffarian et al. 2018). The end result is that only about 17 percent of adults in the United States have ideal cardiovascular health, defined as having at least five of the seven desirable heart healthy behaviors and risk factors (Mozaffarian et al. 2018). This means that the vast majority of adults in the United States need to improve their cardiovascular health. Given the importance of regular physical activity in reducing CVD risk, developing your exercise prescription skills will better enable you to help your clients reduce their risk for a number of NCDs and, more specifically, CVD. In other words, you can make a difference in the lives of others!

WHAT'S THE DIFFERENCE BETWEEN PHYSICAL FITNESS AND HEALTH?

As part of this course, and when you are working with clients in the future, the terms *physical fitness* and *health* will be mentioned frequently. Many people think of them as being somewhat synonymous, with comments like, "I try to stay healthy so I work out." They are certainly related but it is a mistake to think of them as being one-and-the-same. Thus, it is absolutely critical that you understand the similarities and differences between these terms—for your own education but, more importantly, so you can teach your clients the difference. For example, suppose that when initially meeting with a new client, you learn that his primary reason for beginning an exercise program is to "become healthier." As part of this conversation, you ascertain that he was recently diagnosed as pre-diabetic and wants to reduce his risk of becoming diabetic. Type 2 diabetes is a disease that dramatically increases the risk for CVD; it also usually improves with chronic exercise. For this client, his primary motivation for exercising is to improve his health more so than his physical fitness. So, what do you say to him about the association between fitness and health?

In 2008, the seminal *Physical Activity Guidelines for Americans* was published by the U.S. Department of Health and Human Services. These were the first ever federal recommendations for physical activity and as part of their development, the Physical Activity Guidelines Advisory Committee (2008) adopted several definitions based on their assessment of the relevant literature. These definitions were retained in the second edition of the *Guidelines* (2018):

▶ Physical fitness is "the ability to carry out daily tasks with vigor and alertness, without undue fatigue and with ample energy to enjoy leisure-time pursuits and meet unforeseen emergencies." (United States Public Health Service 1996).

▶ Health is "a human condition with physical, social and psychological dimensions, each characterized on a continuum with positive and negative poles. Positive health is associated with a capacity to enjoy life and to withstand challenges; it is not merely the absence of disease. Negative health is associated with morbidity (i.e., illness), and in the extreme, with premature mortality (i.e., death)" (Preamble to the Constitution of the World Health Organization 1946).

Physical fitness has a number of different components and there are discrepancies among experts as to what these components are. The scientific report of the Physical Activity Guidelines Advisory Committee (2018) included cardiorespiratory endurance, muscular strength, endurance and power, flexibility, balance, speed, reaction time, and body composition in its description of physical fitness. It could be argued that some of these components are oriented more toward athletic performance while some are more health-oriented. The American College of Sports Medicine (2018) divides fitness components into health-related and skill-related components. Here, the health-related components are cardiorespiratory endurance, body composition, muscular strength, muscular endurance, and flexibility. The skill-related components are agility, coordination, balance, power, reaction time, and speed.

Clearly, some of the aforementioned are oriented more toward athletic performance, some are more health-oriented and, depending on how they are viewed, some are both. Speed, or the ability to move the body quickly, is important in many athletic endeavors but is not frequently used in everyday life. However, if you are trying to catch a bus, then speed is important! Depending on the sport, muscular strength is often an important contributor to success. But it is also an important aspect of healthy aging. A certain level of strength is needed to enable older adults to remain in their homes rather than having to move into an assisted living community. Here, strength could be defined by how many bags of groceries an older adult can carry from their car into their home. Given how important physical activity and exercise are to reducing NCDs, especially CVD, this textbook is focused more on health-oriented fitness. Here, the components of physical fitness will parallel those of the American College of Sports Medicine (2018): cardiorespiratory fitness, muscular strength and endurance, body composition, and flexibility.

Re-read the definition of "health" given earlier. How is physical fitness related to health? Physical fitness contributes to good health but being healthy is much more than just being physically fit. One can be fit but not healthy and healthy but not fit. A physically fit woman may have a high risk for CVD if she also has elevated lipid levels, is hypertensive, and uses tobacco. Since CVD is a major health risk, then she is not truly healthy because she has increased health risks. Likewise, a person who exercises regularly but struggles with depression, has an eating disorder, or is chronically stressed may be doing well in one health dimension (i.e., physical health) but not in another (i.e., psychological health).

The definition of "health" used here is over seventy years old but is still valid. It focuses not on the absence of disease but more on the capacity to enjoy life and to face the challenges that life brings. In this orientation, it is similar to the newer concept of "wellness." Definitions of wellness vary but most are resonant with the one used by the National Wellness Institute, "Wellness is an active process through which people become aware of, and make choices toward, a more successful existence." Like wellness, becoming physically fit is an active process that is typically the result of a conscious decision to begin exercising. Because of the prevalence of chronic diseases, staying healthy nowadays is also an active process which requires purposeful choices by an individual.

In the earlier example of a new client with pre-diabetes, he has a major health issue. However, his embarking on an exercise program will be quite beneficial

Eight Areas of Physical and Mental Wellness

© John T Takai/Shutterstock.com

toward reducing his risk of developing Type 2 diabetes and, therefore, improving his health. It will also likely have the happy side effect of improving his physical fitness.

WHAT'S THE DIFFERENCE BETWEEN PHYSICAL ACTIVITY AND EXERCISE?

In the same way that confusion exists about the terms physical fitness and health, the terms *physical activity* and *exercise* can be confused. Like physical fitness and health, they are inter-related but not synonymous. For example, when creating an exercise program for a client, it may be more appropriate for the client to change her physical activity habits rather than her exercise habits.

As before, the definitions adopted by the Physical Activity Guidelines Advisory Committee (2018) are salient:

▶ Physical activity is "bodily movement produced by skeletal muscles that results in energy expenditure. The term does not require or imply any specific aspect or quality of movement and encompasses all types, intensities, and domains." In other words, any movement above that seen when resting constitutes physical activity.

▶ Exercise is "physical activity that is planned, structured, repetitive, and designed to improve or maintain physical fitness, physical performance, or health. Exercise encompasses all intensities."

Both terms relate to moving one's body so that energy expenditure is increased above that seen at rest; in other words, the person is doing something that burns calories above-and-beyond that associated with simply being alive. However, exercise has an added focus on physical fitness. Commuting

© connel/Shutterstock.com   © Iakov Filimonov/Shutterstock.com

to work and participating in a group cycling class are both forms of physical activity. But only the group cycling class would be considered exercise *per se* since it is usually only performed with this in mind. So, physical activity is human movement of *any* kind while exercise is physical activity that is effortful enough to increase some aspect of one's fitness and it is performed with this outcome in mind. Of course, there is some overlap. A person who is trying to lose weight may go to a cycling class but may also begin biking to work to burn off a few extra calories!

When working with a client, what considerations may prompt you to ask her to increase her physical activity rather than increasing her exercise? Suppose you have a new client who has been totally sedentary for the past few years (e.g., has a desk job so doesn't move much at work, lives in an apartment so doesn't have to do any yardwork, and does not otherwise get off the couch too often once at home). You may think she'd benefit most from a structured exercise program; however, the effort needed to embark on this program may be too much for the client. In other words, she'd probably quit because the program was too hard. A step in the right direction (literally and figuratively) is simply to ask her to be more active at the office—park further away in the parking lot, take the stairs to her office and, once there, get up and walk around the office every hour. After the client was successful at increasing her physical activity with these small actions, she might be more mentally and physically ready to begin purposefully exercising. This exercise may be in the form of a brisk walk around the neighborhood and, after a few weeks or months, she may be ready for more effortful, or intense, exercise such as jogging. This stepwise progression will be re-visited in Chapter 4.

PUTTING IT ALL TOGETHER

The goals of this chapter were twofold. The first goal was to give you some perspective of the importance of the information to be gained from this textbook and the course that it accompanies. By the time you've finished these learning materials, it is hoped that you'll have a better appreciation of how all your Kinesiology-related coursework is intertwined, be better prepared to successfully challenge a meaningful professional certification, and most importantly, be prepared to help others reduce their risk for CVD and other NCDs via developing reasonable, scientifically-based exercise prescriptions. The second goal was to clarify the meanings of common, yet often misused, terms that are relevant to working with a new client and creating exercise prescriptions. Both physical activity and exercise can be used to improve one's physical health. However, to improve physical fitness, the movement performed by the client must be purposeful and somewhat effortful.

REFERENCES

American College of Sports Medicine. 2018. ACSM's Guidelines for Exercise Testing and Prescription, edited by Deborah Riebe. Philadelphia: Wolters Kluwer.

Gillette L., and J. R. Gillette. "Prepared Students: The Secret's in the Assignment Strategy." Webinar accessed March 10, 2015, http://www.magnapubs.com/online/mentor/how-can-i-effectively-use-class-preparation-assignments-13528-1.html.

Lopez, A. D., T. N. Williams, A. Levin, M. Tonelli, J. A. Singh, P. G. J. Burney, J. Rehm, N. D. Volkow, G. Koob, and C. P. Ferri. 2014. "Remembering the forgotten non-communicable diseases." *BMC Medicine* 12: 200.

Mozaffarian D., E. J. Benjamin, A. S. Go, D. K. Arnett, M. J. Blaha, M. Cushman, S. de Ferranti, et al. 2015. On behalf of the American Heart Association Statistics Committee and Stroke Statistics Subcommittee. "Heart Disease and Stroke Statistics—2015 Update: A Report from the American Heart Association." *Circulation* 131: e29–e322.

Physical Activity Guidelines Advisory Committee. 2008. *Physical Activity Guidelines Advisory Committee Report.* USDHHS, Washington DC.

Preamble to the Constitution of the World Health Organization as adopted by the International Health Conference, New York, June 19–22, 1946; signed on July 22, 1946, by the representatives of 61 states (Official Records of the World Health Organization, no. 2, p. 100) and entered into force on April 7, 1948.

United States Public Health Service, Office of the Surgeon General, National Center for Chronic Disease Prevention and Health Promotion, President's Council on Physical Fitness and Sports. 1996. *Physical Activity and Health: A Report of the Surgeon General.* Atlanta, GA.: U.S. Dept. of Health and Human Services, Centers for Disease Control and Prevention, National Center for Chronic Disease Prevention and Health Promotion; President's Council on Physical Fitness and Sports.

US Burden of Disease Collaboration. 2018. "The State of US Health, 1990–2016: Burden of Diseases, Injuries, and Risk Factors among US States." *JAMA* 319: 1444–72.

U.S. Department of Health and Human Services. 2018. *Physical Activity Guidelines for Americans*, 2nd ed. Washington, DC: U.S. Department of Health and Human Services; 2018.

Whelton P. K., R. M. Carey, W. S. Aronow, D. E. Casey Jr., K. J. Collins, C. Dennison Himmelfarb, S. M. DePalma, S. Gidding, K. A. Jamerson, D. W. Jones, E. J. MacLaughlin, P. Muntner, B. Ovbiagele, S. C. Smith Jr, C. C. Spencer, R. S. Stafford, S. J. Taler, R. J. Thomas, K. A. Williams Sr, J. D. Williamson, J. T. Wright Jr. 2018. ACC/AHA/AAPA/ABC/ACPM/AGS/APhA/ASH/ASPC/NMA/PCNA Guideline for the Prevention, Detection, Evaluation, and Management of High Blood Pressure in Adults: A Report of the American College of Cardiology/American Heart Association Task Force on Clinical Practice Guidelines. *J Am Coll Cardiol* 71: e127–248.

World Health Organization. 2018. *World Health Statistics 2018: Monitoring Health for the SDGs, Sustainable Development Goals.* Geneva: World Health Organization.

CHAPTER 2

CRIPL: An Overview of the Major Components of Working with a Client

©Misunseo/Shutterstock.com

In some ways, being a health/fitness professional is analogous to being a professional carpenter. Many people complete small carpentry-related home projects and as a result, some think they have all the skills needed to do the project well. This may be the case with simple projects. But when the homeowner embarks on an ambitious home renovation, they quickly realize that they lack the skills the professional carpenter has. Likewise, many people have been exposed to exercise concepts through physical education classes, the media, and their own exercise experiences, so they think they know enough to exercise safely and effectively. Their knowledge may be adequate if all they want is a general exercise program. But if they are at risk for chronic diseases, have comorbidities, or need a "next level" exercise program, then they would benefit from working with a health/fitness professional.

In addition, all carpenters have toolboxes, but the toolbox of a more experienced carpenter is likely better equipped than that of a beginner. Health/fitness professionals also have a "toolbox," but this toolbox is the accumulation of their skills, knowledge, and expertise. As exercise professionals become more skilled and more knowledgeable, they add "tools" to their professional "toolbox." For example, an entry-level professional should be able to recognize the major risk factors for cardiovascular disease (CVD). A more experienced personal trainer would have this "tool" but also have the "tool" of being able to help clients modify these risk factors via changing their behaviors.

As with a professional carpenter, a personal trainer's "toolbox" can become cluttered and disorganized. Finding the right tool when it is needed then becomes more difficult which, in turn, makes doing one's job more challenging. The primary goal of this chapter is to introduce a guide, CRIPL, that can help you keep your professional toolbox organized. CRIPL will not replace the professional expertise and judgment, or "tools," you will need when working with a client. However, it should make it easier for you to decide which tools are needed and when they can be put to best use.

There are two other goals of this chapter. The first is to help you understand how to complete preparticipation screening well. Preparticipation screening is a critical step toward reducing the risk of an adverse event occurring in your health/fitness facility. Since the risk of an adverse event is always present in exercise environments, the second goal is to help you understand how to respond to an emergency in your facility.

For example, most exercise professionals would readily recognize that a facility catering to high performance athletes would not be an ideal exercise venue for an eighty-year-old man who was just discharged from physical therapy following a hip replacement. However, what type of facility would be appropriate for him? Or his fifty-year-old son who is overweight, hypertensive, and concerned about his risk for CVD? Or his twenty-five-year-old granddaughter who competes in sprint triathlons and now wants to move up to Olympic triathlon distances? Besides differences in the most appropriate health/fitness facility for each of these clients, are there differences in the skills and expertise needed by the exercise professionals who will be working with each of them?

©racorn/Shutterstock.com

These examples illustrate that when working with a client—especially a new client—there are a number of issues that the health/fitness professional needs to concern themselves with. For example, questions that must be considered include "Is this person an appropriate client for this health/fitness facility?" "Is this health/fitness facility an appropriate outlet for this client?" "Does this person have any health-related conditions that affect his desired exercise program?" "What are this person's goals?" "What should this client's exercise program consist of?" "Is this program realistic for this client?" "Is the help of experts in different fields, like a Registered Dietitian Nutritionist, needed to help this person achieve their goals?" With proper training and adequate experience, addressing these issues and many others that need to be considered becomes second nature. However, getting to the position where these issues *are* second nature can be challenging.

Remembering all the details associated with working with a client can be overwhelming if someone is still learning the art and science of exercise programming. To that end, CRIPL serves as a blueprint to help you remember the important issues to be considered when developing a program for a new client. CRIPL reflects the five important areas to consider and the order in which to do so. These areas are:

Clinical history

Risk factor assessment

Interpreting the data

Prescribing the exercise program

Lifestyle considerations

The term CRIPL was chosen because the phonetic term (i.e., "cripple") is politically incorrect and may therefore be memorable. If desired, a more politically correct acronym, MRIPL (or "Mister Ipple") can be used by replacing "clinical history" with "medical history" (Franke 2005). Regardless, the components of CRIPL form the backbone of this book and will be referred to repeatedly. However, please recognize that there is nothing inherently "special" about the CRIPL acronym and its components. While there are likely other methods that would suffice, CRIPL is used here simply because it *works*. Following the CRIPL method when working with a client will reduce the risk of your overlooking anything important. You may make mistakes of inexperience, which practice and due diligence on your part should reduce, but CRIPL will help you avoid mistakes of ignorance.

Each of the five areas of CRIPL will be described briefly in this chapter and are summarized in Table 2.1. Table 2.1 is the blueprint to follow when working with a client; it is the "organizational chart" for your "professional toolbox." As indicated earlier, a goal of this chapter is to help you understand how to complete preparticipation screening on a new client. Preparticipation screening is encompassed primarily in the "C" of CRIPL. Consequently, "C" will be reviewed extensively in this chapter. The other four areas of CRIPL, or "RIPL," will be expanded upon in subsequent chapters of this book. For example, once a client has undergone preparticipation screening, assessing the client's risk factors for the primary chronic diseases of CVD, or "R", becomes important. Consequently, "R" will be reviewed extensively in the next chapter of this book.

When working with a client, thorough preparticipation screening and following the other principles of CRIPL will help reduce the likelihood of significant emergencies occurring in a health/fitness environment. Nevertheless, despite your best efforts as a health/fitness professional, adverse events will happen. The term, "adverse event," is quite broad and includes issues ranging from relatively minor (e.g., muscle soreness) to severe (e.g., sudden cardiac death). The responses needed by facility staff vary according to the severity of the adverse event. Nevertheless, it is incumbent that the staff be prepared to respond adequately to adverse events, especially life-threatening ones. Consequently, in this chapter, emergency procedures in response to a severe adverse event will also be reviewed.

TABLE 2.1

	Information you need	Items to address	Tips to assist you in addressing these items
C— *Clinical History*	Pre-participation screening information (waiver of risk or informed consent, medical history, medical clearance)	You risk-classified the client based on ALL the following: (1) signs, symptoms of disease, (2) info from 10 components of a good medical history, (3) personal physical feedback, and (4) discussion with client. You should also consider the client's risk factors but will do so with "R" below. Using these tools, you have determined whether the client is appropriate for your facility and vice versa. If they can join your facility, you have determined whether the client has any clinical history which warrants modifying what you would do for him/her and/or how they would function in your facility. You will not perform a fitness assessment until after you've made this determination.	LIST the (1) signs/symptoms of disease and (2) the 10 components of a good medical history. Compare your clients information to these 2 lists and determine if your client has any noteworthy concerns. (3) Look at the personal physician feedback; what did the physician say? (4) Talk to the client about any concerns you may have or to fill in any gaps you may have about their medical history. REMEMBER: you are trying to risk classify this person and decide whether your facility is "right" for him/her and vice versa.
R— *Risk Factor Assessment*	Risk factors	You identified (1) the client's risk factors for CVD, (2) which can be modified and which cannot be, (3) goals for each risk factor and (4) calculated their 10-year risk of developing CVD, (5) determined which risk factor(s) need to be modified first and (6) how their risk for CVD will change with modifying these risk factors. You will address (6) how to modify these risk factors with "L" below.	LIST the (1) CVD risk factors and the criteria for each. Determine what the values (e.g., BP, LDL, etc.) are for your client and if they meet any of these criteria. (2) Identify the nonmodifiable risk factors and (3) what the client's goals should be. Determine the (4) 10-year risk for CVD and (5) prioritize which should be changed first. Finally, (6) estimate how their 10-year risk for CVD will change if the client modifies the risk factors.
I— *Interpreting the Data*	Completed the C & R and you have results from a fitness assessment	You checked (1) to be sure the fitness assessment included all 5 components of fitness, (2) determined if the client underwent a complete assessment, (3) determined if the assessment was done well, (4) determined how your client did on each of these components by comparing them to age- and gender-specific norms, and (5) prioritized the components which most need to be improved.	ANSWER the following: (1) What are the 5 components of fitness? (2) Did the client complete all the components and are items missing? (3) Was the assessment done well or were mistakes made? (4) Do you need to make any calculations (e.g., estimate VO_2max from submax data, calculate ideal body weight) or are all the data there? (5) How does the client compare to their age- and gender-specific peers? (6) Based on this information, which fitness component(s) should the client focus on now? later on?

P— ***Prescribing the Exercise Program***	You have information from C, R, & I	You talked to the client to determine what their goals are. You CAREFULLY (1) balanced the client's goals vs. the client's needs (e.g., what are the goals you think are appropriate?), (2) developed a COMPLETE exercise prescription, which was SPECIFIC to the client and appropriately balancing the goals vs. the needs. If the program was for CV fitness, it included FITT and workloads (minimum, maximum, treadmill, and cycle ergometer). If for weight loss, it included FITT, workloads, and caloric expenditure. If the program was for resistive exercise, it included a needs analysis, acute program variables (choice, order, freq, load, vol, rest) and periodization (classic, undulating, conjugated).	CONSIDER the following: (1) What is the best balance between what the client WANTS to work on (i.e., their goals) vs. what they NEED to work on (i.e., what they were worst on, based on the norms. (2) After doing so, develop an exercise prescription which emphasizes these components and which is specifically designed to best achieve this balance.
L— ***Lifestyle Changes***	You have done all of the above	You identified, both SPECIFICALLY and IN DETAIL, how the client can make the desired lifestyle changes. Depending on the client, this may include how to modify CVD risk factors (using exercise, dietary changes, or other interventions), how to begin a program of regular CV exercise (e.g., beginning stage vs. improvement stage), how to lose weight [exercise program and dietary changes (focusing on behavioral aspects of both)], how to begin a program of resistive exercise (inc. consideration of beginner vs. experienced lifter and acute program variables, periodization). When appropriate, you refer the client to specialist (e.g., Registered Dietitian Nutritionist for dietary or weight loss needs, physician for lipid- or BP-lowering medications, counselor to assist with smoking cessation, stress management, etc.).	ANSWER the following: (1) Did I give the client sufficiently understandable information that they now know what they should do? (2) Was I specific enough (e.g., desired eating habits vs. client's current diet; workloads the client should use)? (3) Are these lifestyle changes integrated into the exercise prescription I developed for the client? (4) Taking into account the client's current lifestyle, are these recommendations reasonable?

MRIPL table adapted from "Covering All the Bases: Working with New Clients" by Warren D. Franke, Ph.D., *ACSM's Health & Fitness Journal*, March/April 2005, Vol. 9, No. 2, pp. 13–17. Reproduced with permission of Wolters Kluwer/Lippincott Williams & Wilkins Health.

OVERVIEW: CLINICAL HISTORY

The primary purpose of "C" is to perform preparticipation screening. The goal is to identify individuals who may be at an increased risk for having an adverse health-related event during exercise (Riebe et al. 2015). The most worrisome adverse events are life-threatening situations. These are usually cardiac-related and manifest as sudden cardiac death or an acute myocardial infarction (a "heart attack"). In relatively younger people, meaning those less than thirty-five or forty years of age, these cardiac-related adverse events are usually due to congenital or hereditary conditions. In other words, the person has had this pathology, such as an abnormally enlarged heart, their entire life (Franklin and Lavie 2011; Goodman, Thomas, and Burr 2011). On the other hand, in middle-age and older adults, over 80 percent of cardiac-related adverse events are due to the CVD of ischemic heart disease. Typically, this event is due to a blood clot blocking blood flow in a coronary artery; this clot formed in response to the rupture of an atherosclerotic plaque (Goodman et al. 2011; Marijon et al. 2015).

Fortunately, the overall risk for significant adverse events during physical activity is quite low. One estimate placed it at 1 to 3 events per 1,000,000 participant-hours (Goodman et al. 2011). Of middle age and older adults who experience sudden cardiac arrest, only about 5 percent of them occur during physical activity (Marijon et al. 2015). For perspective, the overall incidence of sudden cardiac arrest in middle-age exercisers is about the same as that seen in NCAA athletes (Patil and Magalski 2015). The relative rarity of exercise-related cardiac events is good news.

However, these comparisons are misleading. The risk of an adverse event while exercising varies by both the intensity of the exercise and the characteristics of the exerciser. Depending on the circumstances, the risk can be much greater. Several factors affect this risk. First, exercising at more vigorous intensities carries a greater risk than exercising at lower intensities. For example, compared to not exercising at all, an acute bout of vigorous exercise in middle-age and older adults is associated with a 17-fold higher risk of sudden death within an hour of this exercise (Albert et al. 2000). But exercising at a mild-to-moderate intensity has a risk for an acute adverse event that is similar to not exercising at all (Franklin and Levie 2011).

Second, past exercise habits play a role. The risk of an adverse event with a single bout of exercise is higher in a sedentary person than a chronic exerciser (Franklin and Levie 2011; Mittleman and Mostofsky 2011). If the exercise bout is vigorous, the risk is even higher—it may be as much as 100-fold higher in a middle-age, sedentary person doing an acute bout of vigorous exercise (Mittleman et al. 1993)! The good news is that this risk declines with habitual vigorous exercise—the more frequently that an exerciser does vigorous exercise, the lower the overall risk associated with these higher intensities (Franklin 2014; Mittleman et al. 1993; Mittleman and Mostofsky 2011). Of course, the overall benefits of chronic exercise are high enough to offset any short-term risk associated with exercising; over the course of a 24-hour day, the risk of an acute cardiovascular event is lower in exercisers than non-exercisers. Finally, the risk of an adverse event is higher in people with underlying ischemic heart disease (van Teeffelen et al. 2009; Franklin and Lavie 2011). Likewise, people with more CVD risk factors have a statistically higher chance of having an adverse event than people without risk factors (Mittleman and Mostofsky 2011). From a practical perspective, the difference between these two groups is too small to make much of a difference in how you would work with them in a health/fitness setting (Riebe et al. 2015). Consequently, the presence of CVD risk factors *per se* are not considered when performing preparticipation screening.

Recall that there is an estimated risk of an adverse event during exercise of 1 to 3 events per 1,000,000 participant-hours (Goodman et al. 2011). That risk *is* low. But consider this: there were 60,900,000 health club memberships in the United States in 2017 (IHRSA 2018). If each of these members exercised only once a week, that would result in over 3.2 *billion* participant-hours over the course of a year. Because of the number of people at risk for CVD and the number of people who exercise, the net effect is that cardiac-related emergencies are actually quite common. Recent studies found that 17–27 percent of health/fitness facilities had experienced at least one serious emergency within the previous two years (Herbert et al. 2007; McKinnis et al. 2001; Morrey, Finnie, and Hensrud 2002). Over a five-year span, the incidence is closer to 35 percent (Craig 2014).

Consequently, preparticipation screening focuses on determining the likelihood of whether a participant has any factors that may increase the risk of having an exercise-related cardiovascular event. It is a critical step in keeping the risk of cardiac-related adverse events in your facility as low as possible. In essence, preparticipation screening enables you to decide if the client would be appropriate for your health/fitness facility and, conversely, if your health/fitness facility is appropriate for the client. In so doing, you decide whether:

1. *It is appropriate for the client to join your health/fitness facility "as is."* In other words, the client is apparently healthy and does not appear to have any medical issues that would substantively affect their ability to exercise safely. Alternatively, it may be appropriate for them to join your facility but special considerations will need to be made when working with the client. For example, a client who is otherwise healthy except for being moderately hypertensive may be able to perform aerobic exercise without undue concerns but their resistance exercise program may need to exclude lifting heavy weights.

2. *The client needs medical evaluation, or clearance, prior to beginning an exercise program.* Suppose a middle-age adult is joining your facility and tells you that he feels "heartburn" whenever he goes for a brisk walk. Is this really "heartburn" or is it angina associated with ischemia? Medical expertise is needed to make this diagnosis, so follow-up with his personal physician is necessary. Likewise, feedback from the physician of the aforementioned hypertensive client would have been desirable in order to guide you in developing the best exercise program for them.

3. *It is more appropriate for the client to join a medically supervised program.* Most health/fitness facilities are oriented toward working with apparently healthy clients. Someone with significant health issues that place them at higher risk of having an adverse exercise-related event would be better served in a medically supervised facility. An example of this scenario is someone who recently experienced a heart attack and should now go through cardiac rehabilitation. If the middle-age adult (in "2" above) with heartburn was diagnosed with CVD, their physician may refer them into a medically supervised cardiac rehabilitation program as part of his initial medical care. If these symptoms turned out to be due to gastric reflux, or heartburn, and the client did not have any other medical concerns, then the physician might decide that this person is a viable candidate to join your facility.

4. *The client has a medical condition that makes exercise contraindicated until the condition has improved or is controlled.* For example, a potential client has been recently diagnosed with Type 1 diabetes. They are struggling with adequate glucose control but want to begin exercising since they have been told that "working out is good for diabetes." While the latter is correct, exercise is contraindicated in poorly controlled diabetics (American Diabetes Association 2002). So they should not join your facility until this is achieved. Moreover, in situations where exercise may have been contraindicated earlier but now may be feasible, feedback from the client's personal physician is required in order to consider allowing the client to begin exercising.

Preparticipation screening is based on addressing (1) the client's current level of physical activity, (2) whether they have any known cardiovascular, metabolic, or renal disease, (3) whether the client has any signs or symptoms suggestive of cardiovascular, metabolic, or renal disease, and (4) the client's desired exercise intensity (Riebe et al. 2015). Each of these four issues affects the extent to which the client is at risk of having an adverse cardiovascular-related event. The logic model that is recommended by the American College of Sports Medicine to use with preparticipation screening is shown in Figure 2.1.

FIGURE 2.1
ACSM's Exercise Preparticipation Health Screening Logic Model

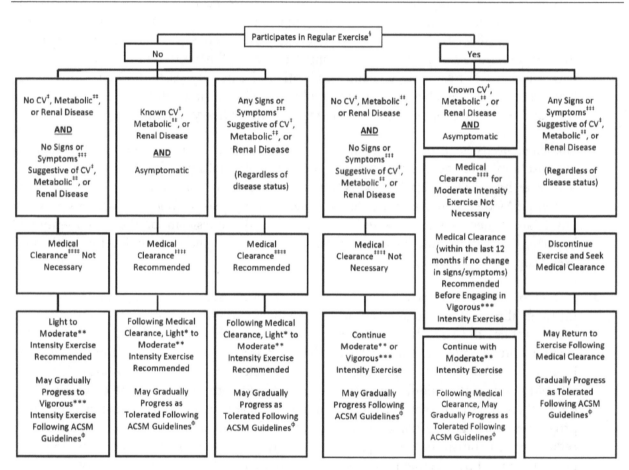

§Exercise participation, performing planned, structured physical activity at least 30 min at moderate intensity on at least 3 d·wk−1 for at least the last 3 months.

*Light-intensity exercise, 30% to <40% HRR or V̇O₂R, 2 to <3 METs, 9–11 RPE, an intensity that causes slight increases in HR and breathing.

**Moderate-intensity exercise, 40% to <60% HRR or V̇O₂R, 3 to <6 METs, 12–13 RPE, an intensity that causes noticeable increases in HR and breathing.

***Vigorous-intensity exercise ≥60% HRR or V̇O₂R, ≥6 METs, ≥14 RPE, an intensity that causes substantial increases in HR and breathing.

‡CVD, cardiac, peripheral vascular, or cerebrovascular disease.

‡‡Metabolic disease, type 1 and 2 diabetes mellitus.

‡‡‡Signs and symptoms, at rest or during activity; includes pain, discomfort in the chest, neck, jaw, arms, or other areas that may result from ischemia; shortness of breath at rest or with mild exertion; dizziness or syncope; orthopnea or paroxysmal nocturnal dyspnea; ankle edema; palpitations or tachycardia; intermittent claudication; known heart murmur; or unusual fatigue or shortness of breath with usual activities.

‡‡‡‡Medical clearance, approval from a health care professional to engage in exercise.

ΦACSM Guidelines, see *ACSM's Guidelines for Exercise Testing and Prescription,* 9th edition, 2014.

Riebe et al, "Updating ACSM's Recommendations for Exercise Preparticipation Health Screening," *Medicine & Science in Sports & Exercise,* 47(11) p. 2473–2479, https://www.ncbi.nlm.nih.gov/pubmed/26473759.

Recall that physically inactive clients have a higher risk for cardiovascular events than active clients. An acute bout of exercise, for anyone of any fitness level, increases this risk. It is increased more in a previously inactive client than an active client. And the relative risk is higher with vigorous intensity exercise than with moderate intensity exercise. However, the absolute risk for the latter is not much different from that of rest. Since the long-term benefits of physical activity far outweigh the short-term risks, the take-home message is that previously inactive clients should be able to safely begin a program of *moderate* intensity exercise. The caveat is that if the client has any known cardiovascular, metabolic (e.g., diabetes) or renal disease, then it is recommended that the client be medically cleared by their health care provider. Likewise, if the client has any signs or symptoms suggestive of the aforementioned, then their health care provider should approve their participating in a light-to-moderate intensity exercise program (Riebe et al. 2015).

With some exceptions, these steps should also be followed when working with a new client who has been exercising. The first exception is if the client has any of these diseases but is asymptomatic, then medical clearance is not necessary if the client will exercise at a moderate intensity. However, medical clearance is recommended if the client wishes to begin a program of vigorous intensity exercise. Second, if the client has any signs or symptoms, then they should discontinue exercising until they receive medical clearance (Riebe et al. 2015).

With preparticipation screening, the most critical component of the "C" in CRIPL is having the potential client complete a health/medical history questionnaire. A well-designed questionnaire will give you information about whether the person has any relevant medical diagnoses, such as cardiovascular, metabolic, or renal disease; the presence of any signs or symptoms suggestive of these diseases; as well as their current and past physical activity habits.

At most health/fitness facilities, where competent professional staff can review the questionnaire responses, a customized form is often developed in-house (Craig 2014). An alternative, premade, choice for a health/medical history questionnaire is the PAR-Q+ (Warburton, Jamnik, and Bredin 2011). In health/fitness facilities, it is the most commonly used non-customized self-guided tool for health/medical history screening (Craig 2014). A user-friendly online version is available (search for "electronic PAR-Q+," currently at www.eparmedx.com). The next most commonly used pre-made alternative is the AHA/ACSM Health/Fitness Facility Preparticipation Screening Questionnaire (Balady et al. 1998). Both questionnaires probe for the presence of signs or symptoms of CVD as well as other health issues. Both are self-guided and completed by the client; consequently, they tend to be conservative in assessing the client's risk for an adverse event and in recommending medical clearance prior to beginning a program of exercise. In the context of CVD, the advantage of the AHA/ACSM questionnaire over the PAR-Q+ is that it explores more completely the presence of CVD risk factors. A disadvantage is that it does not fully assess all the clinically relevant risk factors.

Of course, a fitness center can develop its own medical/health history questionnaire. The internet is replete with examples; a recent search using the term "medical/health history questionnaire" returned over 117 million responses. Good examples are available elsewhere (e.g., ACSM 2019). When either developing a questionnaire or assessing the utility of a pre-existing one, it is recommended that you include the components of a good medical history suggested by the American College of Sports Medicine (2018). These components are medical diagnoses, including past and present conditions; previous physical examination findings, including significant laboratory results; history of symptoms; recent illnesses, hospitalizations, new medical diagnoses, or surgical procedures; orthopedic problems; current medications and drug allergies; social/health habits such as alcohol or tobacco use; physical activity habits; employment status, including physical demands; and family health history. This is a lengthy list of items. However, a medical/health history questionnaire that includes all these items need not be overly long. A well thought-out form, versions of which have been used in a number of high-quality health/fitness facilities for many years, is at the end of this chapter. It is relatively short, can be completed in less than ten minutes by most people, and includes all the aforementioned components of a good medical history (ACSM 2018).

Regardless of the questionnaire used, it should probe for signs and symptoms of cardiovascular, metabolic, and renal diseases. A commonly accepted list of such signs and symptoms is shown in Table 2.2 (ACSM 2018). These signs and symptoms are often seen in the presence of clinically significant CVD, but they are not absolute indicators. For example, a client complaining of "shortness of breath . . . with mild exertion" may simply be very deconditioned while angina-like chest pain could be due to a number of conditions that are not related to CVD (McConaghy and Oza 2013). Thus, a potential client with any of these signs or symptoms needs to receive medical clearance prior to your considering allowing them to join your health/fitness facility.

TABLE 2.2
Major Signs and Symptoms of Cardiovascular and Pulmonary Disease

1. Pain, discomfort, or other anginal equivalent in the chest, neck, jaw, arms, or other areas that may be due to ischemia (i.e., inadequate blood flow to the heart).
2. Shortness of breath at rest or with mild exertion.
3. Dizziness or syncope (fainting), especially with exercise.
4. Orthopnea or paroxysmal nocturnal dyspnea (shortness of breath when supine or when sleeping that is relieved by sitting or standing).
5. Ankle edema.
6. Palpitations (unpleasant awareness of forceful or rapid heartbeat) or tachycardia (rapid heartbeat).
7. Intermittent claudication (ischemic pain in the legs or arms due to peripheral vascular disease).
8. Known heart murmur.
9. Unusual fatigue or shortness of breath with usual activities (may indicate the onset or change status of CVD or metabolic disease).

From the American College of Sports Medicine (2018).

After the new client completes the medical/health history questionnaire, take time to review it thoroughly. Compare the client's responses to the logic model (Figure 2.1) and then decide how to proceed. Can the client be accepted "as is"? Do they need medical clearance before joining your health/fitness facility? Should they be referred to a more medically supervised program? Do they have a health or medical issue that needs to be improved before they can exercise?

If medical clearance is needed in order to join your facility, how do you go about getting it? Sample forms for doing so are readily available on the internet (i.e., an internet search using the term "physician's clearance form for exercise" yielded >7.9 million results) and from quality resources (ACSM 2019; Balady et al. 1998). Regardless of the form that is used, it is critical that you abide by the privacy rules of the Health Insurance Portability and Accountability Act of 1996 (HIPPA; search on "HHS and HIPPA," currently at https://www.hhs.gov/hipaa/index.html). Important HIPPA requirements are (1) the client authorizes the release of medical information from their health care provider to your health/fitness facility, (2) only the minimum amount of protected health information be released that accomplishes the intended purpose, and (3) this information be kept confidential.

A simple method to accomplish the first requirement is to ask the client to deliver the form to their health care provider's office, rather than you doing so, and the client asks for it to be completed.

The request is originating from the office's patient, your client, so no other paperwork or signatures are necessary. To address the second requirement, recall that medical clearance documentation is needed to make sure that the client's health care provider approves their exercising. Thus, the only information you need to receive from the physician is whether the client can exercise safely and, if so, whether any limitations exist that would affect their exercise program. The last requirement, keeping this information confidential, mandates the client's records be kept under lock-and-key. It also mandates that the health/fitness facility employees are careful to avoid disclosing the client's identity if compelled to discuss their information with others. The medical clearance form at the end of this chapter is simple and brief (i.e., the physician only has to answer two "yes–no" questions) yet meets these first two requirements. It is up to you to ensure that the third requirement be met!

Additional paperwork that a new client should complete is a waiver of liability (ACSM 2019). This waiver should contain two distinct sections: an "assumption of risk" section and a "release" section (www.sportrisk.com). An "assumption of risk" without a "release" is also known as an "informed consent." The purpose of the assumption of risk section is to inform the client of the risks associated with participating in a physical activity program. Ideally, these risks would be broadly defined and include all the programs the participant could be involved in at the health/fitness facility (e.g., on a bouldering wall, in a spin class, in a general exercise room, etc.). The participant acknowledges in writing that they are aware of these risks and voluntarily accepts responsibility for participating. The "release" section is where the participant absolves, or releases, the health/fitness facility from responsibility for the consequences of their participation, including negligence on the part of the facility, and waives their right to file a claim or sue the facility. Not all facilities that require an assumption of risk require a release. Regardless, if the client refuses to participate in preparticipation screening, it is critical they complete a full waiver of liability, meaning both an assumption of risk and a release. If they also refuse to sign the waiver, then they should not be allowed to participate in the health/fitness facility to the extent permitted by law.

As with the other documents described here, an internet search will quickly find many examples of waivers. Because of differences among health/fitness facilities, such as equipment, staffing and programming, as well as legal interpretations that differ among states, do not use a premade form and do not attempt to create one on your own. Rather, enlist the assistance of an attorney, preferably one with experience with the health/fitness industry, to prepare a waiver of liability form that is customized to your facility. Recognize that even a well-prepared document may not entirely absolve either the health/fitness facility or its staff from all liability. A client may file a claim if they, or their attorney, feel so inclined. They may have a winnable case if they can show that the actions, or inactions, of the facility or its personnel contributed to harm and that these actions were not explicitly covered by the waiver.

Of course, the best way to reduce either the risk of a participant being injured or the health/fitness facility being sued is to ensure that everyone involved in the operations of a health/fitness facility provides the highest quality services possible. This includes doing one's best to perform thorough preparticipation screening, preventing injuries through rigorous attention to participant safety, having established standards for how participant activities are organized, and careful monitoring of the condition of the facility and equipment. It also includes having effective emergency response plans in place to reduce the extent of any injuries that may occur.

Unfortunately, ~20 percent of health/fitness facilities do not do any preparticipation screening and have reasons for not doing so (Table 2.3; Craig 2014). As described here, the information that preparticipation screening, or the "C" of CRIPL, provides the health/fitness facility can be immensely useful. The "C" can also be done relatively quickly with little to no expense on the part of the facility. Consequently, there are no legitimate reasons for not completing preparticipation screening as part of enrolling a new participant.

TABLE 2.3

Major Reasons Given by Health/Fitness Facilities for Not Requiring
Preparticipation Screening of New Participants

Reason	Frequency (%)
Participants have responsibility for their own health and actions—our facility does not have this responsibility.	29
Screening takes up too much staff time (or lack of staff resources).	15
Fitness facility/franchise policy.	14
Participants would perceive completing screening as a barrier that might cause them to not join the facility or participate in activities.	8
There is no purpose or need for screening.	8
Legal counsel advice (e.g., we have been advised not to conduct screening because it might increase legal liability).	8

Other (most common responses below):
    Required only for personal training and/or other individualized
        fitness/wellness programs
    Do not know why
    It is optional, not required.
	18

From Craig (2014).

OVERVIEW: RISK FACTOR ASSESSMENT

The "R" of CRIPL represents risk factor assessment and refers to determining a client's risk factors for chronic diseases. Most common chronic diseases, such as hypertension, diabetes, and obesity, are either a form of cardiovascular disease (CVD) or a major contributor to the most lethal CVD, ischemic heart disease. The risk factors for these diseases are also risk factors for CVD. Consequently, risk factors for CVD will be the primary focus of "R." Risk factor assessment will be covered in detail in Chapter 3. It is introduced here so you have a better understanding of how it fits into CRIPL. "R" is not an overt part of preparticipation screening, since a client's risk factors are not strongly predictive of their risk for an adverse event (Riebe et al. 2015). However, given the prevalence of CVD risk factors in the United States and how important exercise can be in managing most of these risk factors, it is important that health/fitness professionals assess them in their clients, especially new clients. Consequently, preparticipation screening and risk factor assessment (i.e., "C" and "R") are often completed concurrently, since it is time-efficient to assess the client's risk factors while doing preparticipation screening. Like "C," "R" can be done relatively quickly with little to no expense on the part of the facility.

The overall goal of risk factor assessment is to determine how best to assist the participant in reducing their overall risk for common chronic diseases. The steps for performing risk factor assessment are outlined in "R" of Table 2.1 and, as mentioned previously, will be reviewed as part of Chapter 3. The CVD risk factors that will be emphasized in Chapter 3 are those identified by the American College of Sports Medicine (2018). Be mindful of the fact that the list of factors which contribute to

CVD is continually evolving as are the criteria by which a risk factor is defined (see Lloyd-Jones et al. 2010 and Benjamin et al. 2019 for more complete details). In other words, the current criteria for defining a risk factor may be different five years from now. For example, most people define hypertension as a blood pressure above 140/90. However, before 1988, when treating a hypertensive client, the focus was primarily on lowering elevated diastolic blood pressure (Kotchen 2014). There was not enough clinical evidence to support the medical treatment of an elevated systolic blood pressure. However, that changed in 1988 when the importance of treating elevated systolic blood pressure was codified into the guidelines published by the Joint National Committee on Prevention, Detection, Evaluation, and Treatment of High Blood Pressure. The thresholds for hypertension were defined as either systolic blood pressures of 140 mmHg or diastolic blood pressures of 90 mmHg (James et al. 2014). In response to our increased understanding of the health risks associated with hypertension, these thresholds were lowered in 2017 to 130 mmHg systolic and 80 mmHg diastolic, respectively (Whelton et al. 2018). In other words, risk factor assessment is an evolving process so, moving forward in your professional career, you will need to remain current in how the risk factors are defined.

OVERVIEW: INTERPRETING THE DATA

The "I" of CRIPL is a reminder to review all the relevant information you have on your client as a prelude to developing an exercise prescription for them. Of course, "C" and "R" entail reviewing quite a lot of information. Consequently, "I" is primarily focused on interpreting the results of a fitness assessment and using that information to develop a focused, appropriate exercise prescription. This book assumes that a fitness assessment has been performed on your client; many, but not all, health/fitness professionals administer them. The fitness assessment can be thought of as either the *last* step of preparticipation screening (i.e., at the end of "C" and "R") or the *first* step in "I" or Interpreting the Data. Regardless, the important thing to remember is that you should *not* perform a fitness assessment until *after* you have determined that it is appropriate for the client to join your health/fitness facility.

The first two steps of "I" are (1) to review the fitness assessment for thoroughness and (2) if you did not administer the assessment yourself, attempt to ascertain if the assessment was performed well. "Thoroughness" here means determining if any component of fitness was overlooked. Recall from Chapter 1 that the five components of physical fitness are cardiorespiratory fitness, muscular strength and endurance, body composition, and flexibility. Therefore, review the assessment to determine if all five components were assessed. If not, why not? Was something overlooked during the assessment or, perhaps, is a component of physical fitness purposely ignored in the health/fitness facility? "Performed well" means that you can trust the results to actually reflect the client's physical fitness. These first two steps are important but easy to ignore.

Suppose you are working with a new client who, after undergoing preparticipation screening and being accepted into your health/fitness facility, recently completed a fitness assessment. He has been lifting weights for most of his life and, while already quite muscular, is joining your facility to get more expert guidance as to how to get even stronger. He is 5'9" tall (1.75 m) and weighs 215 pounds (97.5 kg). Your facility uses body mass index (BMI, kg/m^2) as the method to assess body composition. His BMI is 31.8 kg/m^2 which is above the threshold for being considered obese (or 30 kg/m^2). Both you and he are surprised by this outcome, since he looks quite "buff." In other words, you do not trust the results of this component of his assessment. What could be wrong? The fault likely lies with the technique used to assess body composition, BMI. BMI quantifies weight per unit height and not body fatness *per se*. From an epidemiological perspective, a BMI of 30 is a reasonable surrogate measure of obesity (Pasco et al. 2012); however, its ability to correctly identify individuals who are lean but muscular is relatively poor (Romero-Corral et al. 2008). So, BMI is not a good tool to assess obesity in weightlifters like this client. Consequently, you complete skinfold anthropometry assessment of his body composition and determine he is 20 percent body fat. Clearly, blithely trusting the results of the BMI assessment would have resulted in very inaccurate feedback being given to the client: he would have been told he is obese when the reality was quite different. This example illustrates how taking the time to review the extent to which an assessment was thorough and performed well can help keep you from making a grievous error.

Assuming the fitness assessment was acceptable, the next step of "I" is to compare your client's results to age- and sex-specific normative data. It is important to compare your client's results to their peers, since there is an age-associated decline in a number of fitness components. While physical activity or exercise can blunt this decline, it cannot entirely stop it (ACSM 2009). There are also differences in fitness-related performance measures between men and women, and some of these differences appear to be due to their sex (e.g., Joyner 2017). Consequently, it is inappropriate to compare a client to people who are not their peers.

Regardless, completing this step in "I" is not difficult and well worth doing, since it provides you with considerable useful information. First, it enables you to gauge the relative fitness of your client, or how your client compares to other people like them. Relatively speaking, are they in "good" shape, "poor" shape, or somewhere in-between? Second, it helps you decide which components of physical fitness most need to be addressed with the exercise prescription. Based on their fitness assessment, which of the five components of fitness did they perform most poorly on? Is this the component they should focus on most when they start their exercise program? Or is there another component that may be more critical because it will be more beneficial for improving their overall health? Third, it makes it easier to explain to your client what the fitness assessment results mean. Most people have an intuitive understanding of percentiles, which is what is used in most normative data sets. They are analogous to an exam grade, where a lower score is generally worse and a higher score is better. For fitness assessment norms, a score at the 50th percentile is considered average, scores above the 80th percentile are excellent, and scores below the 20th percentile are very poor (Cooper Institute 2013).

Let's look at an example of how normative data can be useful to you when working with a client. Table 2.4 lists fictional normative data for men 50–59 years old. The aforementioned new client is a 52-year-old male, so this table provides the relevant data of people similar to him in age and gender. His results for each of the five components of fitness are circled in the table. Since all five components are represented, the assessment was thorough; in the absence of any other information about the assessment, we don't know if it was performed well.

What is the client's relative fitness? By comparing his absolute scores to the percentile rankings, we can sort his results for each component of the assessment from best to worst:

Muscular Strength	99th percentile
Muscular Endurance	95th "
Body Composition	75th "
Flexibility	50th "
Cardiorespiratory Fitness	20th "

Again, higher rankings suggest a higher level of fitness and scores above the 80th percentile are "excellent" and scores at the 50th percentile are "average." We can quickly ascertain that, compared to other men about his age, he is very fit in his muscular strength and endurance, well above average in his body composition, average in his flexibility, and very poor in his cardiorespiratory fitness. By comparing his results to a large group of his peers, we are able to prioritize what he should focus on with his exercise program. In this case, it is quite evident that his cardiorespiratory fitness most needs to be improved.

TABLE 2.4
Fitness Norms for Males Age 50–59 Years Old

Percentile Ranking	Cardiorespiratory Fitness VO₂ max (ml/kg/min)	Flexibility Sit-n-Reach (inches)	Muscular Endurance Sit-ups (#/min)	Muscular Strength Bench Press 1RM (% of body wt.)	Body Composition Skinfolds (% body fat)
99	52.7	>18.7	>41.2	>103	9.8
95	47.2	18.7	41.2	103.2	13.1
90	45.4	17.7	37.7	95.7	15.7
85	42.8	16.5	34.2	91.2	16.5
80	42.1	16.2	33.7	88.7	18.1
75	40.1	15.2	31.2	85.2	18.4
70	39.7	15.2	29.7	82.7	19.7
65	38.1	14.2	28.2	79.2	19.9
60	37.9	14.2	26.7	77.7	21.0
55	36.3	13.2	25.2	75.2	21.2
50	36.1	13.2	24.7	73.7	22.3
45	34.9	12.2	23.2	71.2	22.4
40	34.3	12.0	22.7	69.7	23.6
35	33.2	10.7	20.2	68.2	23.8
30	32.5	10.7	19.7	66.7	25.0
25	31.2	9.5	18.2	64.2	25.3
20	31.0	9.2	17.7	61.7	26.8
15	29.1	8.0	15.2	58.2	27.4
10	28.1	7.2	13.7	55.7	29.3
5	25.2	5.2	10.2	51.2	30.9
1	21.5	<5.2	<10	<51	35.1

Normative data from Cooper Institute (2013) Adapted by Warren Franke

Recall that this client indicated that he was motivated to join your health/fitness facility in order to get expert guidance as to how to get stronger. Compared to his peers, he is already very strong. However, his cardiorespiratory fitness is quite poor. Besides being the "weak link" in his overall physical fitness, poor cardiorespiratory fitness is associated with several chronic diseases and premature death (Blair and Morris 2009; Ross et al. 2016). Thus, you think your client should, at least initially, focus on working on this rather than improving his already excellent muscular strength.

How do you convince your client to modify his fitness goals? Normative data help. While some of the results of a fitness assessment are esoteric to lay people, expressing them as percentile rankings make the comparisons more intuitive. Much like a grade on an examination, a ranking closer to 100 is better than a ranking closer to 0. Thus, you can tell him that he is stronger than 99 percent of his peers but his cardiorespiratory fitness is better than only 20 percent of them. With these peer comparisons, he can readily comprehend that his cardiorespiratory fitness is worse than any other component of his physical fitness and analogous to a failing grade. He may then be more willing to re-consider his exercise goals and shift his training focus from muscular strength to cardiorespiratory fitness. Thus, the use of normative data made it easier for you to evaluate the results of the fitness assessment, correctly prioritize the exercise prescription, and educate your client about these results.

OVERVIEW: PRESCRIBING THE EXERCISE PROGRAM

As you can see, "I" helps to lay the foundation for developing the exercise program, or the "P" of CRIPL. By using the norms to rank order, and subsequently prioritize, the client's components of physical fitness, you can determine how best to balance what the client *wants* to work on versus what the client *needs* to work on. The aforementioned client *wants* to work on his muscular strength, but based on his fitness assessment, he *needs* to work on his cardiorespiratory fitness. In talking to the client, the normative rankings should make it easier to convince him why this is the case. Hopefully, the client better understands the rationale for focusing on improving his cardiorespiratory fitness more so than improving his already-excellent muscular strength. You can then develop an exercise prescription that is an acceptable middle ground between the two. Fortunately, in the vast majority of cases with real-life clients, the results of the fitness assessment are usually aligned with the client's goals. So, this balancing act of "needs" versus "wants" is not nearly as challenging as this example!

The next step in "P" is to design the exercise program. Learning how to develop complete, focused exercise prescriptions that are specific to the client is the focus of the remainder of much of this book. For now, suffice it to say that developing exercise prescriptions is an art as well as a science. This book will focus on the science of developing exercise prescriptions, or what research suggests are the best methods for developing each component of fitness. The art of exercise prescriptions, or adapting this information to best fit the client's unique circumstances, is largely based on professional experience.

OVERVIEW: LIFESTYLE CHANGES

Finally, the last component of CRIPL, "L" or Lifestyle Changes, reminds you that following an exercise prescription requires changes in the client's behaviors and that an exercise prescription should be more holistic than simply providing an exercise program. Many personal trainers work under the assumption that if they develop a good program, then adhering to it is fairly simple—you tell the client what to do and they happily do it. Unfortunately, it is not nearly as straightforward as that. For perspective, consider that about 50 percent of new exercisers drop out of physical activity intervention research studies (Marcus et al. 2006). This abysmal dropout rate was in interventions *specifically designed* to promote exercise adherence! In typical health/fitness facilities, where these methodologies are usually not employed, the dropout rate is almost certainly higher. If your client is a new exerciser, it is important to recognize that you need to focus as much on exercise adherence as on the details of an exercise prescription. Consequently, the nature and extent of your interactions will likely differ between new and veteran exercisers.

An additional concern with implementing an exercise program is that it is not uncommon for both clients and personal trainers to focus largely on *just* the exercise prescription. While an exercise program should improve a client's physical fitness, it should also help improve their overall health. To that end, the "L" component helps guide you in developing a more holistic wellness prescription while remembering the unique needs of the client. These needs vary from client to client. They may include your considering the steps needed to help the client reduce their risk for chronic diseases if the client has multiple risk factors for CVD or, if the client has not been physically active, considering how best to accommodate the unique needs of a beginning versus a long-term exerciser. In addition, helping the client improve his/her health may entail encouraging them to see a specialist. For example, if your new client is morbidly obese, then enlisting the assistance of a Registered Dietitian Nutritionist is critical to increasing the likelihood of the client successfully losing weight.

In the case of the weightlifting client described previously (Table 2.4), it is important that he recognizes that improving his cardiorespiratory fitness will also result in improvements to his overall health and reductions in his risk for noncommunicable, chronic diseases like CVD. So, it is important for him to work on his cardiorespiratory fitness, even if it may seem tangential to his primary fitness goals. How will he go about adopting these new exercise behaviors? That is a major component of your role in this process—helping this client be successful by helping him learn how to adopt these new behaviors.

In summary, the two primary lifestyle changes that are typically encountered in "L" revolve around helping the client to (1) begin and successfully adhere to a program of regular exercise and (2) modify their health behaviors in order to reduce their risk for the major noncommunicable disease of cardiovascular disease. As with "P," blending these different aspects together into a coherent, cohesive program depends on your professional expertise and is as much an art as a science.

EMERGENCY PROCEDURES: RESPONDING TO AN ADVERSE EVENT

The best way to respond to an adverse event is to prevent it from happening. While emergency procedures are not an overt part of CRIPL, doing CRIPL well is an important contributor to reducing the risk of an adverse event occurring. Adequate preparticipation screening (i.e., the "C" and "R" of CRIPL) will definitely reduce this risk. Likewise, assessing the client's capabilities (i.e., administering a fitness assessment, the "I" of CRIPL) followed by the thoughtful development of an exercise prescription (i.e., the "P" of CRIPL) will help reduce the risk for an adverse event by ensuring that the client is exercising at a level commensurate with their capabilities. Finally, adequate supervision and monitoring of the client as they exercise (i.e., high quality exercise leadership) on safe, well-maintained equipment in a clean, well-lit environment (i.e., the health/fitness facility) will further reduce the risk. Nevertheless, this risk will not be eliminated completely. Therefore, it is critically important to be prepared to respond to an emergency.

From the broad perspective of a health/fitness facility, there needs to be a systematic approach to reducing risk and responding to emergencies. An excellent resource for developing this approach is *ACSM's Health/Fitness Facility Standards and Guidelines* (American College of Sports Medicine 2019). For our purposes here, the focus will be on the expectations of a health/fitness facility catering primarily to low or moderate risk clients.

Recall that the most worrisome adverse events are life-threatening ones and the most common of these is cardiac arrest. For perspective, in a poll of 533 facilities, 35 percent had experienced a cardiac event that required CPR/AED and/or calling 911 within the previous five years (Craig 2014). It is strongly recommended that health/fitness facilities provide staff members the opportunity to be trained and certified in first aid, CPR, and AED use (ACSM 2019). Even if these opportunities are not made available to you by the facility, it is important that you be certified and, more importantly, competent to provide basic care. If your health/fitness facility has an automated external defibrillator (AED), then you should also be competent to use it. Both the American Heart Association (http://www.heart.org/) and American Red Cross (http://www.redcross.org/) offer training courses for CPR and AED skills. Since not all adverse events are life-threatening, such as muscle strains and cuts, you are encouraged to be trained in providing basic first aid. The Red Cross offers a variety of first aid courses.

Developing these individual skills is only part of responding to an emergency. You also need to know how your skills fit into your health/fitness facility's emergency response plan. Every facility should have written emergency response policies and procedures designed to cover the major emergency situations likely to be encountered in the facility. As described in the aforementioned Guidelines (ACSM 2019) and summarized in Table 2.5, these procedures should be reviewed with staff regularly (ideally, every three months) and the emergency response actually rehearsed at least twice annually. Key issues are that the response plan includes steps on how each emergency situation should be handled and each staff member knows his/her responsibilities for each situation. In other words, while it may not be your responsibility to develop the facility's emergency response procedures, it is definitely your responsibility to know what you are expected to do.

If an AED is in the facility, its use should be incorporated into the aforementioned emergency response plan, reviews, and practice drills. Rapid defibrillation is critical to successful recovery from most cardiac arrests. It is essential that the AED be quickly deployed when needed. To that end, the AED needs to be accessible by everyone (including the public), its location well marked, and no more than a 1.5-minute walk (or ~500 feet) to where it is likely to be needed (ACSM 2012). Again, as a staff member, it is absolutely your responsibility to know where the AED is and how to use it.

Finally, health/fitness facilities should have a system in place for documenting incidents (ACSM 2019). Doing so helps to reduce the potential liability of the facility, regardless of whether the incident is minor or major. A written incident report form documents what transpired. While an internet search will quickly reveal hundreds of samples, it is important that the facility's legal counsel approve the form that is used. Regardless of the choice, the form should be completed as soon as possible after the incident. This can be helpful in case litigation occurs and also to determine if further actions need to be taken, such as revising emergency procedures. The incident should be reviewed with the responding staff and facility management to do so. If a major adverse event occurred, the form should be forwarded to the facility's legal counsel and insurance provider so they are apprised of the event. The facility management should also follow up with the affected client to ensure that they can address any questions or concerns that the client may have.

TABLE 2.5
ACSM Standards for Emergency Planning and Policies

1. Facility operators must have written emergency response policies and procedures, which shall be reviewed regularly and physically rehearsed a minimum of twice annually. These policies shall enable staff to respond to basic first-aid situations and other emergency events in an appropriate and timely manner.

2. Facility operators shall ensure that a safety audit is conducted that routinely inspects all areas of the facility to reduce or eliminate unsafe hazards that may cause injury to employees and health/fitness facility members or users.

3. Facility operators shall have a written system for sharing information with members and users, employees, and independent contractors regarding the handling of potentially hazardous materials, including the handling of bodily fluids by the facility staff in accordance with the guidelines of the U.S. Occupational Safety and Health Administration (OSHA).

4. In addition to complying with all applicable federal, state, and local requirements relating to automated external defibrillators (AEDs), all facilities (staffed or unstaffed) shall have as part of their written emergency response policies and procedures a public access defibrillation (PAD) program in accordance with generally accepted practice.

5. AEDs in a facility shall be located to allow a time from collapse, caused by cardiac arrest, to defibrillation of three to five minutes or less. A three-minute response time can be used to help determine how many AEDs are needed and where to place them.

6. A skills review, practice sessions, and a practice drill with the AED shall be conducted a minimum of every six months, covering a variety of potential emergency situations (e.g., water, presence of a pacemaker, children).

7. A staffed facility shall assign at least one staff member to be on duty, during all facility operating hours, who is currently trained and certified in the delivery of cardiopulmonary resuscitation (CPR) and in the administration of an AED.

8. Unstaffed facilities must comply with all applicable federal, state, and local requirements relating to AEDs. Unstaffed facilities shall have as part of their written emergency response policies and procedures a PAD program as a means by which either members and users or an external emergency responder can respond from time of collapse to defibrillation in five minutes or less.

PUTTING IT ALL TOGETHER

The goals of this chapter were threefold. The first goal was to introduce you to a tool, CRIPL, which is designed to help you remember what steps to follow when working with a client as well as the order to follow when doing so. To that end, the bulk of this chapter has been devoted to providing you with an overview of how to use CRIPL. It should help you keep your professional "toolbox" more organized. The "C" and "R" of CRIPL are used to perform preparticipation screening. The second goal was to help you understand how to do preparticipation screening well. Preparticipation screening is the first step in working with a client. This information is critical to helping you decide if the client is an appropriate candidate for your health/fitness facility and vice versa. It is critical that preparticipation screening is something you do with every new client—and do it well. Even under the best of circumstances, including when preparticipation screening has been perfectly performed, adverse events may still occur. Consequently, the third goal of this chapter was to provide you with an overview of how to create an emergency response system in your health/fitness facility and help you understand what your responsibilities may be in the event of an emergency.

The "C" in CRIPL was covered in-depth in this chapter. The remainder of this book is focused on helping you learn how to use the remaining components of CRIPL to best meet the needs of your clients in your role as an exercise professional.

APPENDIX 1.   SAMPLE HEALTH/MEDICAL HISTORY FORM

HEALTH/MEDICAL HISTORY

Today's Date: Feb / 8 / 2019

Personal Information

Name: Joe Keuhl   Age: 51   Date of Birth: Aug / 3 / 1960 Sex: M

Address: 0103 Wallace Dr.   Telephone No: 555-1458

Employer: Auto Parts Store   e-mail address: —

Emergency Information

Personal Physician: Dr. Bill Quackus   Physician's Telephone No: don't know

Physician's Address: _____

Individual to be contacted in case of an emergency: Mary Keuhl

Relationship to you: Wife

Home Address: Same   Home Telephone No: Same

Work Address: _____   Work Telephone No: _____

Do you have medical alert identification? _____ YES X NO

If YES, where is it located? _____

Current Medications (include ALL medications)

Name of Drug	Dosage; Times/day	Why are you on this drug?
baby aspirin	1 / day	heart health
Multivitamin	1 / day	overall health

Physician Visits

Please list the last three (3) times you saw a physician or other health care provider, were hospitalized or had surgery.

When?	Why (flu, surgery, etc.)?	What was done?
June, last year	annual physical	told to diet and exercise

Family History

Have any members of your immediate family had, or currently have, any of the following?

	Heart Disease	Stroke	Diabetes	Sudden Death	Pulmonary Disease	Age of onset
Mother	X (surgery)					72
Father						
Sisters						
Brothers						
Aunts/Uncles						
Grandparents						
Don't know						

Personal Medical History

Do you have any known allergies? _____ YES __X__ NO If YES, please explain: _____

Please check the following disease conditions that you **had** or currently **have**:

____ Heart attack	____ Heart surgery (catheter, bypass)	____ Heart valve problems
____ Angina pectoris	____ Pacemaker or defibrillator	____ Aneurysm
____ Peripheral vascular disease (blockages of blood vessels in legs)		__X__ High blood pressure
____ Deep vein thrombosis/phlebitis	____ Diabetes	__X__ High blood cholesterol
____ Stroke/transient ischemic attacks	____ Anemia	____ High blood triglycerides
____ Abnormal heart rhythm	____ Asthma	____ Emphysema
____ Bronchitis	____ Abnormal lung function	____ Hernia
____ Cancer	____ Infectious mononucleosis	____ Hepatitis
____ Thyroid problems	____ Gout	____ Epilepsy or seizures
____ Rheumatic fever	____ Osteoporosis	____ Depression
____ Eating disorder	____ Other	____ *None*

Please provide dates and explanation to any of the above which you checked, or any OTHER condition you have that is not listed here: _at last check-up, told they were high but don't know what they are._

Do you use tobacco products? __X__ YES _____ NO. If YES, what kind, how much and for how long? _____
Since college but down to ½ pack per day now

What is your cholesterol level? _____ mg/dl _____X_____ don't know

What is your blood glucose level? _____ mg/dl _____X_____ don't know

What is your *resting* blood pressure? _____ mm Hg _____X_____ don't know

Have you experienced, or do you currently experience, any of the following on a *recurring* basis?

	AT REST: YES	NO	**DURING EXERTION:** YES	NO
Discomfort in the chest, jaw, neck or arms		X		X
(such as tightness, pressure, pain, tingling, heaviness, burning, numbness)				
Dizziness, lightheadedness, fainting		X		X
Temporary blurring of vision		X		X
Temporary slurring or loss of speech		X		X
Transient numbness or tingling in arm or leg		X		X
Shortness of breath		X	X	
Rapid or skipped heart beats or palpitations		X	X	
(esp. if associated with physical activity, eating a large meal, emotional upset or cold exposure)				
Leg pain ("cramping")		X		X

If YES to any of the above, please explain: _If I work really hard, I feel these._
If I stop to rest, they go away

Orthopedic/Musculoskeletal Injuries

Please check the following disease or conditions which you had or currently have:

____ Arthritis	____ Muscle weakness	____ Head injury
____ Swollen joints	____ Stiff or painful muscles	X Shoulder injury
____ Painful feet	____ Fractures or dislocations	____ Ankle injury
____ Severe muscle strain	____ Tennis elbow	____ Whiplash or neck
____ Limited range of motion	____ Torn ligaments	injury
in any joint	____ Pinched nerve	____ Slipped disc
____ Bursitis	____ "Trick" knee/knee injury	____ Osteoporosis
____ ANY OTHER condition which affects your mobility		____ *None*

Do any of the above limit your ability to exercise? ____ YES X NO   If YES to any of the above,

please explain: _hurt in high school_

Activity History

Please list any physical or recreational activities that you *currently do* or *have done* on a regular basis.

Activity	Frequency (days/week)	Time (min/session)	How long (years)
Walking	3	20	10 years, but quit 5 years ago

Which of the following best describes your physical activity habits?

____ I am thinking about becoming more active in the next month or so.

 X I am trying to become more active now but have yet to begin.

____ I have begun being more active but started less 3 months ago.

____ I have been physically active and have been that way for more than 3 months.

____ I have been physically active and now need to become even more active.

Diet History

What is do you consider a "good" weight for you? __170__ Lbs. When did you weigh this? __5 yrs ago__ What is the most you have ever weighed? __200__ Lbs. When did you weigh this? __now__ In the past 5 years, how often have you attempted to lose weight? __none__

What diets did you use? __none__

How many meals do you usually eat per day? __3__

How many cups of coffee or caffeinated beverages do you drink per day? __8__

How many servings (1 shot, glass of wine, 12 oz of beer) do you drink per week? __14__

On average, how often do you eat the following foods *per week?*

__5__ cheeses (cheddar, American, etc.)   __1__ eggs (alone or in foods)   __3__ poultry

__5__ fast foods (McDonalds, etc.)   __0__ fried foods (non fast foods)   __0__ non diet pop

__10__ snack foods (chips, cookies, desserts, "junk" food, etc)

Vocational History

What is your present occupation? __Manager, Auto parts store__

Years at present occupation: __15__

Hours worked per day: __varies - work 60-60 hrs/week__ Days per week: _____ Shift: _____

How would you perceive the **average** *physical* demands of your job (check one):

__X__ light   _____ fairly light   _____ somewhat hard   _____ hard   _____ very hard

Briefly describe what your job involves: __making decisions, working with employees and customers__

Approximately what percentage of your day is spent:

__50%__ sitting __50%__ standing   _____ walking   _____ carrying or lifting objects

Please describe any objects you must lift and/or carry at your job: __office stuff, auto parts off of shelves__

Are you exposed to excessive heat, cold, air pollution, or other environmental hazards at your job?

_____ YES __X__ NO If YES, please describe: _____

On a scale of 1 to 10, how would you perceive the **average** *psychological stressfulness* of your **job?**

Severity of stress:

(not at all)   1   2   3   4   5   6   (7)   8   9   10 (very)

Frequency of stress:

(not at all)   1   2   3   4   5   6   (7)   8   9   10 (very)

How would you perceive the **average** *psychological stressfulness* of the rest of your **life?**

(little or no stress)   1   2   (3)   4   5   6   7   8   9   10 (very high)

APPENDIX 2. SAMPLE MEDICAL CLEARANCE FORM

MEDICAL CLEARANCE FORM

A patient of yours, _____,
has expressed an interest in taking part in a program of progressive physical exercise at the (INSERT YOUR HEALTH/FITNESS FACILITY NAME HERE). **The purpose of this form is to make you, the physician, aware that the above individual wishes to start an exercise program and gain your input** so that we can provide this individual with a safe and effective exercise program.

We require general physical fitness assessments of all new clients as well as completion of a medical history. Our participants are generally prescribed an exercise intensity range of 50-85% of their maximal heart rate range. The specific intensity recommended is dependent on factors such as previous exercise history/tolerance, current fitness level, age, physical limitations, and *the feedback we receive from you.*

In order to provide a safe and effective exercise program for your patient, please be kind enough to answer the following questions:

1. Does this individual have any physical limitations/conditions, which you feel warrants the **complete exclusion** of exercise for your patient (yes/no)?

    _____ YES _____ NO

    If "yes," please explain:

    _____

    _____

    _____

2. Does this individual have any physical limitations/conditions which you feel warrants **limiting or modifying** their exercise program (yes/no)?

    _____ YES _____ NO

    If "yes," please explain:

    _____

    _____

    _____

3.   Additional Comments?

    _____

    _____

    _____

    _____

    _____

Physician's Signatur e _____

Name (please print) _____

Date _____

If you have any questions or concerns pertaining to this form and/or your patient's participation in the HEALTH/FITNESS FACILITY program, please feel free to contact YOUR NAME at either PHONE NUMBER or EMAIL ADDRESS. **Thank you for your assistance.**

Please mail the completed form to: YOUR NAME
HEALTH/FITNESS FACILITY NAME
ADDRESS
CITY, STATE ZIP CODE

To be completed by the participant if he/she does not wish to notify their physician:

<u>PHYSICIAN AWARENESS WAIVER</u>

The HEALTH/FITNESS FACILITY encourages all individuals to consult with their personal physician prior to beginning any exercise program. If you choose not to obtain a signed Medical Clearance form, you must sign the following statement.

I, _____ have been informed of the recommendation to obtain a signed Medical Clearance for participation in a progressive exercise/fitness program. Being fully informed of the recommendation for physician's approval, it is my knowing and voluntary decision *not* to seek physician's advice before participant in testing and/or an exercise program.

I fully understand the strenuous nature of this program and accept complete responsibility for my health and well-being in this voluntary exercise program and related testing, and understand that no responsibility is assumed by any employees or affiliates of the HEALTH/FITNESS FACILITY.

_____   _____
Signature   Date

REFERENCES

Albert, C. M., M. A. Mittleman, C. U. Chae, I. M. Lee, C. H. Hennekens, and J. E. Manson. 2000. "Triggering of Sudden Death from Cardiac Causes by Vigorous Exertion." *N Engl J Med*. 343: 1355–61.

———. 2018. *ACSM's Guidelines for Exercise Testing and Prescription*. 10th ed. Baltimore: Wolters Kluwer.

———. 2019. *ACSM's Health/Fitness Facility Standards and Guidelines*. 5th ed. Champaign: Human Kinetics.

American College of Sports Medicine, W. J. Chodzko-Zajko, D. N. Proctor, M. A. Fiatarone Singh, C. T. Minson, C. R. Nigg, G. J. Salem, and J. S. Skinner. 2009. "American College of Sports Medicine Position Stand. Exercise and Physical Activity for Older Adults." *Med Sci Sports Exerc*. 41: 1510–30.

American Diabetes Association. 2002. "Diabetes Mellitus and Exercise." *Diabetes Care* 25: S64–S68.

Balady, G. J., B. Chaitman, D. Driscoll, C. Foster, E. Froelicher, N. Gordon, R. Pate, J. Rippe, and T. Bazzarre. 1998. Recommendations for Cardiovascular Screening, Staffing, and Emergency Policies at Health/Fitness Facilities. *Circulation* 97: 2283–93.

Benjamin, A. S., P. Muntner, A. Alonso, M. S. Bittencourt, C. W. Callaway, A. P. Carson, A. M. Chamberlain, et al. 2019. On Behalf of the American Heart Association Council on Epidemiology and Prevention Statistics Committee and Stroke Statistics Subcommittee. "Heart Disease and Stroke Statistics—2019 Update: A Report from the American Heart Association." *Circulation* 139: e1–e473.

Blair, S. N., and J. N. Morris. 2009. "Healthy Hearts—And the Universal Benefits of Being Physically Active: Physical Activity and Health." *Annals of Epidemiology* 19: 253–256.

Cooper Institute. 2013. *Physical Fitness Assessments and Norms for Adults and Law Enforcement*. Dallas: Cooper Institute.

Craig, A. C. 2014. "A National Investigation of Pre-Activity Health Screening Procedures in Fitness Facilities: Perspectives from American College of Sports Medicine Certified Health Fitness Specialists." *Graduate Theses and Dissertations*. http://scholarcommons.usf.edu/etd/5461.

D'Agostino, R. B. Sr., R. S. Vasan, M. J. Pencina, P. A. Wolf, M. Cobain, J. M. Massaro, and W. B. Kannel. 2008. General Cardiovascular Risk Profile for Use in Primary Care: The Framingham Heart Study. *Circulation* 117: 743–53.

Eichler, K., M. A. Puhan, J. Steurer, and L. M. Bachmann. 2007. "Prediction of First Coronary Events with the Framingham Score: A Systematic Review." *American Heart Journal* 153: 722–731.e8.

Franke, W. D. 2005. "Covering All Bases: Working with New Clients." *ACSM's Health & Fitness Journal* 9: 13–17.

Franklin, B. A. 2014. "Preventing Exercise-Related Cardiovascular Events: Is a Medical Examination More Urgent for Physical Activity or Inactivity?" *Circulation* 129: 1081–84.

Franklin, B. A., and C. J. Lavie. 2011. "Triggers of Acute Cardiovascular Events and Potential Preventive Strategies: Prophylactic Role of Regular Exercise." *Physician and Sportsmedicine* 39: 11–21.

Goff, D. C. Jr., D. M. Lloyd-Jones, G. Bennett, S. Coady, R. B. D'Agostino Sr., R. Gibbons, P. Green-land, et al. 2014. "2013 ACC/AHA Guideline on the Assessment of Cardiovascular Risk: A Report of the American College of Cardiology/American Heart Association Task Force on Practice Guidelines." *J Am Coll Cardiol* 63: 2935–59.

Goodman, J. M., S. G. Thomas, and J. Burr. 2011. "Evidence-Based Risk Assessment and Recommendations for Exercise Testing and Physical Activity Clearance in Apparently Healthy Individuals." *Appl Physiol Nutr Metab.* 36: S14–32.

Herbert, W. G., D. L. Herbert, K. J. McInnis, P. M. Ribisl, B. A. Franklin, M. Callahan, A. W. Hood. 2007. "Cardiovascular Emergency Preparedness in Recreation Facilities at Major US Universities: College Fitness Center Emergency Readiness." *Prev Cardiol* 10: 128–33.

IHRSA. 2018. "Latest Data Shows U.S. Health Club Industry Serves 70.2 Million." Accessed January 30, 2019. https://www.ihrsa.org/publications/the-2017-ihrsa-health-club-consumer-report/.

James, P. A., S. Oparil, B. L. Carter, W. C. Cushman, C. Dennison-Himmelfarb, J. Handler, and D. T. Lackland, et al. 2014. "2014 Evidence-Based Guideline for the Management of High Blood Pressure in Adults: Report from the Panel Members Appointed to the Eighth Joint National Committee (JNC 8)." *JAMA* 311: 507–20.

Joyner, M. J. 2017. "Physiological Limits to Endurance Exercise Performance: Influence of Sex." *J Physiol* 595: 2949–54.

Lloyd-Jones, D. M., Y. Hong, D. Labarthe, D. Mozaffarian, L. J. Appel, L. Van Horn, K. Greenlund, et al. 2010. On Behalf of the American Heart Association Strategic Planning Task Force and Statistics Committee. "Defining and Setting National Goals for Cardiovascular Health Promotion and Disease Reduction: The American Heart Association's Strategic Impact Goal through 2020 and Beyond." *Circulation* 121: 586–613.

Marcus, B. H., D. M. Williams, P. M. Dubbert, J. F. Sallis, A. C. King, A. K. Yancey, B. A. Franklin, D. Buchner, S. R. Daniels, R. P. Claytor. 2006. "Physical Activity Intervention Studies: What We Know and What We Need to Know: A Scientific Statement from the American Heart Association Council on Nutrition, Physical Activity, and Metabolism (Subcommittee on Physical Activity); Council on Cardiovascular Disease in the Young; and the Interdisciplinary Working Group on Quality of Care and Outcomes Research." *Circulation* 114: 2739–52.

Marijon. E., A. Uy-Evanadao, K. Reinier, C. Teodorescu, K. Narayanan, X. Jouven, K. Gunson,, J. Jui, and S. S. Chugh. 2015. "Sudden Cardiac Arrest During Sports Activity in Middle Age." *Circulation* 131: 1384–91.

McConaghy, J. R., and R. S. Oza. 2013. "Outpatient Diagnosis of Acute Chest Pain in Adults." *American Family Physician* 87: 177–82.

McInnis, K., W. Herbert, D. Herbert, J. Herbert, P. Ribisl, and B. Franklin. 2001. Low Compliance with National Standards for Cardiovascular Emergency Preparedness at Health Clubs. *Chest* 120: 283–88.

Mittleman, M. A., M. Maclure, G. H. Tofler, J. B. Sherwood, R. J. Goldberg, and J. E. Muller. 1993. "Triggering of Acute Myocardial Infarction by Heavy Physical Exertion." *N Engl J Med* 329: 1677–1783.

Mittleman, M. A., and E. Mostofsky. 2011. "Physical, Psychological and Chemical Triggers of Acute Cardiovascular Events: Preventive Strategies." *Circulation* 124: 346–54.

Morrey, M. A., S. B. Finnie, D. D. Hensrud, and B. A. Warren. 2002. Screening, Staffing, and Emergency Preparedness at Worksite Wellness Facilities. *Medicine and Science in Sports and Exercise* 34: 239–44.

Pasco, J. A., G. C. Nicholson, S. L. Brennan, and M. A. Kotowicz. 2012. "Prevalence of Obesity and the Relationship between the Body Mass Index and Body Fat: Cross-Sectional, Population-Based Data. *PLoS ONE.* 7: e29580. doi:10.1371/journal.pone.0029580.

Patil, H. R., and A. Magalski. 2015. "Sudden Cardiac Arrest during Sports Activity in Middle Age." Accessed January 30, 2019. https://www.acc.org/latest-in-cardiology/articles/2015/09/29/11/34/sudden-cardiac-arrest-during-sports-activity-in-middle-age.

Riebe, D., B. A. Franklin, P. D. Thompson, C. E. Garber, G. P. Whitfield, M. Magal, and L. S. Pescatello. 2015. Updating ACSM's Recommendations for Exercise Preparticipation Health Screening. *Med Sci Sports Exerc.* 47: 2473–79.

Romero-Corral, A., V. K. Somers, J. Sierra-Johnson, R. J. Thomas, K. R. Bailey, M. L. Collazo-Clavell, T. G. Allison, J. Korinek, J. A. Batsis, and F. Lopez-Jimenez. 2008. "Accuracy of Body Mass Index to Diagnose Obesity in the US Adult Population." *Int J Obes (Lond)* 32: 959–66.

Ross R., S. N. Blair, R. Arena, T. S. Church, J-P Després, B. A. Franklin, W. L. Haskell, L. A. Kaminsky, B. D. Levine, C. J. Lavie, J. Myers, J. Niebauer, R. Sallis, S. S. Sawada, X. Sui, and U. Wisløff; on behalf of the American Heart Association Physical Activity Committee of the Council on Lifestyle and Cardiometabolic Health; Council on Clinical Cardiology; Council on Epidemiology and Prevention; Council on Cardiovascular and Stroke Nursing; Council on Functional Genomics and Translational Biology; and Stroke Council. 2016. "Importance of Assessing Cardiorespiratory Fitness in Clinical Practice: A Case for Fitness as a Clinical Vital Sign: A Scientific Statement from the American Heart Association." *Circulation* 134: e653–e699

van Teeffelen, W. M., M. F. de Beus, A. Mosterd, M. L. Bots, W. L. Mosterd, J. Pool, P. A. Doevendans, and D. E. Grobbee. 2009. "Risk Factors for Exercise-Related Acute Cardiac Events. A Case-Control Study." *British Journal of Sports Medicine* 43: 722–25.

Warburton, D. E., V. K. Jamnik, S. S. D. Bredin, and N. Gledhill. 2011. On Behalf of the PAR-Q+ Research Collaboration. International Launch of the PAR-Q+ and ePARmed-X+. "The Physical Activity Readiness Questionnaire (PAR-Q+) and Electronic Physical Activity Readiness Medical Examination (ePARmed-X+)." *Health & Fitness Journal of Canada* 4: 3–23.

Whelton P. K., R. M. Carey, W. S. Aronow, D. E. Casey, Jr., K. J. Collins, C. Dennison Himmelfarb, S. M. DePalma, S. Gidding, K. A. Jamerson, D. W. Jones, E. J. MacLaughlin, P. Muntner, B. Ovbiagele, S. C. Smith Jr., C. C. Spencer, R. S. Stafford, S. J. Taler, R. J. Thomas, K. A. Williams Sr., J. D. Williamson, J. T. Wright Jr. 2018. 2017 ACC/AHA/AAPA/ABC/ACPM/AGS/APhA/ASH/ASPC/NMA/PCNA Guideline for the Prevention, Detection, Evaluation, and Management of High Blood Pressure in Adults: A Report of the American College of Cardiology/American Heart Association Task Force on Clinical Practice Guidelines. *J Am Coll Cardiol* 71: e127–248.

CHAPTER 3

Understanding Cardiovascular Disease and Helping Your Clients Reduce Their Risk

OVERVIEW

This book is focused on helping you develop the exercise programming skills needed to be successful when working with apparently healthy clients in a high quality health/fitness facility. So, you may be asking yourself, "If this book is oriented toward healthy clients, why is there a chapter on cardiovascular disease?" This is a reasonable question. The answer was hinted at in Chapter 2 but, in a nutshell, cardiovascular disease (CVD) is epidemic in the United States and you are ideally positioned to help change that. In the United States, over 121 million adults have at least one of the conditions that comprise CVD. This represents about 48 percent of the adult population (Benjamin et al. 2019). CVD is the most prevalent noncommunicable disease in the United States. The net effect is that many of your clients are likely either living with some form of CVD or are at an increased risk for developing it. For many of them, one of the motivations for beginning to exercise, and working with you, will be reducing this risk. Consequently, you should have the knowledge and skills needed to help them.

Because of this need, this chapter has four goals related to the aforementioned. First, it is hoped that your understanding of how CVD affects overall health in the United States will be enhanced. Second, you will understand how the process underlying how the most lethal CVD, ischemic heart disease, occurs and in so doing, will understand why CVD risk factors affect this risk. Third, you will learn what the major risk factors are for these diseases and how you can help a client modify them. Finally, you will learn how CRIPL can be used to help you understand how risk factor assessment and risk factor modification fit into the context of working with a client.

CVD has been the leading cause of deaths in the United States in every year since 1900, but for 1918 when the influenza pandemic occurred (Piness 1920). In assessing the lethality of CVD, consider this: cancer is the second leading cause of death, and eliminating all cancers would increase the average life expectancy by approximately three years. While this would be wonderful, it pales in contrast to the seven years gained by eliminating all forms of CVD (Mozaffarian et al. 2015).

Health/fitness professionals can play a major role in helping to reduce this profound, and increasing, negative influence CVD has on the quantity and quality of life. This is because the leading causes of death and years of life lost due to disability are all risk factors for CVD: poor diet, tobacco use, hypertension, high body mass index, and diabetes (US Burden of Disease Collaborators 2018). These risk factors are all related to lifestyle behaviors, which health/fitness professionals can help their clients change. As Sun Tzu said in his *The Art of War* over 2,500 years ago, "Know your enemy and know yourself and you can fight a hundred battles without disaster" (Sun Tzu 2002). If you know the "enemy" of CVD and know how you can help your clients through risk factor modification, then you are well-prepared to successfully "fight the battle" of reducing the epidemic of CVD—and helping your clients live longer and healthier lives.

As suggested by Sun Tzu, the first step in understanding CVD is to know what it is. CVD is not just one disease but a name given to a constellation of diseases that affect the cardiovascular system. The American Heart Association's definition of CVD includes "rheumatic fever/rheumatic heart disease, hypertensive diseases; ischemic (coronary) heart disease; pulmonary heart disease and diseases of pulmonary circulation; other forms of heart disease; cerebrovascular disease (stroke); atherosclerosis; other diseases of arteries, arterioles, and capillaries; diseases of veins, lymphatics, and lymph nodes not classified elsewhere; other unspecified disorders of the circulatory system and (when data are available) congenital cardiovascular defects" (Benjamin et al. 2019). This list is lengthy because it is so encompassing. However, each of these diseases varies considerably in the number of people who have it; consequently, the likelihood that you will encounter people with them varies, too. The two conditions you *are* most likely to encounter are the two most prevalent ones—hypertension and ischemic, or coronary, heart disease.

Hypertension is the most common CVD since 46 percent of adults ≥20 years of age in the US, or 116.4 million people, have elevated blood pressure. The second most common is ischemic heart disease which affects 6.7 percent, or 18.2 million, of adults. A related CVD is strokes. An estimated 7 million adults report having had a stroke and almost 800,000 people have a stroke each year (Benjamin et al. 2019). Most strokes (87 percent) are ischemic strokes, or "heart attacks in the brain." The pathology underlying an ischemic stroke is essentially the same as for ischemic heart disease. Therefore, it is mentioned here because reducing the risk of strokes entails the same methods to reduce the risk of ischemic heart disease.

The risks associated with hypertension, ischemic heart disease, and stroke are intertwined. Hypertension is a disease in its own right, accounting for about 10 percent of deaths due to CVD each year (Benjamin et al. 2019). Eliminating hypertension could reduce CVD mortality by over 30 percent (Patel et al. 2015). Hypertension is also a major risk factor for ischemic heart disease (IHD) and stroke. While hypertension is much more prevalent, IHD is, by far, the leading cause of death in the United States (US Burden of Disease Collaborators 2018). IHD and stroke account for over 60 percent of CVD deaths in the US (43.2 and 16.9 percent, respectively; Benjamin et al. 2019). Ischemic heart disease is also the worldwide leading disease for disability (Murray and Lopez 2013). In the United States, it is the leading cause of years of life lost due to premature death (US Burden of Disease Collaborators 2018). Because of the widespread impact that IHD has, it is not uncommon for people to refer to "CVD" or "heart disease" in casual conversations when they are really talking about IHD.

Ischemic heart disease is characterized by the accumulation of atherosclerotic plaque in the lining of the coronary arteries (Figure 3.1). This phenomenon also occurs in the arteries of the brain. The lumen of the artery, or the opening through which blood flows, becomes progressively narrowed.

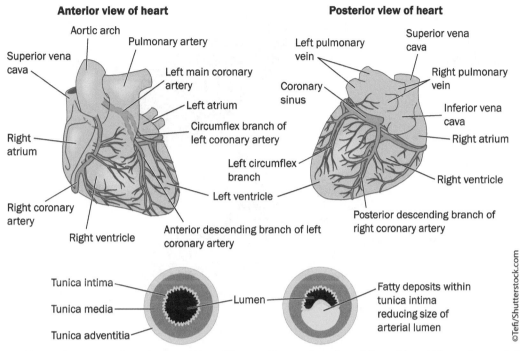

Figure 3.1   Major Coronary Arteries and How Plaque Formation Can Affect Blood Flow through Them

Eventually, blood flow through the coronary artery and into the heart muscle, or myocardium, becomes impaired. This reduced blood flow can lead to an imbalance between the heart's demand for oxygen and the ability to meet that demand via oxygen-rich blood. This imbalance between myocardial oxygen demand and oxygen supply is called ischemia.

Ischemia is often, but not always (Conti, Bavry, and Petersen 2012), accompanied by chest discomfort, or angina pectoris. The sensation of angina varies from person to person, but it is typically characterized as a pressure, fullness, tightness, dull ache or pain in the chest. It may not be localized over the heart but may be felt in the neck, jaw, shoulder, back, or arm. Angina is an "alarm signal" in that portions of the affected myocardium will begin to die if the ischemia is prolonged. The more severe the ischemia, the quicker that myocardial cell death begins. For perspective, with very severe ischemia caused by a total blockage of a coronary artery, myocardial cells begin to die after approximately fifteen minutes and most of the affected cells have died after sixty minutes of ischemia (Jennings 2013). While this cell death is commonly called a heart attack, it is more correctly termed a myocardial infarction, or MI.

As a health/fitness professional, you will probably spend quite a bit of time helping clients reduce their risk for CVD, in general, and IHD, in particular. Your focus will be on risk factor modification. To fully understand why risk factor modification is important, you need to understand atherogenesis, or "know your enemy." The following section will, therefore, provide a brief overview of the process of atherogenesis.

ATHEROGENESIS

A more correct term for the plaque that ultimately leads to a blockage in coronary arteries is "atheroma." Consequently, the process by which plaque formation occurs is called atherogenesis and a common synonym for the presence of these plaques is atherosclerosis. The predominant components of an atheroma vary over its lifespan but include an accumulation of lipids, smooth muscle cells, and other fibrous tissue (Figure 3.2). Not surprisingly, considerable effort has been devoted to understanding

NORMAL ARTERY

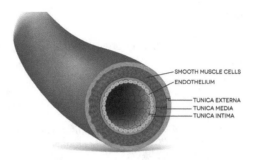

ENDOTHELIAL DISFUNCTION

CHRONIC ENDOTHELIAL INJURY LEADS TO ENDOTHELIAL DISFUNCTION

LOW DENSITY LIPOPROTEIN (LDL) MIGRATES IN TO THE INTIMA AND OXIDIZES

MONOCYTES AND LIMPHOCYTES MIGRATES IN TO THE INTIMA

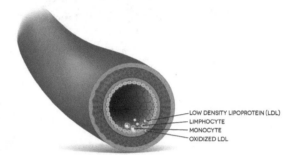

FATTY STREAK FORMATION

MONOCYTES TRANSFORMS INTO THE MACROPHAGES AND "EATS"
OXIDIZED LDL THEN TRANSFORMS INTO THE FOAM CELLS

SMOOTH MUSCLE CELLS MIGRATES INTO THE INTIMA AND ENGULF LIPID

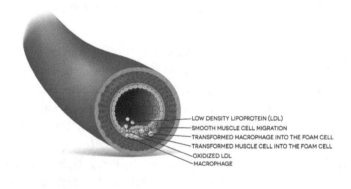

**STABLE (FIBROUS) PLAQUE
FORMATION**

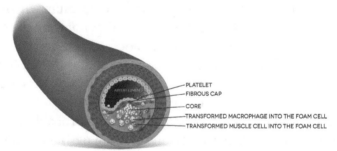

UNSTABLE PLAQUE FORMATION

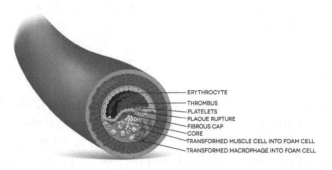

FIGURE 3.2   Progression of Atherosclerosis

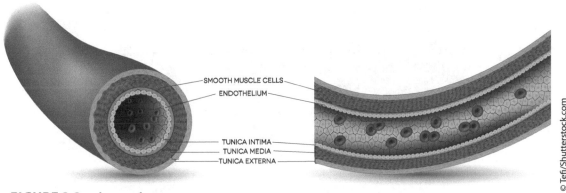

FIGURE 3.3   Artery Anatomy

the mechanisms underlying atherogenesis. In the 1970s, there were at least six hypotheses about the pathogenesis of atherosclerosis (Cowan 1982). Today, the preponderance of evidence supports the response-to-injury hypothesis (Ross and Glomset 1976a, 1976b) such that current research efforts are primarily focused on enhancing our understanding of this process.

Arteries, such as the coronary arteries, consist of three layers (Figure 3.3). The innermost layer, called the tunica intima, is comprised primarily of a single layer of endothelial cells. If an artery is thought of as a garden hose, then the lining of the hose, which is contacted by the water flowing through it, is the intima. The opening through which water flows in a hose, or blood in an artery, is called the lumen. The middle layer of the artery, or tunica media, consists primarily of smooth muscle cells (SMC) embedded in a complex extracellular matrix. Constriction and dilation of the blood vessel are mediated by these SMC contracting and relaxing. The outermost layer of the artery, or tunica adventitia, is analogous to the exterior of the garden hose and contains mast cells, nerve endings, and microvessels (Libby, Ridker, and Hansson 2011).

All the cell types that are involved in atherogenesis have functions which support the normal functioning of the blood vessel. However, in response to chronic, repeated injury to the endothelial cells, these normal functions become skewed which leads to atheroma development (Table 3.1).

TABLE 3.1		
Cell Type	**Normal Role**	**Atherosclerotic Role**
Endothelial Cells	Production of mediators of vascular homeostasis	Activation mediates inflammatory cell recruitment
	Signal transduction	Loss of normal function facilitates smooth muscle cell migration and thrombosis
Smooth Muscle Cells	Vessel contractility	Form fibrous cap, synthesis of extracellular matrix, stabilize lesion Responsible for re-stenosis
Monocytes/ macrophages	Secret cytokines and growth factors	Migrate into core of plaque Form foam cells after scavenging modified lipids Secrete matrix-digesting enzymes that destabilize plaque
Platelets	Mediate thrombosis at sites of vascular injury	Cause thrombosis and embolization at sites of plaque erosion/rupture
From Douglas and Channon (2014)		

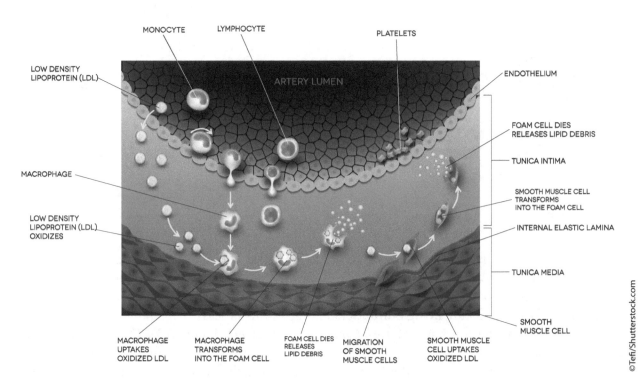

Figure 3.4   Early Development of an Atherosclerotic Plaque, or a Fatty Streak

In a normally functioning blood vessel, blood and its constituent components flow by endothelial cells (Figure 3.3). Unfortunately, many common CVD risk factors, such as high levels of low density lipoproteins in the bloodstream, cause oxidative stress. This stress ultimately leads to endothelial damage (Wu et al. 2017). This damage induces endothelial cells to release adhesion molecules, with vascular cell adhesion molecule-1 (VCAM-1) being a noteworthy one (Falk 2006). These adhesion molecules increase the "stickiness" of the endothelial cells. This causes leukocytes, primarily monocytes but some T lymphocytes, to adhere to them. These cells are components of the body's immune system and, in the early stages of atherogenesis, this endothelial cell activation mimics the body's innate immune response (Hopkins 2013). In other words, many of the contributors to atherogenesis are part of the otherwise-normal inflammatory responses to injury and infection that are mediated by the immune system. This is why the "response-to-injury hypothesis" mentioned earlier is no longer viewed as a hypothesis *per se* but, rather, the way atherogenesis occurs.

Chemoattractants, such as chemokines, entice the attached monocytes to migrate below the endothelial cells (left-hand side of Figure 3.4). The damaged endothelial cells also have changes in their permeability such that low-density lipoprotein cholesterol (LDL) can more easily pass by the endothelial cells and enter into the sub-endothelial space, or the space just below the endothelium but above the tunica media. These LDL become oxidized (oxLDL) and, in so doing, become major chemokines. Monocyte chemotactic protein-1 (MCP-1) is another important chemokine (Falk 2006); MCP-1 can be released by endothelial cells, smooth muscle cells, and endothelial cells. Other inflammatory components of the immune system, such as the cytokine macrophage-colony-stimulating factor (M-CSF), cause the monocytes to differentiate into macrophages (Hansson, Robertson, and Söderberg-Nauclér 2006). Macrophages are a type of white blood cell that normally engulf and digest foreign substances such as cellular debris, microbes, and other pathogens. Unfortunately, with atherogenesis, these macrophages engulf oxLDL. Because they now have scavenger receptors rather than normal LDL receptors, they take up oxLDL in considerable excess of what would be considered "normal." Cholesterol, originating from the oxLDL molecules, accumulates in these macrophages and results in the formation of foam cells, or lipid-filled macrophages. When foam cells accumulate, they form a fatty streak (Figure 3.4); fatty streaks are the first evidence of atherogenesis that can be seen with the naked eye. Several different cytokines, such as interferon-γ, also act on the macrophages to release a number of pro-inflammatory mediators that can exacerbate all the aforementioned processes. Fatty streak development begins at an early age, in childhood.

Over time, some of these foam cells die and release their accumulated lipids. The plaque develops a necrotic core. This core consists of cellular debris and an accumulated pool of the extracellular lipids that were released when the foam cells died. This necrotic core can grow to occupy 30–50 percent of the volume of the arterial wall (Insull 2009). Besides this necrotic core, part of the maturation of the atheroma includes an increased incorporation of smooth muscle cells into the plaque. In other words, the plaque transitions from being a fatty streak, and consisting of mostly lipids, to being a fibrous plaque and having an increasingly larger proportion of fibrous tissues such as smooth muscle cells and collagen (Figure 3.5; Falk 2006). This transition includes the development of a fibrous cap that is over the necrotic core and just under the endothelium (Insull 2009). As the plaque matures, calcification occurs by a number of mechanisms (Nakahara et al. 2017) such that the plaques begin to accumulate deposits of calcium. Calcification is a marker of atherosclerosis. Calcification can be assessed clinically via a computed tomography, or CT, scan. Higher coronary artery calcium scores are associated with greater risk of coronary events, such as a myocardial infarction (Detrano et al. 2008).

For this transition from fatty streak-to-fibrous plaque to occur, several inflammatory cytokines and growth factors, such as MCP-1, facilitate both the migration of SMCs from the tunica media into the intima and the subsequent proliferation of the SMCs (Rudijanto 2007). These SMCs become intermixed with the foam cells to form an intermediate lesion—not quite a fatty streak but not quite a mature, fibrous atheroma. The SMCs also synthesize most of the extracellular matrix molecules, or fibrous tissue, that are found in these maturing lesions. There are several types of these extracellular matrix molecules (e.g., collagen, elastin, proteoglycans) and some of them contribute to forming the fibrous cap overlying the atheroma (right-hand side of Figure 3.5). Eventually, this atheroma can become large enough to interfere with adequate blood flow through the coronary arteries. A mature plaque is characterized by a substantial necrotic core, involvement of SMCs into the plaque, and a robust fibrous cap overlying it (Figure 3.5; Douglas and Channon 2014). The transition from a fatty streak to a mature fibrous plaque can begin in teenagers and young adults. Mature fibrous plaques are typically seen in middle-age and older adults. Compared to people with few CVD risk factors, people with numerous risk factors typically experience a more rapid progression to the larger, fibrous plaques (Insull 2009).

Depending on the structural integrity of the aforementioned fibrous cap, the plaque may be "stable" or "unstable." The fibrous cap of a stable plaque has considerable amounts of connective tissue. The shoulders of the plaque, which is where the fibrous cap merges with the adjacent normal endothelial cells, are relatively thick (Figure 3.5). The likelihood of this stable plaque breaking open is relatively low, because the shoulders are so sturdy. Unfortunately, components of the immune system, such as macrophages, T cells, and mast cells, can produce several types of molecules that lead to a weakening of the fibrous cap shoulders. This is due to reductions in the amount of connective

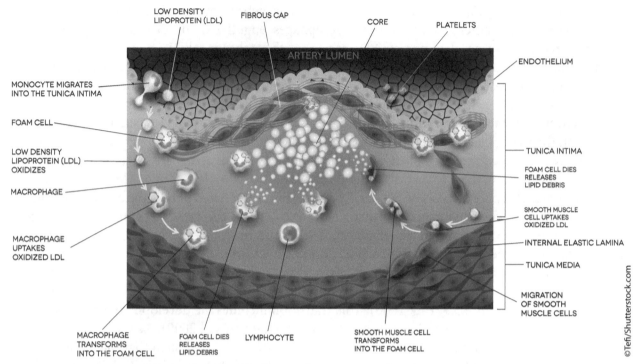

Figure 3.5 Stable Plaque Formation in the Human Artery

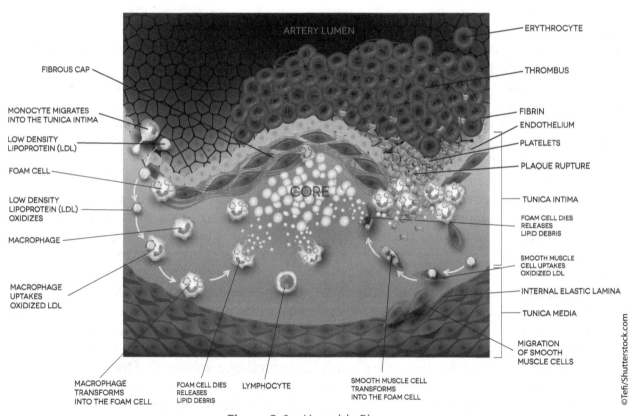

Figure 3.6 Unstable Plaque

tissue in the cap (Hansson, Robertson, and Söderberg-Nauclér 2006; Libby, Ridker, and Hansson 2011). Most myocardial infarctions occur when the fibrous cap becomes damaged, either by cracks or fissures forming on the surface or by erosion of the overlying endothelial cells (Figure 3.6; Hansson, Robertson, and Söderberg-Nauclér 2006). This exposes the underlying plaque to the bloodstream. Platelets are in the bloodstream and become activated by encountering this plaque. They subsequently form a clot, or thrombus, which can hinder blood flow (Figure 3.6). Most heart attacks, or myocardial infarctions, are the result of a plaque rupture leading to clot formation that, in turn, occludes blood flow through the lumen of the artery. This occlusion causes ischemia that can quickly lead to the MI.

Unfortunately, this disruption can also occur in plaques that are relatively immature, such as fatty streaks or intermediate lesions. Because they do not have significant amounts of fibrous tissue and lack a robust overlying cap, these plaques tend to be more fragile than stable mature plaques. Moreover, they often are not large enough to hinder blood flow through the artery. As such, they typically do not cause any symptoms, such as angina, so the person is often completely unaware they have ischemic heart disease (IHD). Consequently, the first symptom the person may experience is sudden cardiac death.

The process of atherogenesis is summarized in Figure 3.7 (Wang et al. 2012) on the following two pages. As will be shown in the next section of this chapter, this process can either be initiated or exacerbated by CVD risk factors. By understanding how atherogenesis unfolds, you will have a better understanding of why these risk factors are just that—factors that increase the risk of developing IHD. You will also begin to appreciate why risk factor modification is so critical to reducing the development of clinically significant CVD and IHD in your clients.

Figure 3.7   (a) Normal artery with occasional circulating lipids. (b) Early fatty streak formation with dysfunctional endothelial cells, lipid insudation and the macrophages transformation into foam cells. (c) Early atherosclerotic plaque with a fibrous cap, smooth muscle migration, and macrophage infiltration. The vascular wall is starting to remodel to accommodate the plaque. (d) Unstable atherosclerotic plaque with extensive infiltration by T-lymphocytes, a thin fibrous cap, and a necrotic core. (e) Older plaques can become stable after forming a thick fibrous cap with lots of calcifications. While these plaques can be large, they have a relatively low risk of rupture. (f) Plaque complication. An unstable plaque may erode or rupture. This plaque shows erosion of the surface that bulges into the bloodstream. An acute thrombus is forming at the endothelial cell erosion—a collection of fibrin and platelets is seen. This could lead to occlusion of the vessel. This erosion could lead to angina pectoris or an acute myocardial infarction, especially in regions with insufficient collaterals. (g) Plaque complication. The unstable plaque has ruptured at one shoulder area, where the fibrous surface had become thin (because of the effects of inflammatory cells), with release of plaque debris and hemorrhage into the plaque as well as the formation of overlying thrombus. These changes can lead to occlusion and myocardial infarction.

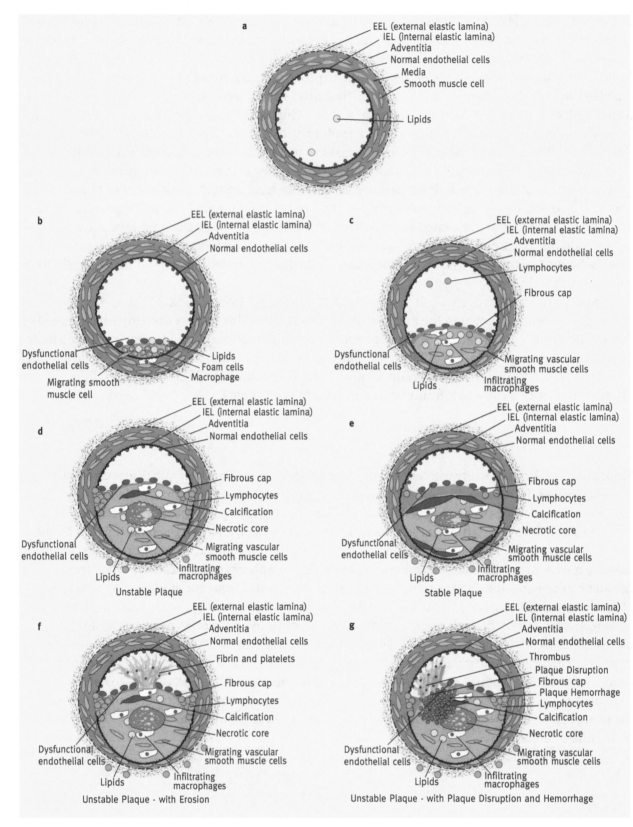

Figure and figure caption from Wang and colleagues (2012).

THE MAJOR CVD RISK FACTORS

Atherogenesis is an incredibly complex process and our understanding of how it happens is continually being refined. Our understanding of factors which contribute to atherogenesis is likewise an ongoing process. Consequently, the list of major CVD risk factors and the criteria at which they become a risk factor is also evolving. For example, in 1960, a desirable serum total cholesterol was thought to be <260 mg/dl (Kannel et al. 1961) but we now know that <200 mg/dl is a more appropriate goal. Prior to 1997, a fasting plasma glucose value of 140 mg/dl or higher was the criteria for diabetes but was lowered to 126 mg/dl in recognition of the pathogenesis of diabetes (Expert Committee 1997). And, as described previously, in 2017, the criteria blood pressures for hypertension were lowered from 140 and 90 mmHg (systolic and diastolic, respectively) to 130 and 80 mmHg (Whelton et al. 2018). Nevertheless, it has long been recognized that most CVD risk factors are modifiable and can be improved with the adoption of appropriate healthy behaviors. The current list of CVD risk factors are in Table 3.2 (ACSM 2018) on the previous page.

TABLE 3.2	
CVD Risk Factors and Desired Values for an Adults	
Risk Factor	**Desired Value**
Age	Men <45 yrs, Women <55 yrs
Family History	No first degree relative (i.e., parents, offspring, siblings) of client with a diagnosis of heart disease or sudden death before the age of 55 if relative is male or 65 if female.
Blood pressure*	<120/<80 mm Hg
Current smoking	Never or quit
Dyslipidemia *†	Total cholesterol: <200 mg/dL Low-density lipoprotein (LDL) cholesterol: < 100 mg/dL High-density lipoprotein (HDL) cholesterol: >40 mg/dl
Obesity	Body mass index <25 kg/m2
Prediabetes/ Diabetes Melltus*	Fasting plasma glucose <100mg/dL
Physical activity	>150 min/wk moderate intensity or >75 min/wk vigorous intensity or a combination
* And not on medications to achieve the desired value † Elevations in cholesterol or LDL is a risk factor and low HDL is another, separate risk factor	
American College of Sports Medicine, *Guidelines for Exercise Testing and Prescription,* Tenth Edition. © 2018 by Wolters Kluwer Health. Reprinted by permission.	

The American Heart Association (AHA) promotes improving cardiovascular health while preventing CVD. The AHA considers ideal cardiovascular health as being the simultaneous presence of four health behaviors and three health factors, or outcomes (Lloyd-Jones et al. 2010), collectively called "Life's Simple 7" (Table 3.3).

While the AHA has striven to reduce CVD mortality throughout its existence, the Simple 7 reflects an increased emphasis on improving overall cardiovascular health via behavior change or "promoting health" rather than just improving CVD risk factors. In other words, while reducing, say, a client's total cholesterol to <200 mg/dl is a goal as a CVD risk factor (Table 3.2), the Simple 7 emphasizes achieving this goal through adopting healthy lifestyle behaviors (Table 3.3) as opposed to simply taking a lipid lowering medication. It is important to recognize that these health behaviors have a robust, positive influence on overall CVD risk above and beyond just the outcome of improved risk factors like a lowered total cholesterol (Folsom et al. 2011). These differences between the two tables may seem subtle, but they should influence your approach to working with a client. So take a minute to consider them.

As a health/fitness professional, it is important that you know the goal values for each risk factor, or what the desired outcome is, so you can educate your clients. However, your client will also need to know how to achieve these goals. You can help your client do so by teaching them how to adopt healthy lifestyle behaviors. For perspective, about 80 percent of all CVD could be prevented if the Simple 7 were achieved by everyone (Mozaffarian et al. 2015). Unfortunately, only about 18 percent of adults in the US have ideal levels in at least five of these seven goals and less than 1 percent have ideal levels in all seven (Benjamin et al. 2019). Clearly, you will not lack for clients that need your help. Thus, the following sections will be devoted to helping you understand the major CVD risk factors.

TABLE 3.3	
The American Heart Association's "Life's Simple 7"	
Goal	**Definition of Ideal Health**
Health Behaviors (goal behaviors)	
• Not smoking	Never or quit 12 mo ago
• Sufficient physical activity	>150 min/wk of moderate intensity or >75 min/wk of vigorous intensity or some combination
• A healthy diet pattern	4–5 components of the 5 assessed
• Normal weight	Body mass index <25 kg/m2
Health Factors (goal outcomes achieved in the absence of drug treatment)	
• Optimal total cholesterol	<200 mg/dl
• Optimal blood pressure	<120/<80 mm Hg
• Optimal glucose	<100 mg/dl
From https://www.heart.org/en/healthy-living/healthy-lifestyle/my-life-check--lifes-simple-7 and Lloyd-Jones et al., (2010)	

© Lauren Lesley Studio/Shutterstock.com

Age

The death rate due to CVD increases with age. For example, in 2016, only about 20,000 people under the age of 45 died due to CVD. This increased in a stepwise fashion with each additional decade of life such that over 500,000 people aged 75 and over died from CVD (Benjamin et al. 2019). Heart disease morbidity increases with age too. In 2016, about 10 percent of men between the ages of 45–54 reported a history of heart disease. This prevalence was 16.4 percent in men 55–64 years and 33.9 percent in men aged 65 and over (National Center for Health Statistics 2018). Women are typically stricken with CVD about ten years later than men and often with greater lethality. A significant contributor to this delay is the protective effects associated with higher estrogen levels in premenopausal women (Meyer and Barton 2016). To a lesser extent, part of the difference may be due to younger men frequently having worse risk factor profiles than similarly-aged women (Anand et al. 2008; Jousilahti et al. 1999). Regardless, the criteria where age becomes a CVD risk factor is 45 years for men and 55 years for women. After these ages, the risk for IHD increases similarly in both sexes (McSweeney et al. 2016). Since aging is inevitable, it is an unmodifiable risk factor.

Family History

The risk for CVD is increased if the client has a history of the disease within their first-degree relatives, meaning parents, siblings, and their children. First-degree relatives share about 50 percent of their genetic variation among each other and CVD is increasingly recognized as having a genetic component. The risk increases with either increases in the number of relatives with CVD or decreases in the age at which their relatives were diagnosed. For example, compared to someone without a family history, having a parent experiencing a myocardial infarction increases a client's risk

© Rohit Seth/Shutterstock.com

by about 62 percent but, if this occurred to both parents, by more than twice that (Chow et al. 2011). If the parent was relatively young, this risk is increased even more. Some of this association is likely behavioral (e.g., siblings were raised by the same parents and learned unhealthy lifestyle habits from those parents) (Yusuf et al. 2004). Nevertheless, the genetic component remains even after considering other CVD risk factors (Chow et al. 2011; Mozaffarian et al. 2015) and is associated with a 70 percent increased risk in women and 100 percent increase in men (Lloyd-Jones et al. 2004).

Besides the risk of developing CVD, the likelihood of developing modifiable CVD risk factors also has a genetic component. For example, there is a heritable component to being physically active, unhealthy body weight, smoking, food preferences, elevated blood lipids, hypertension, and diabetes (Benjamin et al. 2019). The criteria for when family history becomes a risk factor is if a first-degree relative was diagnosed with ischemic heart disease, coronary revascularization, or sudden death before the age of fifty-five if a male relative or sixty-five if female. These differences in age of the relatives accounts for the previously discussed sex-related age differences in CVD onset. Since one's genes cannot be changed, family history is considered an unmodifiable risk factor.

When working with a client, it is important to be mindful of the importance of age and family history in contributing to the client's overall risk for CVD. However, these risk factors are unmodifiable so the client cannot change them. Fortunately, the risk factors to be reviewed in the subsequent sections of this chapter are modifiable. Both you and the client should put more time and effort into addressing these.

Hypertension

Recall that hypertension is the most common cardiovascular disease and a potent risk factor for ischemic heart disease (IHD). It is also the leading cause of disease-related disability in the world (Murray and Lopez 2013). In the United States, hypertension ranks among the top three causes (Murray et al. 2013). Almost half of adult Americans are hypertensive and of these people, almost 35 percent are unaware they have high blood pressure (Benjamin et al. 2019). African Americans have among the highest prevalence

of hypertension in the world (57.6 percent for males, 53.2 percent for females). Not surprisingly, hypertension is a major contributor to the increased prevalence of IHD and stroke seen in African Americans (Mozaffarian et al. 2015). While the prevalence of hypertension rises dramatically with age, the negative effects of hypertension are seen in younger people, too. In adults younger than forty years old, those with Stage 1 hypertension experienced ~25 percent higher incidence of ischemic heart disease over the next ten years compared to normotensive adults (Son et al. 2018).

An optimal BP is <120/80. The risk for IHD and stroke increases linearly with increases in either systolic or diastolic blood pressure. It is doubled for every 20 mmHg increase in systolic or 10 mmHg diastolic blood pressure (Chobanian et al. 2003). Consequently, the current criteria for defining someone as hypertensive is (a) having blood pressures >130 mmHg systolic or >80 mmHg diastolic (either/or, need not be both), (b) taking antihypertensive medication, or (c) having been told at least twice by a physician or other health professional that they have high blood pressure (Table 3.4; Whelton et al. 2018). Individuals with elevated, yet not hypertensive, blood pressures are at an increased risk because of the aforementioned linear increase.

It has been estimated that completely eliminating hypertension would reduce CVD-related mortality by about 30 percent and 38 percent in men and women, respectively (Patel et al. 2015). While it is doubtful that this goal can be achieved, several lifestyle choices affect the development of hypertension and improving these will help lower blood pressure. These modifications are especially effective in clients with either an elevated blood pressure or Stage 1 hypertension. They are also beneficial for many of the other modifiable risk factors that are reviewed in this chapter.

TABLE 3.4
Categories of Blood Pressure (BP) in Adults

BP Category	Systolic BP		Diastolic BP
Normal	<120 mm Hg	and	<80 mm Hg
Elevated	120–129 mm Hg	and	<80 mm Hg
Stage 1 Hypertension	130–139 mm Hg	or	80–89 mm Hg
Stage 2 Hypertension	>140 mm Hg	or	>90 mm Hg
Clients with SBP and DBP in 2 categories should be classified into the higher BP category.			

Reproduced with permission of ELSEVIER INC. from the *Journal of the American College of Cardiology*, 71(19), 2018 by American College of Cardiology. Permission conveyed through Copyright Clearance Center, Inc.

The first modification is eating healthy, meaning embracing a heart-healthy pattern of eating rather than focusing on individual dietary components. Specifically, the ideal heart-healthy diet would emphasize an "intake of vegetables, fruits, and whole grains; include low-fat dairy products, poultry, fish, legumes, nontropical vegetable oils, and nuts; and limit intake of sweets, sugar-sweetened beverages, and red meats" (Eckel et al. 2014). This diet, commonly called DASH or Dietary Approaches to Stop Hypertension, differs only modestly from what is generally considered to be a healthy eating pattern following current USDA guidelines (Table 3.5). Healthy eating patterns are covered in much more detail in Chapter 8.

An additional dietary recommendation for hypertensives is to reduce sodium intake to < 2400 mg/d or about 1 teaspoon of table salt; reducing it to < 1500 mg/d will likely lower BP even more and should be the ultimate goal for a hypertensive (Eckel et al. 2014). Increasing potassium intake helps to blunt the effect of sodium on blood pressure (Whelton et al. 2018). The second lifestyle modification is regular physical activity (Eckel et al. 2014). This will be discussed in detail in

TABLE 3.5
Comparison of Dietary Intakes between DASH and Standard Recommended Healthy Eating Pattern for a 2000 Calorie per Day Diet

	DASH	Healthy Eating Pattern
Grains and grain products	6–8	6 oz-eq
Vegetables	4–5	2.5 cups
Fruits	4–5	2 cups
Lowfat dairy products	2–3	3 cups
Lean meats, poultry, and fish	≤6	5.5 oz-eq
Nuts, seeds, and dry beans	4–5/week	(part of "Lean meat, poultry, and fish")
Fats and oils	2–3	6 tsp
Sweets	<5/week	267 discretionary calories

From USDHHS and USDA (2015).

Chapter 4, but for now, suffice it to say that current recommendations are 150 minutes of moderate intensity exercise or 75 minutes of vigorous exercise or some combination of the two (USDHHS 2018). Body mass index is strongly associated with hypertension, with some studies suggesting a nearly linear relationship between BMI and BP (Whelton et al. 2018). Consequently, the third recommendation is to achieve and maintain a healthy weight, defined as a body mass index < 25 kg/ m² (Chobanian et al. 2003). Finally, moderate alcohol consumption, defined as one to two drinks per day depending on body weight, may help lower BP (Chobanian et al. 2003).

These guidelines work well for everyone. However, if your client is hypertensive and a person of color, then it is especially critical that you assist them in reducing their high blood pressure. Morbidity and mortality due to hypertension tends to be higher in Hispanic Americans and African Americans than in whites. This is because, in Hispanic Americans, there is a greater prevalence of a lack of awareness and treatment. Blacks tend to be as aware of their hypertension as whites yet hypertension is often more severe and less responsive to some medications (Benjamin et al. 2019). Regardless of a client's race or ethnicity, if they have been prescribed medications to lower their hypertension, they should still embrace these lifestyle modifications in order to lower their overall risk for CVD.

Current Smoking

Smoking is lethal. Worldwide, it kills over 7 million people annually (Benjamin et al. 2019). Smokers die at least ten years earlier, on average, than people who have never smoked (Jha et al. 2013). Smoking, including exposure to secondhand smoke, is second only to hypertension in its impact on disease-related disability in the world (Murray and Lopez 2013). In the United States, it is the leading cause of disability-adjusted life years (U.S. Burden of Disease Collaborators 2018). This is in spite of the fact that the number of cigarette smokers in the US in 2017 was at its lowest in over fifty years (Wang et al. 2018). In women, the IHD risk due to smoking is higher than that of men, by ~25 percent (Huxley and Woodward 2011).

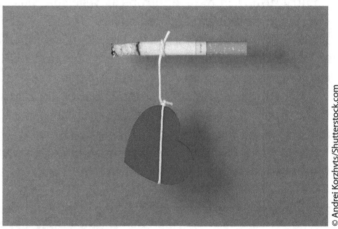

While cigarettes are most commonly mentioned in discussions about IHD, tobacco ingestion of *any* kind contributes to this risk (Piano et al. 2010). For example, in one study, cigarette smoking tripled the risk for a myocardial infarction while chewing tobacco doubled the risk (Teo et al. 2006). E-cigarettes, while only a relatively recent addition to cigarette alternatives, already appear to contribute to CVD risk (Bhatnagar 2016; Olfert et al. 2018). This may be due to e-cigarette users being exposed to tobacco-related toxicants. Exclusive e-cigarette users have higher levels of chemicals such as nicotine and metals like lead and cadmium in their bodies, albeit at lower concentrations than cigarette smokers (Goniewicz et al. 2018). Unfortunately, e-cigarettes are perceived as a safer alternative to cigarettes; for perspective, since 2011, cigarette use in high school students has declined to 8.0 percent while e-cig use has increased sevenfold to 11.3 percent (National Center for Health Statistics 2018). Nevertheless, cigarette smoking *per se* has received the most attention.

There is a dose response relationship between tobacco use and CVD risk. The risk changes due to the number of cigarettes smoked, how long the person has smoked, and the depth of inhalation. The latter is typically not considered in epidemiologic studies because it is difficult to quantify accurately. Smoking any number of cigarettes daily sharply increases IHD and stroke risk and the risk associated with smoking just one cigarette per day was almost half that associated with smoking twenty cigarettes per day (Hackshaw et al. 2018). Another large review study found that, compared to not smoking, the risk is doubled with ten cigarettes per day and quadrupled in people who smoke at least a pack a day (Teo et al. 2006). Regardless, it is clear that the risk of heart disease from smoking one cigarette daily is *not* 1/20 the risk of smoking twenty cigarettes, which is a pack per day. In addition, the risk for IHD-related death increases the longer a person has smoked; in smokers fifty-five to seventy-four years of age, about two-thirds of the IHD deaths can be attributed to smoking (USDHHS 2014). However, since younger people have a lower prevalence of IHD than older adults, younger smokers have a relatively higher risk for IHD compared to their nonsmoking peers.

Because of the aforementioned dose-response relationship, smoking is quantified in terms of pack-years. Pack-years is calculated as the product of the number of packs of cigarettes smoked daily and the number of years smoked. Recall that a pack holds twenty cigarettes. So someone who smoked ten cigarettes daily for twenty years would have a ten pack-year history (1/2 pack × 20 years = 10 pack-years) as would someone who smoked a pack per day for ten years (1 pack × 10 years = 10 pack-years). Of course, not all tobacco users smoke just cigarettes. When working with these individuals, an online resource may be helpful (search for "Smoking Pack Years," currently at http:// smokingpackyears.com). It considers other types of tobacco products, such as cigars, pipes, and cigarillos, in estimating pack-years.

Passive smoking, or exposure to secondhand smoke, increases both IHD risk and stroke risk by about 25 percent (USDHHS 2014). This risk may be as much as 65 percent higher based on studies that actually measured exposure rather than relying on the less-accurate self-report measure (Lv et al. 2015). About 34,000 nonsmokers die prematurely each year due to IHD as a consequence of passive smoking (USDHHS 2014). Just as with direct smoking, this increase varies by the amount of exposure. Nevertheless, the risk is relatively more severe at lower levels of exposure, where nonsmokers are physiologically more sensitive to the negative effects of tobacco. Not surprisingly, municipalities that enact smoke-free laws have a marked reduction in CVD events (Tan and Glants 2012). One study found a 25 percent reduction following the implementation of smoke-free policies in restaurants and bars and this rose to 46 percent when workplace policies were included (Mayne et al. 2018).

Tobacco use contributes to atherogenesis in a host of ways. Chemicals in the tobacco can damage endothelial cells, promote inflammation, increase the number and activity of macrophages, increase platelet aggregation and promote thrombosis, and increase myocardial demand for oxygen while causing coronary vasoconstriction (USDHHS 2014). Sadly, this list is not all-inclusive. Fortunately, tobacco use is a modifiable risk factor. As alluded to earlier, there is no strong evidence to suggest that smoking less makes a substantive difference in CVD risk (Mozaffarian et al. 2015) so stopping altogether is the desired goal.

Tobacco is highly addictive and quitting is very challenging for most people. But given how harmful tobacco use is, it is worth it. Quitting has positive effects in the short-term (e.g., lessened myocardial demand for oxygen, reduced coronary vasoconstriction) and, over the long-term, will lead to a reduced risk for IHD and other CVD. The risk is elevated for several years after quitting and may remain elevated for up to twenty years in formerly-heavy smokers (Teo et al. 2006). This effect varies by age, too, in that smokers who quit before the age of thirty-five live about as long as never-smokers while smokers who quit near age sixty-five gain about four years of life compared to smokers (Jha et al. 2013). For perspective, these older adults would have gained ~11.5 years if they'd have never smoked. If you are developing a program to help others, a good resource to investigate is the American Lung Association's "Freedom from Smoking" program (currently at www.freedomfromsmoking.org); it can be delivered online, via telephone counseling, and in small groups. Facilitator training is also available.

For the purposes of estimating CVD risk, tobacco use is viewed dichotomously—either "yes" or "no." Despite the data suggesting persistent effects of tobacco use and the dose-response relationship between tobacco use and CVD, the latter includes former smokers regardless of their pack-year history.

Dyslipidemia

Four lipid categories are routinely considered when determining CVD risk. They are total cholesterol, low density lipoproteins (LDL), high density lipoproteins (HDL), and triglycerides. Early in our understanding of risk factors for atherosclerosis, serum total cholesterol was recognized as a major contributor to IHD (Kannel et al. 1961). As our understanding became more complete, the other three lipids were included and are considered important today. Nevertheless, as will be discussed here, our understanding of the role that different lipids play in atherogenesis is far from complete. What is considered clinically important now may be quite different five or ten years from now.

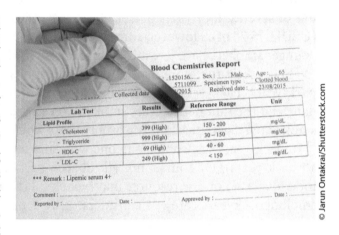

Cholesterol and triglycerides are insoluble in water and, in order to be transported through the bloodstream, are bound up with proteins in complex particles called lipoproteins (Table 3.6). Lipoproteins have a central core of cholesterol esters and triglycerides, which are hydrophobic, around which are accumulations of free cholesterol, phospholipids, and apolipoproteins that are hydrophilic (Feingold and Grunfeld 2018; Superko 2009). Traditionally, lipoproteins have been categorized by their density (Table 3.6) which varies due to the different proportions of their constituent components, such as cholesterol. A total cholesterol measurement is the sum of all the cholesterol fractions of all these lipoproteins.

While lipoproteins are commonly considered categorically, or as discrete types, they are better viewed as being on a continuum since, even within categories, they vary in composition, size, density, and function (Miller et al. 2011). For example, chylomicrons and VLDL will change in size based on the quantity of triglycerides that are in them. If someone ate a high fat meal, then the chylomicrons and VLDL subsequently produced by the liver would have more triglycerides in them and be relatively larger (Feingold and Grunfeld 2018). If these triglycerides were removed by, say, skeletal muscle and adipose tissue for fuel, then the resultant lipoproteins would become smaller. The smaller chylomicrons are now called chylomicron remnants and the smaller VLDL are now called VLDL remnants or, more commonly, IDL. Importantly, smaller lipoproteins (<70 nm in size) freely pass through the endothelial layer and help initiate atherogenesis (Ference et al. 2019). Larger particles do not. As a result, smaller particles of the same category of lipoprotein, such as chylomicron remnants and IDL, can contribute to heart disease while larger particles, such as chylomicrons and VLDL, do not. These size differences are true for all the categories of lipoproteins. Thus, not all LDL are identical nor are all HDL. Nevertheless, in terms of IHD, the most important categories of lipids are LDL and HDL.

Based on the earlier review of the process of atherogenesis, it should be clear now that LDL is heavily involved in the development of IHD. It is the "bad lipoprotein" since, of the lipoproteins,

TABLE 3.6

Categories of Lipoproteins Based on Density Ranges (g/mL) and
Percentage of Cholesterol Contained in Each

Lipoprotein	Density (g/mL)	Cholesterol (%)	Major Lipids
Chylomicrons	<0.94	4–8	triglycerides, cholesterol
Chylomicron remnants	0.940–1.006	15–25	cholesterol
Very low-density lipoproteins (VLDL)	0.940–1.006		triglycerides
Intermediate density lipoprotein (IDL, also called VLDL remnants)	1.006–1.020	38	triglycerides, cholesterol
Low density lipoprotein (LDL)	1.020–1.063	42–52	cholesterol
High density lipoproteins (HDL)	1.063–1.200	15–16	cholesterol, phospholipids

Densities from Superko (2009), cholesterol percentages from Voet and Voet (2010), and major lipids from Feingold and Grunfeld (2018).

it carries the greatest proportion of cholesterol and is the most atherogenic. This is also why early research found high levels of serum cholesterol to be associated with IHD—the high total cholesterol likely reflected an increased LDL. HDL is the "good lipoprotein" since, beginning in the mid-1970s, it became appreciated that high concentrations of HDL are prospectively associated with a reduced risk for IHD (Gordon et al. 1977; Gordon et al. 1989). Regardless of other risk factors, higher levels of HDL are associated with greater reductions in risk (Cooney et al. 2000). For that reason, a HDL >60 mg/dL is considered a negative risk factor. An important mechanism by which HDL reduces risk for IHD is via its ability to remove cholesterol from cells, called reverse cholesterol transport (Feingold and Grunfeld 2018; Fielding and Fielding 1995).

Elevated triglyceride levels are also associated with an increased risk for CVD (Miller et al. 2011). However, the extent to which high triglycerides are an independent risk factor remains debatable. Some research supports this assertion and some suggests otherwise. For example, when the lipoproteins that contain a lot of triglycerides, meaning chylomicrons and VLDL, are broken down into remnant particles, the resulting remnant particles are quite atherogenic (Ference et al. 2019; Miller et al. 2011). This may explain why many people who have an elevated triglyceride level often also have high LDL and low HDL; elevations in the former are causally related to the latter. However, other research suggests that elevated triglycerides are not a risk factor once other risk factors, like LDL and HDL, are considered. The rationale is that all three may be skewed due to poor lifestyle choices which lead to obesity (Miller et al. 2011). Here, several studies have found a greater prevalence of elevated triglycerides in people with higher body mass index levels. Regardless of how elevated triglycerides are mechanistically associated with CVD, they need to be included in any CVD risk assessment.

Table 3.7 provides a listing of when these risk factors become most worrisome and what the desirable, or goal, levels are for these risk factors. Recall that "total cholesterol" reflects all the total

TABLE 3.7
Desirable and Undesirable Lipid Ranges

Lipid	Desirable (mg/dL)	High Risk (mg/dL)
Total Cholesterol	<200	>240
Low-density lipoproteins	<100*	≥190
High-density lipoproteins	≥60**	<40
Triglycerides	≤150	≥500
TC/HDL ratio	<4.5	
LDL/HDL ratio	<3.0	

* Depending on the global risk for CVD, the most correct recommendation is to reduce LDL-C 30–50 percent below baseline (Stone et al. 2014); <100 mg/dL is a generalized approximation of this outcome and may provide the most benefit (NCEP, 2002).

** HDL-C above 60 is considered a "negative" risk factor because of its protective effects (American College of Sports Medicine 2014)

cholesterol carried within all these lipoproteins. Since LDL has the greatest proportion of cholesterol, a high total cholesterol value is most likely due to an elevated LDL. In other words, a high total cholesterol, in the absence of any other information, would be interpreted as reflecting an increased risk for CVD that is probably due to an increased LDL. However, this is not always the case. A markedly elevated HDL could result in a high total cholesterol value. In this case, and if HDL had not been measured, then the client might be erroneously concerned that their risk for IHD was increased due to an elevated total cholesterol. While this situation is uncommon, it most definitely happens. In addition, when assessing CVD risk, the combination of LDL and VLDL, termed "non-HDL cholesterol" is more atherogenic than either of these lipoproteins alone (Grundy et al. 2018). This is because the non-HDL number includes a number of lipoproteins that are highly atherogenic besides LDL and VLDL, such as IDL and chylomicron remnants. The take-home message here is to assess as many of the lipoproteins as you can afford to do so—not just total cholesterol.

Nevertheless, of the four lipid categories described in Table 3.7, only three are actually measured as part of a routine laboratory blood lipid panel. The three are total cholesterol, HDL, and triglycerides. LDL are not routinely measured. This is for a variety of reasons (Mora 2009; Superko 2009) including the added expense associated with performing the actual laboratory procedure needed to measure LDL (Mora 2009; Superko 2009). Consequently, LDL is typically estimated rather than measured. The most common formula (Friedewald, Levy, and Fredrickson 1972) for doing so is:

$$LDL = Total\ cholesterol - HDL - (Triglycerides/5)$$

where the concentration of VLDL is estimated as triglycerides/5. This formula works reasonably well for most clients but is far from perfect (Sniderman et al. 2003). It is not usable when the client's triglyceride levels are above 400 mg/dL and it is also inaccurate at lower LDL levels, especially LDL <70 mg/dl (Grundy et al. 2018). In these situations, a physician may be inclined to measure LDL directly rather than estimate it. For these reasons, there is support (Miller et al. 2011), albeit not universal (Stone et al. 2014), for using non-HDL (non-HDL = total cholesterol – HDL) as a surrogate marker of atherogenic lipids. In general, a goal non-HDL is 30 mg/dl higher than the LDL goal.

Regardless of these caveats, when assessing a client's lipid profile, the first step is to determine how the client's lipids compare to the "Desirable" column in Table 3.7. If a client has any lipid values that are outside the "Desirable" column, then efforts need to be made to improve them. Moreover, if any of the client's values are in the "Very High" category, then the client should talk to their personal physician to rule out other issues, such as a familial hyperlipidemia, besides a suboptimal lifestyle. A second consideration is the relative balance of the "bad cholesterol" to the "good cholesterol." Numerous studies suggest that either the TC/HDL or LDL/HDL ratio provide information about a client's risk that neither TC, LDL, nor HDL can provide individually (Elshazly et al. 2015; Millan et al. 2009). Consequently, determine these ratios for your client; goal values for TC/HDL and LDL/HDL are <4.5 and <3.0, respectively (Millan et al. 2009). Because of the aforementioned concerns with the accuracy of LDL assessments, the TC/HDL ratio may be preferable to the LDL/HDL ratio when determining a client's CVD risk.

If the client's lipid profile is less than desirable, the next step is determining how to improve it. Here, the medical community is strongly encouraged to focus on reducing LDL (Grundy et al. 2018). Besides encouraging lifestyle changes, a client's physician may therefore also prescribe lipid lowering medications, such as a statin. Factors that often prompt such a decision are if the client has an elevated LDL (e.g., > 160 mg/dL), is diabetic, or has an increased risk of developing CVD in the next ten years based on the ACC/AHA Risk Algorithm (described later in this chapter) (Grundy et al. 2018). Regardless, lifestyle changes should be an important component of any efforts to improve a lipid profile, since lifestyle behaviors are an important part of the AHA's Simple 7.

Perhaps not too surprisingly, the lifestyle changes that should lower LDL and raise HDL are virtually identical to those that will improve hypertension (Eckel et al. 2014). First, the client should follow a healthy eating pattern (discussed in Chapter 8) or the similar DASH-type eating pattern described previously. As with improving hypertension, the emphasis is on an "intake of vegetables, fruits, and whole grains; include low-fat dairy products, poultry, fish, legumes, nontropical vegetable oils, and nuts; and limit intake of sweets, sugar-sweetened beverages, and red meats" (Eckel et al. 2014). This behavior is for a lifetime. So it should be adapted to fit the client's caloric needs, their personal and cultural preferences, and also considering other medical conditions such as diabetes. In addition, the client should strive to have a diet that results in less than 10 percent of calories from saturated fat and a reduction in calories derived from *trans* fats. These dietary changes are challenging for many people, so do not hesitate to enlist the assistance of a Registered Dietitian Nutritionist in helping your client be successful. An internet search using the term "local RDN" will help you find one (the current website is at http://www.eatright.org/find-an-expert). Second, the client should engage in a program of regular physical activity that is consistent with the latest federal recommendations (USDHHS 2018)—at least 150 minutes per week of moderate intensity exercise, or 75 minutes per week of vigorous intensity exercise or a combination of the two (discussed in detail in Chapter 4). Finally, the client should strive to achieve a healthy weight, defined as a body mass index <25 kg/m². While these recommendations are focused on improving a lipid profile, they are consistent with the dietary guidelines recommended for everyone (USDA 2015; USDHHS 2014).

Recall that while lipoproteins are described categorically (Table 3.7), they really are more on a continuum. Each of the lipoproteins consist of subfractions which differ in their density, composition, and size (German et al. 2006) and which affect their role in IHD. For example, LDL particles vary somewhat in the concentration of cholesterol that are carried. Smaller, denser LDL particles carry less cholesterol than larger, more buoyant LDL particles. However, the dense LDL particles are more atherogenic, probably because they cross the endothelial cell wall more readily and are more readily oxidized (Mudd et al. 2007). Thus, if two clients have the same LDL but one has more of the denser particles, he will have a greater risk for IHD than the other client with more of the "fluffy" particles (Mudd et al. 2007). Unfortunately, these differences will be missed with routine blood work since the assessed lipid levels do not necessarily equate to lipoprotein particle levels. All the LDL particles will be lumped into the category of LDL on the client's blood lipid panel. Likewise, there are subtypes of HDL with HDL2 containing relatively more cholesterol than HDL3 and being associated with increases in IHD (Superko 2009). Again, these differences will be missed with routine blood work.

Given that there are subfractions of each important lipoprotein which appear to contribute more to IHD risk, why are the subfractions not measured routinely? The answer to this question is complex and, if ten experts were asked, you may get ten different answers. However, part of the response may be that the research isn't definitive enough yet to support routinely measuring a specific set of subfractions or lipoprotein particles (Mudd et al. 2007). Many of these additional laboratory tests are expensive so it is not cost-effective to analyze all the potentially relevant subfractions. Another part of the answer may be that, even if the appropriate subfractions were identified and assessed, this added insight probably would not actually change the treatment for the client with elevated LDL. While there are exceptions, for the vast majority of people, it would not. The recommended course of action may change in the future, but for now, the currently recommended treatment is aggressive reduction of LDL using both lifestyle changes and medications, when needed (Eckel et al. 2014; Grundy et al. 2018). The lifestyle changes which will do this should also lower triglycerides and raise HDL.

Obesity

Chapter 8 of this book is devoted to the topic of obesity and weight control, including the negative health implications. Consequently, this section will provide only a brief CVD-focused overview.

Let's begin with what "obesity" is. The Centers for Disease Control and Prevention defines it as "weight that is higher than what is considered as a healthy weight for a given height" (from https://www.cdc.gov/obesity/adult/defining.html). Operationally, the CDC assesses this with body mass index (BMI,

© Monkey Business Images/Shutterstock.com

calculated as weight in kilograms/height in meters squared, or kg/m^2). Based on large-scale studies of the association between BMI and measures of health, the current definitions of healthy weight are given in Table 3.8. BMI is the preferred method of assessing obesity by the World Health Organization (WHO 1995) and is the most common method used for epidemiological studies where large numbers of people are assessed. Mathematically, for average height males and females, a BMI of 30, or the threshold for being considered as "obese," means the client is about 30 to 35 pounds heavier than they would weigh at a BMI of 25. For the majority of people, this extra weight is very likely due to extra fat.

However, as described in Chapter 2 and discussed in more detail in Chapter 8, BMI is far from being an ideal method to assess how healthy a client's weight may be (Romero-Corral et al. 2008). BMI disregards what the weight is—fat, muscle, or something else. Consequently, BMI may misrepresent a client's body composition. For example, BMI assessments of professional and aspiring professional

TABLE 3.8 Health-Related Criteria for Obesity	
Method	**Criteria**
Body Mass Index (kg/m²)	
Underweight	<18.5
Desirable	18.5–24.9
Overweight	25–29.9
Obese	≥30.0
Class 1	30.0–34.9
Class 2	35.0–39.0
Class 3	≥40.0
Waist Circumference (use if BMI <35)*	
Desirable	<102 cm (male), <88 cm (female)
Unhealthy	>102 cm > 88 cm
Body Composition (% body fat)	
Obese male	>25%
Obese female	>35%

Adapted from Cornier et al 2011.

* Most people with BMI >35 will already exceed these criteria because of their excess weight.

football players suggests that linebackers and running backs are morbidly obese when more direct measures of body composition suggest they have desirable levels of body fat (Dengel et al. 2014; Provencher et al. 2018). Clearly, more direct assessments of body composition are needed to truly determine unhealthy levels of "fatness."

Nevertheless, using the definition of a BMI > 30 kg/m², obesity is associated with an increased risk of CVD in large-scale studies (Benjamin et al. 2019; Jiang et al. 2013; Prospective Studies Collaboration 2009; Riaz et al. 2018) and, since 1998, obesity has been classified as a CVD risk factor by the American Heart Association (Eckel et al. 1998). However, the nature and extent of how obesity contributes to CVD is hotly debated. It is too simplistic to state that "a BMI > 30 kg/m² contributes to CVD." There is much more to this relationship than just body weight.

A very important, but often overlooked, component of this debate is accurately defining what a "healthy weight" means. In other words, when is a specific body weight unhealthy? While a BMI of 30 kg/m² is the accepted threshold of being obese, an increasing number of studies do not find obesity to be markedly associated with an increased mortality until BMI exceeds 30 or even 35 kg/m² (Flegal et al. 2013; Yi et al. 2017). Moreover, in people who have CVD, better outcomes are often seen in patients who are overweight or mildly obese than in the normal weight patients (Oktay et al. 2017; Ortega et al. 2016). Consequently, a "healthy weight" for one person may be an "unhealthy weight" for another person, even if both people have the same BMI.

Another part of the debate about this relationship is the extent to which the inclusion of other CVD risk factors reduces the association between obesity and CVD. In other words, is it having an excessive amount of body fat that is the risk factor or is it the other risk factors that an obese person also has that raises their risk for CVD? Many studies (Burke et al. 2008; Emerging Risk Factors Collaboration 2011a; Ortega et al. 2016) suggest that the other risk factors play an important role. While CVD risk factors are common among US adults, the prevalence of risk factors is higher in people who are overweight or obese (Flegal 2006; Saydah et al. 2014). Put another way, overweight people tend to have more CVD risk factors than people with a desired BMI and obese people tend to have even more risk factors.

It is important to note that studies with better, more comprehensive assessments of other risk factors often *do* find a weaker association of obesity with CVD. This finding has led some experts to conclude that obesity is not a risk factor *per se* but is simply an "innocent bystander" to the insidious effects of these other CVD risk factors. This conclusion is likely an overstatement of what is actually the case. First, obese people without other CVD risk factors (often called "metabolically healthy but obese") have a risk for CVD that is higher than their normal weight peers (Ortega et al. 2016). They are also relatively rare in that only about 10 percent of obese people can be considered metabolically healthy (Nichols et al. 2017). Second, the lifestyle behaviors that often lead to someone becoming excessively heavy are also lifestyle behaviors that lead to the majority of the modifiable CVD risk factors—meaning unhealthy eating and not enough physical activity. Nevertheless, metabolically healthy but obese people have a risk for CVD that is lower than their obese peers who do have other risk factors (Ortega et al. 2016). Third, fat cells are metabolically active and may contribute importantly to atherogenesis directly, perhaps by triggering chronic low-grade inflammation in the blood vessels that is a major contributor to atherogenesis (Gregor and Hotamisligril 2011; Parto and Lavie 2017). Fat cells also contribute to CVD risk indirectly, through their influence on the development of other risk factors such as hypertension and diabetes (Bastien et al. 2014; Chrostowska et al. 2013). *Where* the fat cells are located is important, too. Fat around the internal organs, or visceral adipose tissue, is more worrisome than subcutaneous fat. For example, people with a normal BMI but a high waist-to-hip ratio (an indirect measure of visceral adiposity) have a higher mortality than people who are overweight or obese but have a normal waist-to-hip ratio (Sahakyan et al. 2015).

Another factor in the debate about the criticality of obesity to CVD is the role that cardiorespiratory fitness plays in moderating the effects of obesity. Regardless of one's weight, physical activity and, even more so, physical fitness reduce the risk of CVD. Obese, physically inactive adults have a markedly elevated risk for CVD compared to people who have either only one or neither of these two risk factors (Farrell et al. 2014; Lee et al. 1999; Li et al. 2006). Importantly, an increasing number of high-quality studies support the assertion that cardiorespiratory fitness can largely "normalize" the risk of premature death associated with obesity (Barry et al. 2014). In other words, everything else being equal, fit-but-fat individuals have a lower risk of dying prematurely than unfit-normal weight individuals and an overall risk that is almost the same as people who are fit but normal weight.

The mechanisms underlying this finding remain unclear. The current thinking is that fitter people tend to have lower levels of most CVD risk factors and, within the population of heavy people, fitter people tend to also have lower levels of CVD risk factors. Unfortunately, the prevalences of physical inactivity and low fitness are higher in the obese than in the normal weight (Wei et al. 1999) so obesity may be a CVD risk factor partly because of its association with physical inactivity and low fitness. Nevertheless, fit-but-fat people enjoy an almost "normal" CVD risk. It is important to understand, also, that "fit" in this context is better described as "not unfit." This is because, in almost all the relevant studies assessing the fit-but-fat paradigm, "fit" was defined as simply not being in the *bottom 20 percent* of cardiorespiratory fitness of all the people participating in the studies. Here the "fit" category was not just people of better-than-average fitness; rather, it included the other 80 percent of people in these studies! Unfortunately, the number of obese individuals who are in this fit-but-fat category is only about 20 percent of the total number of people who are considered obese (Ortega et al. 2016) and only about 9 percent of obese individuals have above average levels of cardiorespiratory fitness (Duncan 2010).

Importantly, when cardiorespiratory fitness is factored into this assessment, the fit-but-fat people *without* other CVD risk factors do *not* have an elevated risk for CVD compared to their normal weight peers. Since only about 10 percent of people with obesity do not have other risk factors (Nichols et al. 2017) and only about 9 percent have above average fitness (Duncan 2010), the number of people who are fit-but-fat and with no CVD risk factors is relatively small.

A key unanswered question is, "Is there a level of fatness where the negative health effects of excessive weight offset the positive health effects of being fit?" Based on the research, if someone has a BMI between 25 and 35 kg/m², but doesn't have any significant risk factors for CVD and is not unfit, then their excess weight is of no substantive health consequence at all. At higher levels of BMI, the answer remains uncertain. As mentioned previously, fit-fat individuals are relatively uncommon (Duncan 2010; Ortega et al. 2016) and even fewer also have no significant CVD risk factors. The take-home message is that, when working with an obese client, it is far, far more important to focus on changing important lifestyle behaviors, like exercise and a healthy diet, than focusing on the person's weight.

Prediabetes and Diabetes Mellitus

Diabetes mellitus (DM) is a term given to a number of health conditions that are characterized by inadequate regulation of blood glucose. A normal fasting blood glucose level is <100 mg/dL. A fasting blood glucose >126 mg/dL is the threshold for DM and clients with values of 100 to <126 mg/dL are said to have an impaired fasting glucose or be prediabetic. A client who is learning for the first time that they have either DM or is prediabetic should be referred to their personal physician for more definitive assessment. This will likely include

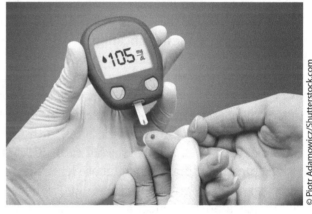

measurement of their glycated hemoglobin levels (A_{1c}); an A_{1c} > 6.5 is indicative of DM while a value > 5.7 suggests prediabetes (Fox et al. 2015). Chronic elevations of glucose in the blood produce higher than normal amounts of glycated hemoglobin; consequently, an elevated A_{1c} reflects average glucose levels over the preceding three months.

Unfortunately, prediabetes and diabetes are common as is ignorance of having the disease. While over 26 million adults have diagnosed diabetes in the US, about 92 million people are prediabetic, and an additional 9.4 million are diabetic and do not know it (Benjamin et al. 2019). While these numbers are staggering, they are expected to rise such that, by 2020, over half of all adults in the United States will have an abnormal fasting glucose (Huffman et al. 2012). About 90–95 percent of diabetics have Type 2 DM (T2DM), characterized by insulin resistance rather than a failure to produce enough insulin.

The risk for premature death is much higher in diabetics than nondiabetics. For example, forty-year-old diabetics typically die about six to seven years younger than their nondiabetic counterparts with CVD being the underlying cause ~60 percent of the time (Emerging Risk Factors Collaboration 2011b). Much like hypertension, there appears to be a relatively continuous association between increases in glucose levels and risk for premature death. For perspective, a fasting glucose of 126 mg/dL is associated with about a twofold higher risk for CVD-related mortality (ERFC 2011b). Because of this, it is critical that diabetics do their best to keep their glucose levels as normal as possible.

Diabetics, especially those with T2DM, typically have other risk factors for CVD. This clustering of risk factors commonly includes obesity, dyslipidemia, and hypertension (Fox et al. 2015). About 66 percent of diabetics are obese (Fryar and Frenk 2014). Likewise, 65 percent of diabetics have elevated LDL and over 70 percent are hypertensive (Centers for Disease Control and Prevention 2014). These co-morbidities certainly contribute to the increased risk for CVD. For example, the metabolically active adipocytes seen with obesity likely contribute to the low-level chronic inflammatory pro-atherogenic state seen with T2DM (van Gaal et al. 2006). In diabetics and compared to nondiabetics, the increased LDL are also more likely to be of the especially atherogenic small, dense type (Dokken 2008; Laakso 2010). There is a genetic component to DM; in one large study, the risk for developing DM increased 6.1-fold if both parents had diabetes (Meigs et al. 2000).

Regardless of these other risk factors, T2DM contributes to atherosclerosis. The lynchpin to this contribution, and the hallmark of T2DM, is insulin resistance. This contributes to atherogenesis in a variety of ways—endothelial dysfunction, an over-activated inflammatory response, more activated leukocytes (white blood cells), and a hypercoagulable state (Dokken 2008; Laakso 2010). In addition, the resulting hyperglycemia leads to an increased production of reactive oxygen species, or "free radicals" (Brownlee 2005; Dokken 2008; Laakso 2010). Through at least four different pathways, this increased oxidative stress is a major contributor to the damage which occurs to both small and large blood vessels (i.e., microvascular and macrovascular damage, respectively). It is for all these reasons that it is imperative that clients with T2DM do all they can to reduce their overall risk for CVD via aggressive risk factor modification.

The risk for DM increases in proportion to the number of other risk factors a client has (Joseph et al. 2016). The lifestyle changes that will improve the previously reviewed CVD risk factors should improve T2DM. Because of this, intensive risk factor modification via lifestyle changes is a standard of treatment (Buse et al. 2007; Fox et al. 2015). Both weight loss and physical activity improve T2DM (Aguiar et al. 2014; Orozco et al. 2008), although it remains uncertain if one is preferable over the other (Orozco et al. 2008; Sénéchal et al. 2014). However, in one study, after controlling for several risk factors including fasting glucose level, low fitness levels were much more related to CVD deaths than was body weight (Church et al. 2005). Of the different types of physical activity, aerobic exercise clearly has a positive effect although more limited research also supports the efficacy of resistance training (Yang et al. 2014). The net effect is that the recommendations provided for dyslipidemia and hypertension in this chapter are consistent with those recommended for T2DM (Fox et al. 2015). But regular physical activity is a critical component of a successful program to combat T2DM. Regardless of a client's activity level, reducing sedentary time is also important (Biswas et al. 2015).

Because of the complexities of T2DM and the critical role the client has in managing their diabetes (Powers et al. 2015), a team-based approach should be taken in working with the client. You, the health/fitness professional, should work in cooperation with the client's personal physician and other health professionals, such as a certified diabetes educator or a registered dietitian nutritionist, to optimize care for the client.

Physical Activity

Physical inactivity is a major risk factor for CVD (Benjamin et al. 2019). It has direct effects on CVD risk, meaning that in-and-of-itself, being inactive increases risk because of how it directly affects the human body. It also has indirect effects, wherein inactivity may contribute to other CVD risk factors, like obesity and diabetes (Figure 3.8).

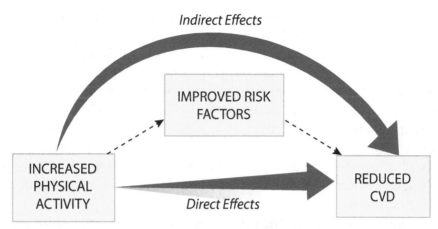

Figure 3.8   How Increases in Physical Activity Can Reduce CVD Risk

In a study of factors contributing to acute myocardial infarctions in fifty-two countries, physical inactivity could be "blamed" for ~25 percent of these events, when the interaction of inactivity and several other major risk factors were included in the analyses (Yusuf et al. 2004). However, when only physical inactivity was considered, meaning most of these risk factors were statistically excluded from consideration, this attribution was 12 percent. This 12 percent reflects the direct effect of inactivity on CVD risk and the increase from 12 to 25 percent illustrates the indirect effect via inactivity's influence on other risk factors. Another example of the direct effect is shown in Figure 3.9. In this large-scale study, when the contribution of all the other modifiable risk factors were considered in the statistical analyses, low cardiorespiratory fitness accounted for the greatest proportion of mortality, mostly CVD-related (Blair 2009). Parenthetically, one of the direct effects by which physical activity and cardiorespiratory fitness reduce CVD risk is by reducing pro-atherogenic inflammatory mediators (Lee et al. 2010). The important message here is that inactive clients who become more fit will have a reduced risk for CVD even if their other risk factors remain unchanged (Farrell et al. 1998; Sui, LaMonte, and Blair 2007).

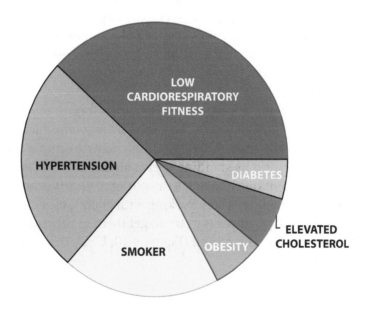

FIGURE 3.9   Attributable fractions (%) for all-cause deaths in 40,842 men and 12,943 women in the Aerobics Center Longitudinal Study. The attributable fractions are the mean for both genders after adjustment for age and each other item in the figure. Figure modified from Blair (2009).

When you read the previous paragraph, you may have noticed that one study focused on physical activity while the other study focused on cardiorespiratory fitness. Physical activity and physical fitness were defined in Chapter 1. Cardiorespiratory fitness is an element of overall physical fitness but relates to how well the cardiovascular and respiratory systems can supply oxygen to muscles during sustained physical activity. Compared to their less fit peers, higher fit clients can meet the metabolic demands of higher exercise workloads and will have a higher VO_2 max (see Table 2.2 of Chapter 2 for comparisons of fitness levels). While there is a marked genetic component to VO_2 max in sedentary subjects (Bouchard et al. 1998) and in the magnitude of the response to exercise training (Bouchard et al. 1999), an increase in physical activity should lead to an increase in VO_2 max. Nevertheless, while they are interrelated, the terms "physical activity" and "cardiorespiratory fitness" are not synonymous.

Increases in either physical activity or cardiorespiratory fitness will reduce the risk for CVD in a linear fashion (Williams 2001). This is true across the spectrum from very low (Farrell et al. 2015) to very high (Feldman et al. 2015) levels of fitness. So within the constraints of what is realistically achievable and when specifically focusing on CVD risk, more really is better. For example, in a study of over 120,000 people followed for about eight years, the factors contributing to mortality among the lowest fit was compared to the highest fit (least fit 25 percent versus most fit 2.3 percent). Here, cardiorespiratory fitness was more important than any CVD risk factor (Mandsager et al. 2018). Moreover, there did not appear to be an upper limit of cardiorespiratory fitness where further improvements were not associated with further reductions in risk.

While more is better, there is a dose-response relationship between physical activity, or physical fitness, and risk of CVD. At higher levels of activity (the "dose"), the benefits of the activity (the "response") are not as robust as seen at lower levels. For example, someone who is inactive but begins to exercise a total of 100 minutes per week will have about a 25 percent reduced risk of dying from CVD because of this 100-minute increase. However, someone who is exercising 400 minutes per week at a moderate-to-vigorous intensity and increases that to 500 minutes per week will not have a markedly reduced risk because of this additional 100 minutes (2018 Physical Activity Guidelines Advisory Committee 2018). Consequently, the greatest reduction in CVD mortality is seen when clients move out of the bottom 20th percentile for either activity or fitness (Lee et al. 2010) or, put another way, they exercise enough to raise their VO_2 max above ~18 ml/kg/min (Ross et al. 2016). This level of fitness is still quite low but, importantly, at least half of the reduction in CVD-related mortality due to physical inactivity occurs when these least fit people become slightly more fit (Ross et al. 2016). Put another way, the clients who benefit most from becoming more active are those who were previously the least active.

Even sedentary clients who do not work out *per se* but become less inactive by, say, using a standing workstation or trying to walk more at work will enjoy a reduced risk of premature death (Ekelund et al. 2016; Katzmarzyk et al. 2009). Getting clients to move more throughout the day, even if these changes are as modest as standing versus sitting at work, taking the stairs versus the elevator, or walking to an adjacent office to talk to a colleague versus sending them an email, will be beneficial for the client. Consequently, when working with clients, especially those who are resistant to becoming more physically active, *Step 1* is to try to get them to move more and sit less throughout the day—*any* activity is better than none at all (Figure 3.10; USDHHS 2018).

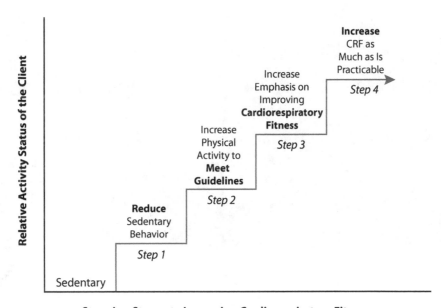

Stepping Stones to Improving Cardiorespiratory Fitness

FIGURE 3.10   Steps to Follow When Working with a Client, Based on Their Current Level of Physical Activity

If you are working with a client who is inactive but is willing to become more active, then *Step 2* is to support them in their efforts to do so. They should work toward meeting the goal expressed in the *Physical Activity Guidelines for Americans* (USDHHS 2018)—150 minutes of moderate intensity exercise, or 75 minutes of vigorous intensity exercise, or some combination of the two. An example of 150 minutes of moderate intensity exercise would be a 30-minute walk done 5 days a week while 75 minutes of vigorous exercise could be jogging for 25 minutes 3 days a week. "Moderate" and "vigorous" are relative terms—what may be moderate intensity exercise for a fit person may be vigorous intensity exercise for an unfit person. Nevertheless, in the present context, moderate intensity exercise is defined as any activity requiring between 3 to 5.9 metabolic equivalent units (METs) while activities requiring 6 METs or more are considered vigorous (USDHHS 2018). For perspective, 1 MET is the equivalent of the average resting VO_2 of humans. Therefore, a 3 MET activity would require a metabolic demand, or VO_2, that is three times greater than that of being awake but resting. A fast walk, shooting a basketball, light carpentry, or heavy house cleaning are examples of moderate intensity exercise. Examples of vigorous intensity exercise are jogging, playing basketball, carrying heavy loads, or backpacking (Haskell et al. 2007). Achieving this goal level of physical activity will definitely ensure that the client is not in the bottom 20th percentile of activity. Moreover, considerable research supports the notion that "it's not too late to start" meaning unfit individuals who become fit will have a reduced risk for CVD, even if they had been unfit for many years (Lee et al. 2011).

© Marida/Shutterstock.com

If your client is achieving this recommended level of physical activity, then *Step 3* (Figure 3.10) of reducing their CVD risk via physical activity is to shift their training to an emphasis on improving their cardiorespiratory fitness. This emphasis is due to the repeated finding that, everything else being equal, increases in cardiorespiratory fitness are considerably more beneficial to reducing CVD risk than are increases in physical activity (Lee et al. 2010; Williams 2001). Methods of increasing VO_2 max will be reviewed in detail in Chapter 4 but, for the moment, suffice it to say that increasing fitness requires either spending more time exercising, exercising at a higher relative intensity, or both.

Within broad constraints, there is no upper limit to the reduced risk of premature mortality enjoyed by increases in cardiorespiratory fitness (Feldman et al. 2015; Mandsager et al. 2018). Consequently, *Step 4* is to encourage your client to become as fit as they are willing to be. From a health perspective, more is better. Recall that there is a dose-response effect to the health benefits associated with improvements in cardiorespiratory fitness, meaning the increase in CVD-related benefits becomes progressively smaller as the client becomes increasingly fitter (Lee et al. 2010; 2018 Physical Activity Guidelines Advisory Committee 2018). Consequently, a fit person may not view these smaller additional gains as being worth the investment of more time and energy. From a pragmatic perspective, if the client is not willing to devote any additional time exercising, then encourage them to spend more time exercising at a vigorous, rather than a moderate, exercise intensity. Ideally, the client would expend at least 1,000 kilocalories per week in physical activity (Lee and Skerrett 2001).

Are There Other Risk Factors?

As mentioned earlier, our understanding of what contributes to atherogenesis is continually evolving. Consequently, the list of risk factors continues to evolve. There are a number of health concerns that may predispose a person to developing CVD. However, the current evidence is not sufficient for these health concerns to be routinely considered as risk factors.

Two promising risk factors are a coronary artery calcification score (CAC) and a measure of high sensitivity C-reactive protein (hsCRP). A CAC score is computed using an imaging device, such as a CT scan, to determine the presence of calcification in the walls of the coronary arteries. High CAC scores imply more advanced atheromas and greater risk for an adverse cardiac event (Mori et al. 2018). After taking into account traditional CVD risk factors, even relatively low CAC scores are associated with an increased risk (Desai et al. 2013). C-reactive protein is a marker of inflammation; recall that atherogenesis has a major pro-inflammatory component (Ridker 2016). Both risk factors are definitely associated with CVD. However, questions remain about the clinical utility of both risk factors and the extent to which they should be used in the routine clinical assessment of CVD risk (Lin et al. 2018).

Other risk factors can be considered as "predisposing" or "emerging" risk factors. One of these is chronic mental stress. Several psychological factors, such as depression, anxiety, social isolation, and chronic stress, have long been known to contribute to IHD (Rozanski et al. 1999). Moroever, acute stress, such as anger (Mostofsky et al. 2013) or emotionally traumatic events (Steptoe and Brydon 2009), can trigger an acute cardiac event. Chronic kidney disease affects almost 15 percent of adult Americans and it is increasingly recognized as being associated with the development of CVD (Benjamiin et al. 2019). Frequently, people with chronic kidney disease have multiple traditional CVD risk factors and these risk factors also contribute to the kidney disease. An additional example of another predisposing risk factor is poor sleep (Benjamin et al. 2019). Both short sleep (<7 hr/ night) and long sleep (>8 hr/night) are associated with increased risks of dying. Obstructive sleep apnea is also associated with an increased risk of dying (Fu et al. 2017). Consequently, if your client has one or more of these health issues, they may have an increased risk for CVD. However, for now, it remains difficult to determine the magnitude of this risk.

The point here is that, in the future, the list of CVD risk factors that are routinely assessed when working with a client may change. Consequently, it is important that, as you move forward in your career, you continue to remain educated as to what are the CVD risk factors.

WORKING WITH A CLIENT TO REDUCE CVD RISK

It can be challenging to determine how best to help your client reduce their risk for CVD and, as part of this effort, convey all this information to your client. You are encouraged to use the CRIPL rubric that was introduced in Chapter 2 to help guide you in these efforts. Table 3.9 is a "working summary" of how to act on the central elements of "R" and "L" in CRIPL to help your client reduce her risk for CVD. Recall that the "R" in CRIPL is "Risk Factor Assessment" and the "L" refers to "Lifestyle Changes." Both "R" and "L" embody what you will do to assist your client to reduce their risk for CVD. With "R," you focus on identifying the client's risk factors. With "L," you consider the behaviors, or lifestyle factors, the client needs to adopt in order to do so.

©Robert Kneschke/Shutterstock.com

The first step of "R" in CRIPL is to identify the client's risk factors for CVD. Identifying whether someone does or does not have a particular risk factor is not difficult; simply compare the participant's information to the list of risk factors provided in Table 3.2. For a minimal level of risk classification, total the number of risk factors the participant has and note whether they have two or more risk factors. An HDL value >60 mg/dl is a *negative* risk factor because it confers reduced CVD risk; therefore, if present, it would be *subtracted* from the total. If information about a specific risk factor is not known, assume the participant has that risk factor. Finally, blend this information into that gained as part of "C" to complete your preparticipation screening.

While this methodology will suffice for preparticipation screening, several other issues must be considered if the client needs to reduce their risk for CVD. These are outlined in the "R" section of CRIPL in Table 3.9. First, identify which of the client's risk factors are modifiable. Advancing age and family history are nonmodifiable risk factors so, by definition, cannot be changed. While these

TABLE 3.9	
Element	**How to Proceed**
Elements from "R" or "Risk Factor Assessment"	
1. Identify the client's risk factors for CVD.	List the risk factors and criteria for each, compare your client's risk factor information to this information.
2. Which can be modified and which cannot be?	Make this determination for your client.
3. Goals for each risk factor.	Determine the desired values for your client for each of his/her risk factors.
4. Calculate client's 10-year risk developing CVD.	Use either of the risk factor algorithms (Framingham, ACC/AHA algorithms) to identify the client's 10-year risk for CVD.
5. Determine which risk factor(s) need to be modified first.	This is a judgment call. Which risk factors appear the worst? Which would respond quickly? In general, tobacco use and diabetes are good candidates for action.
6. How will the client's risk for CVD change with modifying these risk factors?	Using the risk algorithm, determine how the 10-year risk will change after modifying the risk factors.
Elements from "L" or Lifestyle Changes	
1. Identify specifically and in detail how the client can make the desired changes.	First, remember that you are working with your client in finding solutions to their health risks. You are not telling them what to do but helping them make this decision. Second, once they've identified the risk factor(s) to act on, be sure to (a) use simple, or layman's, terms when explaining what the client needs to do and (b) integrate all these actions into one cohesive message to the client. Methods for helping the client adopt behavior changes will be reviewed in Chapter 8.

certainly affect overall CVD risk, neither you nor the client can do anything about them. However, the modifiable risk factors *can* be improved, so the next step is to determine reasonable goals for the client's modifiable risk factors. Ideally, the client would achieve the "desired values" of Table 3.2, although intermediate goals may be needed if the client has markedly elevated risk factors.

After identifying the client's modifiable risk factors and the goal values for each, you should calculate the client's overall risk for CVD. There is an interactive effect for risk factors, meaning the presence of multiple risk factors has a more-than-additive effect on a client's true risk for CVD. A simple, effective method for estimating a client's overall risk for CVD, and one that accounts for this interaction, is a risk score algorithm.

A number of risk scores are available, each using different combinations of CVD risk factors to predict CVD-related outcomes (Goff et al. 2014). Recently, the American College of Cardiology and the American Heart Association jointly published guidelines on risk assessment (Goff et al. 2014) including an easy-to-use online tool to calculate the ten-year risk for developing clinically significant atherosclerotic CVD. It can be found by using the search term "ASCVD Risk Estimator Plus" which is currently at http://tools.acc.org/ASCVD-Risk-Estimator-Plus/#!/calculate/estimate. This algorithm is probably the one best validated for use in the United States (Muntner et al. 2014) and, unlike the Framingham risk scores, takes into account differences in risk due to the client's race or ethnicity.

An alternative choice would be the risk scores from the ongoing Framingham Heart Study (www.framinghamheartstudy.org). These are perhaps the most widely used algorithms in the United States and, while not perfect, work well (Eichler, Puhan, Steurer, and Bachmann 2007). Several risk scores have emanated from this long-standing, ongoing study, but the one shown in Figure 3.11 can be used to estimate an apparently healthy client's ten-year risk for having a CVD event (D'Agostino et al. 2008). As with the ASCVD Risk Predictor Plus, an easy-to-use online version is available using the search term "Framingham General CVD risk prediction" (https://www.framinghamheartstudy.org/fhs-risk-functions/cardiovascular-disease-10-year-risk/).

Both risk scores can be used to estimate the likelihood that the client will have a clinically significant CVD event or diagnosis in the next ten years. However, the ASCVD score is increasingly used over the Framingham score. Consider the risk of a 55 year old white male, with a BP of 128/84, a total cholesterol of 228 mg/dl, HDL of 42 mg/dl, and LDL of 142 mg/dl. He is not a diabetic, nonsmoker, and not on any medications other than a medication for hypertension. He would have very different estimates of having a CVD event in the next ten years—7.6 percent with the ASCVD risk predictor, but 14.4 percent using the Framingham method. Both algorithms are based on high quality research but the risk estimates differ due to the use of differing definitions of a CVD event and differing methodologies in their development. In both cases, this person's risk is about 2.7 to 2.9 times the optimal, or best achievable, risk.

The categories of what constitutes low, intermediate, and high risk for a CVD event in the next ten years also differ between algorithms. The ASCVD algorithm defines high risk >20%, intermediate = 7.5–19.9%, borderline = 5–7.4%, and very low <5%. The Framingham algorithm defines high risk as being >20%, intermediate = 10.1–19.9% risk, and low <10%. These categories are not absolute predictors, meaning you should use them as a guideline of how to work with your client. Moreover, you need to consider the effects of risk factors which were not included in the algorithm. For example, neither body composition nor physical activity is included in either algorithm and both can affect CVD risk. Despite this limitation, you can use either algorithm with a reasonable degree of confidence. However, pick one and stick with it—they are not interchangeable.

Figure 3.11   Sample Estimate of Ten-Year Risk for Developing CVD Using the Framingham Risk Algorithm.

General CVD Risk Prediction Using Lipids

Sex:
● M ○ F

Age (years):
55

Systolic Blood Pressure (mmHg):
128

Treatment for Hypertension:
○ Yes ● No

Current smoker:
○ Yes ● No

Diabetes:
○ Yes ● No

HDL:
42

Total Cholesterol:
228

Calculate

Your Heart/Vascular Age: 62

10 Year Risk

Your risk	14.4%
Normal	10.1%
Optimal	5.4%

An advantage of these risk score algorithms is that, besides determining the client's overall risk for CVD, you can estimate how this risk will change if the client modified his risk factors. The final step in the "R" of CRIPL is to do just that. In Figure 3.11, you can see that the client has an elevated blood pressure and elevated total cholesterol and LDL (he may have other risk factors that were not included here but, for the moment, let's assume that is not the case.) How would his ten-year risk change if he improved either his blood pressure or his lipids, or both? The "what if" scenarios can be easily explored using the risk scores. In Figure 3.12, we can see that improving his systolic blood pressure to 118 mmHg reduces his ten-year risk from 7.6 percent to 6.6 percent while decreasing his total cholesterol to 190 mg/dL and LDL to 130 mg/dL is about equally effective, lowering his risk to 6.1 percent. However, improving both lowers his risk to 5.3 percent. His risk is still above what is considered optimal for a man his age but is much better than before. The point here is that you can play "what if" scenarios to determine what it would take for him to lower his risk even more. Regardless, these data can help the client decide, with your input, what lifestyle changes to make. In this case, lowering either his blood pressure or his lipids will have about the same influence on reducing his risk for CVD. If he thinks he could be more successful with making the lifestyle changes needed to improve one of these risk factors, as opposed to the other, then he may want to begin with that one.

The "L" component of CRIPL, or "Lifestyle Changes," is intended to serve as a reminder to you as to how best to help the client make these changes (Table 3.9). Recall that the lifestyle changes associated with improving each risk factor were reviewed in the relevant sections of this chapter. Did you explain to the client what lifestyle changes they should make? Did you help the client prioritize which lifestyle change(s) to make first? Were you specific enough that they could successfully begin these changes? Is your client receptive to these suggestions? Do you need to do any goal-setting to help the client succeed? The key with "L" is that your client needs to be in control of the decision-making process. It is up to them to decide how best to proceed. Your role is to assist them in this decision-making process and provide them with the information, tools, and motivation to be successful.

PUTTING IT ALL TOGETHER

The goals of this chapter were fourfold. The first goal was to increase your understanding of how CVD and IHD affect overall health in the United States and, in so doing, help you realize how you can play a major role in reducing this epidemic. The second goal was to help you learn about how IHD happens, meaning the process of atherogenesis. This is important since, if you understand how CVD and IHD happens, then you can better explain to your clients why risk factor modification is so important. The third goal was to help you gain a solid grasp of how the major risk factors contribute to CVD in general and IHD, specifically. This included information related to the criteria at which a risk factor became a risk factor, mechanisms by which a risk factor contributed to atherosclerosis, as well as lifestyle changes which should improve the risk factor. The fourth goal was to re-visit the CRIPL rubric, especially the "R" and "L," to help solidify your understanding of where risk factor assessment and risk factor modification fit into the "big picture" of working with a client.

REFERENCES

2018 Physical Activity Guidelines Advisory Committee. *2018 Physical Activity Guidelines Advisory Committee Scientific Report.* Washington, DC: U.S. Department of Health and Human Services.

Aguiar E. J., P. J. Morgan, C. E. Collins, R. C. Plotnikoff, and R. Callister. 2014. "Efficacy of Interventions That Include Diet, Aerobic and Resistance Training Components for Type 2 Diabetes Prevention: A Systematic Review with Meta-Analysis." *International Journal of Behavioral Nutrition and Physical Activity* 11: 2. doi:10.1186/1479-5868-11-2

American College of Sports Medicine. 2018. *ACSM's Guidelines for Exercise Testing and Prescription.* 10th ed. Baltimore: Wolters Kluwer.

Anand, A. A., S. Islam, A. Rosengren, M. G. Granzosi, K. Steyn, A. H. Yusufali, M. Keltai, R. Diaz, S. Rangarajan, and S. Yusuf. 2008. On behalf of the INTERHEART investigators. "Risk Factors for Myocardial Infarction in Women and Men: Insights from the INTERHEART Study." *Eur Heart J.* 29: 932–40.

Barry, V. W., M. Baruth, M. W. Beets, J. L. Durstine, J. Liu, and S. N. Blair. 2014. "Fitness vs. Fatness on All-Cause Mortality: A Meta-Analysis." *Prog Cardiovasc Dis.* 56: 382–90.

Bastien, M., P. Poirier, I. Lemieux, and J-P Després. 2014. "Overview of Epidemiology and Contribution of Obesity to Cardiovascular Disease." *Progress in Cardiovascular Diseases.* 56: 369–81.

Benjamin, A. S., P. Muntner, A. Alonso, M. S. Bittencourt, C. W. Callaway, A. P. Carson, A. M. Chamberlain, et al. 2019. On behalf of the American Heart Association Council on Epidemiology and Prevention Statistics Committee and Stroke Statistics Subcommittee. "Heart Disease and Stroke Statistics—2019 Update: A Report from the American Heart Association." *Circulation* 139: e1–e473.

Bhatnagar, A. 2016. "E-Cigarettes and Cardiovascular Disease Risk: Evaluation of Evidence, Policy Implications, and Recommendations. *Curr Cardiovasc Risk Rep* 10: 24. https://doi.org/10.1007/s12170-016-0505-6

Biswas A., P. I. Oh, G. E. Faulkner, R. R. Bajaj, M. A. Silva, M. S. Mitchell, and D. A. Alter. 2015. "Sedentary Time and its Association with Risk for Disease Incidence, Mortality, and Hospitalization in Adults: A Systematic Review and Meta-Analysis." *Ann Intern Med.* 162: 123–32.

Blair, S. N. 2009. "Physical Inactivity: The Biggest Public Health Problem of the 21st Century." *Br J Sports Med.* 42: 1–2.

Bouchard, C., P. An, T. Rice, J. S. Skinner, J. H. Wilmore, J. Gagnon, L. Pérusse, A. S. Leon, D. C. Rao. 1999. "Familial Aggregation of VO$_2$max Response to Exercise Training: Results from the HERITAGE Family Study." *J Appl Physiol.* 87: 1003–08.

Bouchard, C., E. W. Daw T. Rice, L. Pérusse, J. Gagnon, M. A. Province, A. S. Leon, D. C. Rao, J. S. Skinner, and J. H. Wilmore. 1998. "Familial Resemblance for VO2max in the Sedentary State: The HERITAGE Family Study." *Med Sci Sports Exerc.* 30: 252–58.

Bray, G. A., C. Bouchard, and W. P. T. James. 1998. *Handbook of Obesity.* New York: Marcel Dekker.

Brownlee, M. 2005. "The Pathobiology of Diabetic Complications: A Unifying Mechanism." *Diabetes* 54: 1615–25.

Burke, G. L., Bertoni, A. G., S. Shea, R. Tracy, K. E. Watson, R. S. Blumenthal, H. Chung, and M. R. Carnethon. 2008. "The Impact of Obesity on Cardiovascular Disease Risk Factors and Subclinical Vascular Disease: The Multi-Ethnic Study of Atherosclerosis." *Arch Intern Med.* 168: 928–35.

Buse, J. B., H. N. Ginsberg, G. L. Bakris, N. G. Clark, F. Costa, R. Eckel, V. Fonseca, et al. 2007. "Primary Prevention of Cardiovascular Diseases in People With Diabetes Mellitus: A Scientific Statement from the American Heart Association and the American Diabetes Association." *Diabetes Care* 30: 162–72.

Centers for Disease Control and Prevention. 2014. *National Diabetes Statistics Report: Estimates of Diabetes and Its Burden in the United States, 2014.* Atlanta: U.S. Department of Health and Human Services.

Chobanian, A. V., G. L. Bakris, H. R. Black, W. C. Cushman, L. A. Green, J. L. Izzo, D. W. Jones, et al. 2003. "Seventh Report of the Joint National Committee on Prevention, Detection, Evaluation, and Treatment of High Blood Pressure." *Hypertension* 42: 1206–52.

Chow, C. K., S. Islam, L. Bautista, Z. Rumboldt, A. Yusufali, C. Xie, S. S. Anand, J. C. Engert, S. Rangarajan, and S. Yusuf. 2011. "Parental History and Myocardial Infarction Risk across the World: The INTERHEART study." *J Am Coll Cardiol.* 57: 619–27.

Chrostowska, M., A. Szyndler, M. Hoffmann, and K. Narkiewica. 2013. "Impact of Obesity on Cardiovascular Health." *Best Practice & Research Clinical Endocrinology & Metabolism* 27: 147–56.

Church, T. S., M. J. LaMonte, C. E. Barlow, and S. N. Blair. 2005. "Cardiorespiratory Fitness and Body Mass Index as Predictors of Cardiovascular Disease Mortality Among Men With Diabetes." *Arch Intern Med.* 165: 2114–20.

Conti, C. R., A. A. Bavry, and J. W. Petersen. 2012. "Silent Ischemia: Clinical Relevance." *J Am Coll Cardiol.* 59: 435–41.

Cooney, M. T., A. Dudina, D. De Bacquer, L. Wilhelmsen, S. Sans, A. Menotti, G. De Backer, et al. 2009. "HDL Cholesterol Protects against Cardiovascular Disease in Both Genders, at All ages and at All Levels of Risk." *Atherosclerosis* 206: 611–16.

Cornier, M.-A., J.-P. Despre´s, N. Davis, D. A. Grossniklaus, S. Klein, B. Lamarche, F. Lopez-Jimenez, et al. 2011. On behalf of the American Heart Association Obesity Committee of the Council on Nutrition, Physical Activity and Metabolism, Council on Arteriosclerosis, Thrombosis and Vascular Biology, Council on Cardiovascular Disease in the Young, Council on Cardiovascular Radiology and Intervention, Council on Cardiovascular Nursing, Council on Epidemiology and Prevention, Council on the Kidney in Cardiovascular Disease, and Stroke Council. "Assessing Adiposity: A Scientific Statement from the American Heart Association." *Circulation* 124: 1996–2019.

Cowan, M. J. 1982. "Pathogenesis of Atherosclerosis." In *Cardiac Nursing*, edited by Sandra L. Underhill, Susan L. Woods, Erika Seiberler Sivarajan, and Carol Jean Halpenny, 103–10. Philadelphia: J.B. Lippincott.

Dengel, D. R. T. A. Bosch, T. P. Burruss, K. A. Fielding, B. E. Engel, N. L. Weir, and T. D. Weston. 2014. "Body Composition and Bone Mineral Density of National Football League Players." *J Strength Cond Res.* 28: 1–6.

Desai, C. S., H. Ning, J. Kang, A. R. Folsom, J. F Polak, C. T. Sibley, R. Tracy, and D. M. Lloyd-Jones. 2013. "Competing Cardiovascular Outcomes Associated with Subclinical Atherosclerosis (from the Multi-Ethnic Study of Atherosclerosis). *Am J Cardiol.* 111: 1541–46.

Detrano, R., A. D. Guerci, J. J. Carr, B. E. Bild, G. Burker, A. R. Folsom, K. Liu, S. Shea, M. Szklo, D. A. Bleumke, D. H. O'Leary, R. Tracy, K. Watson, N. D. Wong, and R. A. Kronmal. 2008. "Coronary Calcium as a Predictor of Coronary Events in Four Racial or Ethnic Groups." *N Engl J Med.* 358: 1336–45.

Dokken, B. B. 2008. "The Pathophysiology of Cardiovascular Disease and Diabetes: Beyond Blood Pressure and Lipids." *Diabetes Spectrum.* 21: 160–65.

Douglas, G., and K. M. Channon. 2014. "The Pathogenesis of Atherosclerosis." *Medicine* 42: 480–84.

Duncan, G. E. 2010. "The 'Fit but Fat' Concept Revisited: Population-Based Estimates using NHANES." *Int J Behav Nutr Phys Act.* 7: 1–5.

Eckel, R. H., J. M. Jakicic, J. D. Ard, J. M. de Jesus, N. Houston Miller, V. S. Hubbard, I.-M. Lee, et al. 2014. "2013 AHA/ACC Guideline on Lifestyle Management to Reduce Cardiovascular Risk: A Report of the American College of Cardiology/American Heart Association Task Force on Practice Guidelines." *J Am Coll Cardiol* 63: 2960–84.

Eckel, R. H., and R. M. Krauss. 1998. "American Heart Association Call to Action: Obesity as a Major Risk Factor for Coronary Heart Disease." *Circulation* 97: 2099–100.

Ekelund, U., J. Steene-Johannessen, W. J. Brown, M. Wang Fagerland, N. Owen, K. E. Powell, A. Bauman, and I-M. Lee for the Lancet Physical Activity Series 2 Executive Committee and the Lancet Sedentary Behaviour Working Group. 2016. "Does Physical Activity Attenuate, or Even Eliminate, the Detrimental Association of Sitting Time with Mortality? A Harmonised Meta-Analysis of Data from More than 1 Million Men and Women." *Lancet* 388: 1302–10.Elshazly, M. B., R. Quispe, E. D. Michos, A. D. Sniderman, P. P. Toth, M. Banach, K. R. Kulkarni, et al. 2015. "Patient-Level Discordance in Population Percentiles of the TC/HDL Ratio Compared with LDL and Non-HDL: The Very Large Database of Lipids Study (VLDL-2B)." *Circulation* 132: 667–76.

Emerging Risk Factors Collaboration. 2011a. "Separate and Combined Associations of Body-Mass Index and Abdominal Adiposity with Cardiovascular Disease: Collaborative Analysis of 58 Prospective Studies." *Lancet* 377: 1085–95.

Emerging Risk Factors Collaboration. 2011b. "Diabetes Mellitus, Fasting Glucose, and Risk of Cause-Specific Death." *N Eng J Med.* 364: 829–41.

Expert Committee on the Diagnosis and Classification of Diabetes Mellitus. 1997. "Report of the Expert Committee on the Diagnosis and Classification of Diabetes Mellitus." *Diabetes Care* 20: 1183–97.

Falk, E. 2006. "Pathogenesis of Atherosclerosis." *J Am Coll Cardio.* 47: C7–C12.

Farrell, S. W., C. E. Finley, W. L. Haskell, and S. M. Grundy. 2015. "Is There a Gradient of Mortality Risk among Men with Low Cardiorespiratory Fitness?" *Med Sci Sports Exerc.* 47: 1825–32.

Farrell, S.W., C.E. Finley, A. W. Jackson, G. L. Vega, and J. R. Morrow, Jr. 2014. "Association of Multiple Adiposity Exposures and Cardiorespiratory Fitness with All-Cause Mortality in Men: The Cooper Center Longitudinal Study." *Mayo Clin Proc.* 89: 772–80.

Farrell, S. W., J. B. Kampert, H. W. Kohl 3rd, C. E. Barlow, C. A. Macera, R. S. Paffenbarger Jr, L. W. Gibbons, and S. N. Blair. 1998. "Influences of Cardiorespiratory Fitness Levels and Other Predictors on Cardiovascular Disease Mortality in Men." *Med Sci Sports Exerc.* 30: 899–905.

Feingold K. R., and C. Grunfeld. 2018. *Introduction to Lipids and Lipoproteins.* Edited by Feingold KR, Anawalt B, Boyce A, et al. MDText.com. https://www.ncbi.nlm.nih.gov/pubmed/26247089

Feldman, D. I., M. H. Al-Mallah, S. J. Keteyian, C. A. Brawner, T. Feldman, R. S. Blumenthal, and M. J. Blaha. 2015. "No Evidence of an Upper Threshold for Mortality Benefit at High Levels of Cardiorespiratory Fitness." *JACC* 65: 629–30.

Fielding, C. J., and P. E. Fielding. 1995. "Molecular Physiology of Reverse Cholesterol Transport." *J Lipid Research* 36: 211–28.

Flegal, K. M. 2006. "Body Mass Index of Healthy Men Compared with Healthy Women in the United States." *International Journal of Obesity* 30: 374–79.

Flegal, K. M., B. K. Kit, H. Orpana, and B. I. Graubard. 2013. "Association of All-Cause Mortality With Overweight and Obesity Using Standard Body Mass Index Categories: A Systematic Review and Meta-Analysis." *JAMA* 309: 71–82.

Folsom, A. R., H. Yatsuya, J. A. Nettleton, P. L. Lutsey, M. Cushman, and W. D. Rosamond. 2011. For the ARIC Study Investigators. "Community Prevalence of Ideal Cardiovascular Health, by the American Heart Association Definition, and Relationship with Cardiovascular Disease." *J Am Coll Cardiol.* 57: 1690–96.

Fox, C. S., S. H. Golden, C. Anderson, G. A. Bray, L. E. Burke, I. H. de Boer, P. Deedwania, et al. 2015. On behalf of the American Heart Association Diabetes Committee of the Council on Lifestyle and Cardiometabolic Health, Council on Clinical Cardiology, Council on Cardiovascular and Stroke Nursing, Council on Cardiovascular Surgery and Anesthesia, Council on Quality of Care and Outcomes Research, and the American Diabetes Association. "Update on Prevention of Cardiovascular Disease in Adults with Type 2 Diabetes Mellitus in Light of Recent Evidence: A Scientific Statement from the American Heart Association and the American Diabetes Association." *Circulation* 132: 691–718.

Friedewald, W. T., R. I. Levy, and D. S. Fredrickson. 1972. "Estimation of the Concentration of Low-Density Lipoprotein Cholesterol in Plasma, without Use of the Preparative Ultracentrifuge." *Clinical Chemistry* 18: 499–502.

Fryar, C. D., and S. M. Frenk. 2014. "Percentage Distribution of Weight Status among Adults Aged >20 Years with Diabetes, by Sex—National Health and Nutrition Examination Survey, United States, 2009–2012." *MMWR* 63: 678.

Fu, Y., Y. Xia, H. Yi, H. Xu, J. Guan, and S. Yin. 2017. "Meta-Analysis of All-Cause and Cardiovascular Mortality in Obstructive Sleep Apnea with or without Continuous Positive Airway Pressure Treatment." *Sleep Breath* 21: 181–89.

Goniewicz, M. L., D. M. Smith, K. C. Edwards, B. C. Blount, K. L Caldwell J. Feng, L. Wang, C. Christensen, B. Amborse, N. Borek, D. van Bemmel, K. Konkel, G. Erives, C. A Stanton, E. Lambert, H. L. Kimmel, D. Hatsukami, S. S. Hecht, R. S. Niaura, M. Travers, C. Lawrence, and A. J. Hyland. 2018. "Comparison of Nicotine and Toxicant Exposure in Users of Electronic Cigarettes and Combustible Cigarettes." *JAMA Network Open* 1: e185937. doi:10.1001/jamanetworkopen.2018.5937

Gordon, D. J., J. L. Probstfield, R. J. Garrison, J. D. Neaton, W. P. Castelli, J. D. Knoke, D. R. Jacobs Jr., S. Bangdiwala, and H. A. Tyroler. 1989. "High-Density Lipoprotein Cholesterol and Cardiovascular Disease. Four prospective studies." *Circulation* 79: 8–15.

Gordon, T., W. P. Castelli, M. C. Hjortland, W. B. Kannel, and T. R. Dawber. 1977. "High Density Lipoprotein as a Protective Factor against Coronary Heart Disease." *Am J Med.* 62: 707–14.

Gregor, M. F., and G. S. Hotamisligil. 2011. "Inflammatory Mechanisms in Obesity." *Annu Rev Immunol.* 29: 415–45.

Grundy S. M., N. J. Stone, A. L. Bailey, C. Beam, K. K. Birtcher, R. S. Blumenthal, L. T. Braun, S. de Ferranti, J. Faiella-Tommasino, D. E. Forman, R. Goldberg, P. A. Heidenreich, M. A. Hlatky, D. W. Jones, D. Lloyd-Jones, N. Lopez-Pajares, C. E. Ndumele, C. E. Orringer, C. A. Peralta, J.

J. Saseen, S. C. Smith Jr, L. Sperling, S. S. Virani, J. Yeboah. 2018. "2018 AHA/ACC/AACVPR/AAPA/ABC/ACPM/ADA/AGS/APhA/ASPC/NLA/PCNA Guideline on the Management of Blood Cholesterol: A Report of the American College of Cardiology/American Heart Association Task Force on Clinical Practice Guidelines." *J Am Coll Cardiol.* Epub ahead of print, doi: 10.1016/j.jacc.2018.11.003

Hackshaw, A., J. K. Morris, S. Boniface, J. Tang, and D. Milenkovi´ç. "Low Cigarette Consumption and Risk of Coronary Heart Disease and Stroke: Meta-Analysis of 141 Cohort Studies in 55 Study Reports." *BMJ* 360: J5855.

Hansson, G. K., A.-K. L. Robertson, and C. Söderberg-Nauclér. 2006. "Inflammation and Atherosclerosis." *Annu Rev Pathol Mech Dis.* 1: 297–329.

Haskell, W. L., I.-M. Lee, R. R. Pate, K. E. Powell, S. N. Blair, B. A. Franklin, C. A. Macera, G. W. Heath, P. D. Thompson, and A. Bauman. 2007. "Physical Activity and Public Health: Updated Recommendation for Adults from the American College of Sports Medicine and the American Heart Association." *Med Sci Sports Exerc.* 39: 1423–34.

Hubert, H. B., M. Feinleib, P. M. McNamara, and W. P. Castelli. 1983. "Obesity as an Independent Risk Factor for Cardiovascular Disease: A 26-Year Follow-Up of Participants in the Framingham Heart Study." *Circulation* 67: 968–77.

Huffman, M. D., S. Capewell, H. Ning, C. M. Shay, E. S. Ford, and D. M. Lloyd-Jones. 2012. "Cardiovascular Health Behavior and Health Factor Changes (1988–2008) and Projections to 2020: Results From the National Health and Nutrition Examination Surveys." *Circulation* 125: 2595–2602.

Huxley, R. R., and M. Woodward. 2011. Cigarette Smoking as a Risk Factor for Coronary Heart Disease in Women Compared with Men: A Systematic Review and Meta-Analysis of Prospective Cohort Studies. *Lancet* 378: 1297–1305.

Insull, Jr., W. 2009. "The Pathology of Atherosclerosis: Plaque Development and Plaque Responses to Medical Treatment." *Am J Med.* 122: S3–S14.

James, P. A., S. Oparil, B. L. Carter, W. C. Cushman, C. Dennison-Himmelfarb, J. Handler, and D. T. Lackland, et al. 2014. "2014 Evidence-Based Guideline for the Management of High Blood Pressure in Adults: Report From the Panel Members Appointed to the Eighth Joint National Committee (JNC 8)." *JAMA.* 311: 507–20.

Jennings, R. B. "Historical Perspective on the Pathology of Myocardial Ischemia/Reperfusion Injury." *Circulation Research* 113: 428–38.

Joseph, J. J., J. B. Echouffo-Tcheugui, M. R. Carnethon, A. G.. Bertoni, C. M. Shay, H. M. Ahmed, R. S. Blumenthal, M. Cushman, and S. H. Golden. 2016. "The Association of Ideal Cardiovascular Health with Incident Type 2 Diabetes Mellitus: The Multi-Ethnic Study of Atherosclerosis." *Diabetologia* 59: 1893–1903.

Jousilahti, P., E. Vartiainen, J. Tuomilehto, and P. Puska. 1999. "Sex, Age, Cardiovascular Risk Factors, and Coronary Heart Disease: A Prospective Follow-Up Study of 14,786 Middle-Aged Men and Women in Finland." *Circulation* 99: 1165–72.

Kannel, W. B., T. R. Dawber, A. Kagan, N. Revotskie, and J. Stokes 3rd. 1961. "Factors of Risk in the Development of Coronary Heart Disease—Six Year Follow-Up Experience. The Framingham Study." *Ann Intern Med.* 55: 33–50.

Katzmarzyk, P. T., T. S. Church, C. L. Craig, C. Bouchard. 2009. "Sitting Time and Mortality from All Causes, Cardiovascular Disease, and Cancer." *Med Sci Sports Exerc.* 41: 998–1005.

Lee, C. D., S. N. Blair, and A. S. Jackson. 1999. "Cardiorespiratory Fitness, Body Composition, and All-Cause and Cardiovascular Disease Mortality in Men." *Am J Clin Nutr.* 69: 373–80.

Lee, D.-C., E. G. Artero, X. Sui, and S. N. Blair. 2010. "Mortality Trends in the General Population: The Importance of Cardiorespiratory Fitness." *J Psychopharmacol* 24, Supplement 4: 27–35.

Lee, D.-C., X. Sui, E. G. Argero, I.-M. Lee, T. S. Church, P. A. McAuley, F. C. Stanford, H. W. Kohl III, and S. N. Blair. 2011. "Long-Term Effects of Changes in Cardiorespiratory Fitness and Body Mass Index on All-Cause and Cardiovascular Disease Mortality in Men: The Aerobics Center Longitudinal Study." *Circulation.* 124: 2483–90.

Lee, I.-M., and P. J. Skerrett. 2001. "Physical Activity and All-Cause Mortality: What Is the Dose-Response Relation?" *Med Sci Sports Exerc.* 33: S459–S471.

Libby, P., P. M. Ridker, and G. K. Hansson. 2011. "Progress and Challenges in Translating the Biology of Atherosclerosis." *Nature* 47317: 317–25.

Lin, J. S., C. V. Evans, E. Johnson, N. Redmond, E. L. Coppola, N. Smith. 2018. "Nontraditional Risk Factors in Cardiovascular Disease Assessment: Updated Evidence Report and Systematic Review for the US Preventive Services Task Force." *JAMA* 320: 281–97.

Lloyd-Jones, D. M., B.-H. Nam, R. B. D'Agostino Sr., D. Levy, J. M. Murabito, T. J. Wang, P. W. F. Wilson, and C. J. O'Donnell. 2004. "Parental Cardiovascular Disease as a Risk Factor for Cardiovascular Disease in Middle-Aged Adults: A Prospective Study of Parents and Offspring." *JAMA* 291: 2204–11.

Lloyd-Jones, D. M, Y. Hong, D. Labarthe, D. Mozaffarian, L. J. Appel, L. Van Horn, K. Greenlund, S. Daniels, G. Nichol, G. F. Tomaselli, D. K. Arnett, G. C. Fonarow, P. M. Ho, M. S. Lauer, F. A. Masoudi, R. M. Robertson, V. Roger, L. H. Schwamm, P. Sorlie, C. W. Yancy, W. D. Rosamond; on behalf of the American Heart Association Strategic Planning Task Force and Statistics Committee. 2010. "Defining and Setting National Goals for Cardiovascular Health Promotion and Disease Reduction: The American Heart Association's Strategic Impact Goal through 2020 and Beyond." *Circulation* 121: 586–613.

Lv, X., J. Sun, Y. Bi, M. Xu, J. Lu, L. Zhao and Y. Xu. 2015. "Risk of All-Cause Mortality and Cardiovascular Disease Associated with Secondhand Smoke Exposure: A Systematic Review and Meta-Analysis." *Int J Cardiol.* 199: 106–15.

Mandsager, K., S. Harb, P. Cremer, D. Helan, S. E. Nissen, and W. Jaber. 2018. "Association of Cardiorespiratory Fitness with Long-Term Mortality among Adults Undergoing Exercise Treadmill Testing." *JAMA Network Open* 1(6): e183605. doi:10.1001/jamanetworkopen.2018.3605

Mayne S. L, R. Widome, A. J. Carroll, P. J. Schreiner, P. Gordon-Larsen, D. R. Jacobs, Jr., and K. N. Kershaw. 2018. "Longitudinal Associations of Smoke-Free Policies and Incident Cardiovascular Disease." *Circulation* 138: 557–66.

Meigs, J. B., L. A. Cupples, and P. W. F. Wilson. 2000. "Parental Transmission of Type 2 Diabetes—The Framingham Offspring Study." *Diabetes.* 49: 2201–07.

Meyer M. R., and M. Barton. 2016. "Estrogens and Coronary Artery Disease: New Clinical Perspectives." *Adv Pharmacol.* 77: 307–60.

Millan, J., X. Pinto, A. Munoz, M. Zuniga, J. Rubies-Prat, L. F. Pallardo, L. Masana, et al. 2009. "Lipoprotein Ratios: Physiological Significance and Clinical Usefulness in Cardiovascular Prevention." *Vascular Health and Risk Management* 5: 757–65.

Miller, M., N. J. Stone, C. Ballantyne, V. Bittner, M. H. Criqui, H. N. Ginsberg, and A. C. Goldberg, et al. 2011. On behalf of the American Heart Association Clinical Lipidology, Thrombosis, and Prevention Committee of the Council on Nutrition, Physical Activity and Metabolism, Council on Arteriosclerosis, Thrombosis and Vascular Biology, Council on Cardiovascular Nursing, and Council on the Kidney in Cardiovascular Disease. "Triglycerides and Cardiovascular Disease: A Scientific Statement from the American Heart Association." *Circulation* 123: 2292–333.

Mora, S. 2009. "Advanced Lipoprotein Testing and Subfractionation Are Not (Yet) Ready for Routine Clinical Use." *Circulation* 119: 2396–404.

Mori, H., S. Torii, M. Kutyna, A. Sakamoto, A. V. Finn, and R. Virmani. 2018. "Coronary Artery Calcificiation. What Does It Really Mean?" *J Am Coll Cardioll Img.* 11: 127–42.

Mozaffarian, D., E. J. Benjamin, A. S. Go, D. K. Arnett, M. J. Blaha, M. Cushman, and S. de Ferranti, et al. 2015. On behalf of the American Heart Association Statistics Committee and Stroke Statistics Subcommittee. "Heart Disease and Stroke Statistics—2015 Update: A Report from the American Heart Association." *Circulation* 131: e29–e322.

Mudd, J. O., B. A. Borlaug, P. V. Johnston, B. G. Kral, R. Rouf, R. S. Blumenthal, and P. O. Kwiterovich Jr. 2007. "Beyond Low-Density Lipoprotein Cholesterol: Defining the Role of Low-Density Lipoprotein Heterogeneity in Coronary Artery Disease." *J Am Coll Cardiol.* 50: 1735–41.

Muntner, P., L. D. Colantonio, M. Cushman, D. C.Goff Jr., G. Howard, V. J. Howard, B. Kissela, E. B. Levitan, D. M. Lloyd-Jones, and M. M. Safford. 2014. "Validation of the Atherosclerotic Cardiovascular Disease Pooled Cohort Risk Equations." *JAMA* 311: 1406–15.

Murray, C. J. L., C. Atkinson, K. Bhalla, G. Birbeck, R. Burstein, D. Chou, and R. Dellavalle, et al. 2013. "The State of US Health, 1990–2010: Burden of Diseases, Injuries, and Risk Factors." *JAMA* 310: 591–608.

Murray, C. J. L., and A. D. Lopez. 2013. "Measuring the Global Burden of Disease." *N Engl J Med.* 369: 448–57.

Nakahara T., M. R. Dweck, N. Narula, D. Pisapia, J. Narula, and H. W. Strauss. 2017. "Coronary Artery Calcification: From Mechanism to Molecular Imaging." *J Am Coll Cardiol Img.* 10: 582–93.

National Center for Health Statistics. 2018. *Health, United States, 2017: With Special Feature on Mortality.* Hyattsville, MD.

National Heart, Lung, and Blood Institute, 2012. *Morbidity and Mortality: 2012 Chart Book on Cardiovascular, Lung, and Blood Diseases.* Bethesda, MD.

Nichols G. A., M. Horberg, C. Koebnick, D. R. Young, B. Waitzfelder, N. E. Sherwood, M. F. Daley, and A. Ferrara. 2017. "Cardiometabolic Risk Factors Among 1.3 Million Adults With Overweight or Obesity, but Not Diabetes, in 10 Geographically Diverse Regions of the United States, 2012–2013." *Prev Chronic Dis.* 14: 160438. doi:https://doi.org/10.5888/pcd14.160438

Oktay, A. A., C. J. Lavie, P. F. Kokkinos, P. Parto, A. Pandey, and H. O. Ventura. 2017. "The Interaction of Cardiorespiratory Fitness with Obesity and the Obesity Paradox in Cardiovascular Disease." *Prog Card Disease.* 60: 30–44.

Olfert, I. M., E. DeVallance, H. Hoskiinson, K. W. Branyan, S Clayton, C. R. Pitzer, D. P. Sullivan, M. J. Breit, Z. W. P. Klinkhachorn, W. K Mandler, B. H. Erdreich, B. S. Ducatman, R. W. Bryner, P. Dasgupta, and P. D. Chantler. 2018. "Chronic Exposure to Electronic Cigarettes Results in Impaired Cardiovascular Function in Mice." *J Appl Physiol.* 124: 573–82.

Orozco, L. J., A. M. Buchleitner, G. Gimenez-Perez, M. Roqué i Figuls, B. Richter, and D. Mauricio. 2008. "Exercise or Exercise and Diet for Preventing Type 2 Diabetes Mellitus." *Cochrane Database of Systematic Reviews* 2008, 3. Art. No.: CD003054. doi:10.1002/14651858.CD003054.pub3

Ortega, F. B., C. J. Lavie, and S. N. Blair. 2016. "Obesity and Cardiovascular Disease." *Circ Res.* 118: 1752–70.

Parto, P., and C. J. Lavie. 2017. "Obesity and Cardiovascular Diseases." *Curr Probl Cardiol.* 42: 376–94.

Patel, S. A., M. Winkel, M. K. Ali, K. M. V. Narayan, and N. K. Mehta. 2015. "Cardiovascular Mortality Associated with 5 Leading Risk Factors: National and State Preventable Fractions Estimated from Survey Data." *Ann Intern Med.* 163: 245–53.

Piano, M. R., N. L. Benowitz, G. A. FitzGerald, S. Corbridge, J. Heath, E. Hahn, T. F. Pechacek, and G. Howard. 2010. "Impact of Smokeless Tobacco Products on Cardiovascular Disease: Implications for Policy, Prevention, and Treatment. A Policy Statement from the American Heart Association." *Circulation* 122: 1520–44.

Piness, G. 1920. "Review of 1918 Census of Causes of Ceath." *Cal State J Med.* 18: 121.

Powers, M. A., J. Bardsley, M. Cypress, P. Duker, M. M. Funnell, A. Hess Fischl, M. D. Maryniuk, L. Siminerio, and E. Vivian. 2015. "Diabetes Self-Management Education and Support in Type 2 Diabetes: A Joint Position Statement of the American Diabetes Association, the American Association of Diabetes Educators, and the Academy of Nutrition and Dietetics." *J Acad Nutr Diet.* 115: 1323–34.

Prospective Studies Collaboration. 2009. "Body-Mass Index and Cause-Specific Mortality in 900,000 Adults: Collaborative Analyses of 57 Prospective Studies." *Lancet* 373: 1083–96.

Provencher, M. T., J. Chala, G. Sanchez, M. E. Cinque, N. I. Kennedy, J. Whalen, M. D. Price, G. Moatshe, and R. F. LaPrade. 2018. "Body Mass Index versus Body Fat Percentage in Prospective National Football League Athletes: Overestimation of Obesity Rate in Athletes at the National Football League Scouting Combine." *J Strength Cond Res.* 32: 1013–19.

Riaz H., M. S. Khan, T. J. Siddiqi, M. S. Usman, N. Shah, A. Goyal, S. S. Khan, F. Mookadam, R. A. Krasuski, and H. Ahmed. 2018. "Association between Obesity and Cardiovascular Outcomes: A Systematic Review and Meta-Analysis of Mendelian Randomization Studies." *JAMA Network Open* 1: e183788. doi:10.1001/jamanetworkopen.2018.3788

Ridker, P. M. 2016. "A Test in Context. High-Sensitivity C-Reactive Protein." *J Am Coll Cardiol.* 67: 712–23.

Romero-Corral, A., V. K. Somers, J. Sierra-Johnson, R. J. Thomas, K. R. Bailey, M. L. Collazo-Clavell, T. G. Allison, J. Korinek, J. A. Batsis, and F. Lopez-Jimenez. 2008. "Accuracy of Body Mass Index to Diagnose Obesity in the US Adult Population." *Int J Obes (Lond).* 32: 959–66.

Ross R., S. N. Blair, R. Arena, T. S. Church, J-P. Després, B. A. Franklin, W. L. Haskell, L. A. Kaminsky, B. D. Levine, C. J. Lavie, J. Myers, J. Niebauer, R. Sallis, S. S. Sawada, X. Sui, U. Wisløff; on behalf of the American Heart Association Physical Activity Committee of the Council on Lifestyle and Cardiometabolic Health; Council on Clinical Cardiology; Council on Epidemiology and Prevention; Council on Cardiovascular and Stroke Nursing; Council on Functional Genomics and Translational Biology; and Stroke Council. 2016. "Importance of Assessing Cardiorespiratory Fitness in Clinical Practice: A Case for Fitness as a Clinical Vital Sign: A Scientific Statement from the American Heart Association." *Circulation* 134: e653–99.

Ross, R., and Glomset, J. A. 1976a. "The Pathogenesis of Atherosclerosis (First of Two Parts)." *N Engl J Med.* 295: 369–77.

Ross, R., and J. A. Glomset. 1976b. "The Pathogenesis of Atherosclerosis (Second of Two Parts)." *N Engl J Med.* 295: 420–25.

Rozanski, A., J. A. Blumenthal, and J. Kaplan. 1999. "Impact of Psychological Factors on the Pathogenesis of Cardiovascular Disease and Implications for Therapy." *Circulation* 99: 2192–217.

Sahakyan, K. R., V. K. Somers, J. P. Rodriguez-Escudero, D. O. Hodge, R. E. Carter, O. Sochor, T. Coutinho, M. D. Jensen, V. L. Roger, P. Singh, and F. Lopez-Jiminez. 2015. "Normal-Weight Central Obesity: Implications for Total and Cardiovascular Mortality." *Ann Intern Med.* 163: 827–35.

Saydah, S., K. McKeever Bullard, Y. Cheng, M. K. Ali, E. W. Gregg, L. Geiss, and G. Imperatore. 2014. "Trends in Cardiovascular Disease Risk Factors by Obesity Level in Adults in the United States, NHANES 1999–2010." *Obesity* 22: 1888–95.

Sénéchal, M., J. Slaght, N. Bharti, and D. R. Bouchard. 2014. "Independent and Combined Effect of Diet and Exercise in Adults with Prediabetes." *Diabetes, Metabolic Syndrome and Obesity: Targets and Therapy* 7: 521–29.

Sniderman, A. D., D. Blank, R. Zakarian, J. Bergeron, and J. Frohlich. 2003. "Triglycerides and Small Dense LDL: The Twin Achilles Heels of the Friedewald Formula." *Clinical Biochemistry* 36: 499–504.

Son, J. S., S. Choi, K. Kim, S. M. Kim, D. Choi, G. Lee, S. Jeong, S. Y. Park, Y. Kim, J. Youn and S.M. Park. 2018. "Association of Blood Pressure Classification in Korean Young Adults According to the 2017 American College of Cardiology/American Heart Association Guidelines with Subsequent Cardiovascular Events." *JAMA* 320: 1783–92.

Steptoe, A. and L. Brydon. 2009. "Emotional Triggering of Cardiac Events." *Neuroscience and Biobehavioral Reviews* 33: 63–70.

Stone, N. J., J. G. Robinson, A. H. Lichtenstein, C. N. Bairey Merz, C. B. Blum, R. H. Eckel, and A. C. Goldberg. 2014. "2013 ACC/AHA Guideline on the Treatment of Blood Cholesterol to Reduce Atherosclerotic Cardiovascular Risk in Adults: A Report of the American College of Cardiology/American Heart Association Task Force on Practice Guidelines." *Circulation* 129, suppl 2: S1–45.

Sui, X., M. J. LaMonte, and S. N. Blair. 2007. "Cardiorespiratory Fitness as a Predictor of Nonfatal Cardiovascular Events in Asymptomatic Women and Men." *Am J Epidemiol.* 165: 1413–23.

Sun, Tzu. 2002. *The Art of War.* Translated by L Giles. Mineola: Dover Publications.

Superko, H. R. 2009. "Advanced Lipoprotein Testing and Subfractionation Are Clinically Useful." *Circulation* 119: 2382–95.

Teo K. K., S. Ounpuu, S. Hawken, M. R. Pandey, V. Valentin, D. Hunt, R. Diaz, W. Rashed, R. Freeman, L. Jiang, X. Zhang, S. Yusuf on behalf of INTERHEART Study Investigators. 2006. "Tobacco Use and Risk of Myocardial Infarction in 52 Countries in the INTERHEART Study: A Case-Control Study. *Lancet* 368: 647–58.

US Burden of Disease Collaborators. 2018. "The State of US Health, 1990–2016: Burden of Diseases, Injuries, and Risk Factors among US States." *JAMA* 319: 1444–72.

U.S. Department of Health and Human Services. 2014. *The Health Consequences of Smoking—50 Years of Progress. A Report of the Surgeon General.* Atlanta: U.S. Department of Health and Human Services, Centers for Disease Control and Prevention, National Center for Chronic Disease Prevention and Health Promotion, Office on Smoking and Health.

U.S. Department of Health and Human Services. 2018. *Physical Activity Guidelines for Americans.* 2nd ed. Washington, DC: U.S. Department of Health and Human Services.

U.S. Department of Health and Human Services and U.S. Department of Agriculture. 2015–2020 Dietary Guidelines for Americans. 8th ed. December 2015. http://health.gov/dietaryguidelines/2015/guidelines/.

Voet, D., and J. G. Voet. 2010. *Biochemistry. 4th ed.* Hoboken: Wiley.

Wang, T. W., K. Asman, A. S. Gentzke, K. A. Cullen, E. Holde-Hayes, Reyes-Guzman, A. Jamal, L. Neff, and B. A. King. 2018. "Tobacco Product Use among Adults—United States." 2017. *MMWR Morb Mortal Wkly Rep.* 67: 1225–32.

Wang, T., D. Palucci, K. Law, B. Yanagawa, J. Yam, and J. Butany. 2012. "Atherosclerosis: Pathogenesis and Pathology." *Diagnostic Histopathology* 18: 461–67.

Wei, M., J. B. Kampert, C. E. Barlow, M. Z. Nichaman, L. W. Gibbons, R. S. Paffenbarger, Jr. S. N. Blair. 1999. "Relationship between Low Cardiorespiratory Fitness and Mortality in Normal-Weight, Overweight, and Obese Men." *JAMA* 282: 1547–53.

Whelton, P. K., R. M. Carey, W. D. Aronow, D. E. Casey Jr, K. J. Collins, C. Dennison Himmelfarb, S. M. DePalma, S. Gidding, K. A. Jamerson, D. W. Jones, E. J. MacLaughlin, P. Muntner, B. Ovbiagele, S. C. Smith Jr, C. C. Spencer, R. S. Stafford, S. J. Taler, R. J. Thomas, K. A. Williams Sr., J. D. Williamson, and J. T. Wright Jr. 2018. "2017 ACC/AHA/AAPA/ABC/ACPM/AGS/APhA/ASH/ASPC/NMA/PCNA Guideline for the Prevention, detection, Evaluation, and Management of High Blood Pressure in Adults: A Report of the American College of Cardiology/American Heart Association Task Force on Clinical Practice Guidelines." *J Am Coll Cardiol.* 71: e127–248.

Williams, P. T. 2001. "Physical Fitness and Activity as Separate Heart Disease Risk Factors: A Meta-Analysis." *Med Sci Sports Exerc.* 33: 754–61.

World Health Organization. 1995. "*Physical Status: The Use and Interpretation of Anthropometry. Report of a WHO Expert Committee.*" World Health Organ Tech Rep Ser 854: 1–452.

Wu M-Y., C-J. Li, M-.F Hou, and P-Y. Chu. 2017. "New Insights into the Role of Inflammation in the Pathogenesis of Atherosclerosis." *Int J Mol Sci.* 18: 2034. doi:10.3390/ijms18102034

Yang, Z., C. A. Scott, C. Mao, J. Tang, and A. J. Farmer. 2014. "Resistance Exercise Versus Aerobic Exercise for Type 2 Diabetes: A Systematic Review and Meta-Analysis." *Sports Med.* 44: 487–99.

Yi, S-W., H. Ohrr, S-A. Shing, and J-J. Yi. 2015. "Sex-Age-Specific Association of Body Mass Index with All-Cause Mortality among 12.8 Million Korean Adults: A Prospective Cohort Study. *Int J Epidemiol.* 44: 1696–1705.

Yusuf, S., S. Hawken, Ôunpuu, T. Dans, A. Avezum, F. Lanas, M. McQueen, et al. 2004. On behalf of the INTERHEART Study Investigators. "Effect of Potentially Modifiable Risk Factors Associated with Myocardial Infarction in 52 Countries (The INTERHEART Study): Case-Control Study." *Lancet* 364: 937–52.

CHAPTER 4

Exercise Prescription for Developing Cardiorespiratory Fitness

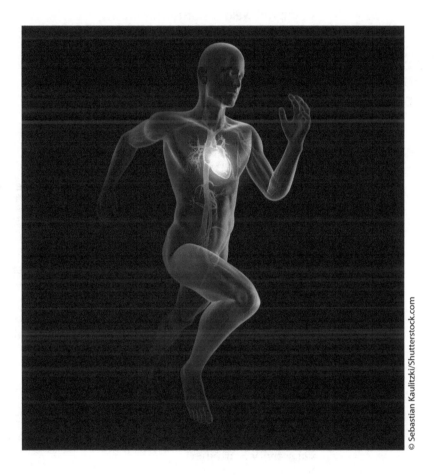

© Sebastian Kaulitzki/Shutterstock.com

OVERVIEW

In Chapter 3, the benefits of physical activity and cardiorespiratory fitness for reducing a client's risk for cardiovascular disease were reviewed. However, the benefits of being physically active extend far beyond just cardiovascular disease. A summary of these benefits is provided in Table 4.1. The important point here is that being physically active has far-reaching benefits for everyone. A second important point, touched on in Chapter 3, is that the amount of physical activity needed to derive substantial health benefits is relatively modest—any activity will help. The 2018 Physical Activity Guidelines for Americans recommends that everyone perform at least 75 minutes of vigorous intensity physical activity weekly, or 150 minutes of moderate intensity activity, or some combination, preferably with the activity spread over the week (USDHHS 2018). From a health perspective, an

TABLE 4.1		
Physical Activity-Related Health Benefits for the General Population		
CHILDREN		
3 to < 6 years of age	Improved bone health and weight status	
6 to 17 years of age	Improved cognitive function (ages 6–13 years)	
	Improved cardiorespiratory and muscular fitness	
	Improved bone health	
	Improved cardiovascular risk factor status	
	Improved weight status or adiposity	
	Fewer symptoms of depression	
ADULTS, ALL AGES		
All-cause mortality	Lower risk	
Cardiometabolic Conditions	Lower cardiovascular incidence and mortality (including heart disease and stroke)	
	Lower incidence of hypertension	
	Lower incidence of Type 2 diabetes	
Cancer	Lower incidence of bladder, breast, colon, endometrium, esophagus, kidney, stomach, and lung cancers	
Brain Health	Reduced risk of dementia	
	Improved cognitive function	
	Improved cognitive function following bouts of aerobic activity	
	Improved quality of life	
	Improved sleep	
	Reduced feelings of anxiety and depression in healthy people and in people with existing clinical syndromes	
	Reduced incidence of depression	
Weight Status	Reduced risk of excessive weight gain	
	Weight loss and the prevention of weight regain following initial weight loss when a sufficient dose of moderate-to-vigorous physical activity is attained	
	An additive effect on weight loss when combined with moderate dietary restriction	
OLDER ADULTS		
Falls	Reduced incidence of falls	
	Reduced incidence of fall-related injuries	
Physical Function	Improved physical function in older adults with and without frailty	
From 2018 Physical Activity Guidelines Advisory Committee (2018).		

optimal dose is 150–300 minutes of moderate-to-vigorous physical activity (2018 Physical Activity Guideline Committee 2018).

In Chapter 3, you were encouraged to use a four-step approach in deciding what physical activity behaviors to emphasize to your client (Figure 4.1). This chapter will focus primarily on Step 3 of this

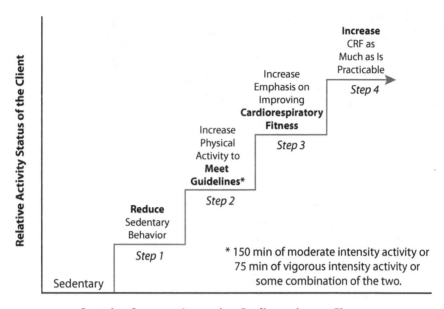

Stepping Stones to Improving Cardiorespiratory Fitness

Figure 4.1   Approach to Use When Working with a Client to Improve Cardiorespiratory Fitness

approach, which is developing an exercise prescription for clients who want to improve their cardio-respiratory fitness. Step 3 differs from Step 2 in that Step 2 was focused primarily on using physical activity as a means to improve health.

The term "cardiorespiratory fitness" refers to maximal oxygen uptake, or VO$_2$max. VO$_2$max is the maximal amount of oxygen that can be consumed by a client; a higher VO$_2$max reflects better cardiorespiratory fitness. In a laboratory environment, this is typically determined by measuring a client's VO$_2$ as they complete progressively more intense workloads on a treadmill or cycle ergometer until they are unable to progress to a higher workload. This is commonly referred to as a "graded exercise test," or "exercise tolerance test." Maximal effort is desired but performing supramaximal work as part of this type of protocol does not markedly change a client's VO$_2$max (Hawkins et al. 2007). Outside of a laboratory, such as in a high school physical education class, cardiorespiratory fitness is often assessed using field tests, such as the FitnessGram PACER test, a timed one-mile run or measuring the distance covered in a twelve-minute run.

While a higher VO$_2$max is considered the benchmark measure of better cardiorespiratory fitness, it is often confused with cardiorespiratory endurance and cardiorespiratory performance. Cardiorespiratory endurance refers to how long aerobic exercise can be performed using large muscle groups. Someone who can complete a marathon has better cardiorespiratory endurance than someone who struggles to complete a 5K run. Cardiorespiratory performance generally refers to how fast someone can traverse a specific distance by running, cycling, swimming, or the like. A runner with a personal best marathon time of 2:30 has better cardiorespiratory performance than a marathoner with a best time of 3:00. The field tests performed in a physical education class actually assess performance.

Consequently, cardiorespiratory fitness can be conceptually thought of as "how high," cardiorespiratory endurance is "how long," and performance is "how fast." Not surprisingly, these three measures are inter-related physiologically; VO$_2$max is a very important determinant of cardiorespiratory endurance and performance (Levine 2008). Why? The physiologic adaptations associated with the exercise training needed to improve cardiorespiratory fitness also affect endurance and performance. These adaptations can include increased heart size, cardiac compliance, stroke volume, blood volume, and lactate threshold; an altered utilization of carbohydrates and fats as fuel; and, in the trained muscles, increases in capillary density, mitochondrial density, and oxidative enzymes (Joyner and Coyle 2008; Kenney, Wilmore, and Costill 2012).

As a practical example of the inter-relatedness between fitness, endurance, and performance, consider the two-mile run time used by the U.S. Army to assess cardiorespiratory fitness. A timed run is a measure of cardiorespiratory performance since "how fast" is being assessed. However, it is viewed as an acceptable surrogate for assessing fitness since the association between VO_2max and two-mile run time in soldiers is quite robust (r ~ −0.90; Mello, Murphy, and Vogel 1988). In other words, research supports the common-sense notion that, compared to less fit people, people who are more fit typically can run a certain distance faster.

On the other hand, it is important to remember that, while cardiorespiratory fitness, endurance, and performance are interrelated, they are not synonymous (Levine 2008). Individual clients vary in each parameter. Take the example of a 55-year-old man with a VO_2max of 54 ml/kg/min and his fastest time for a 1.5-mile run is 14:34. Table 4.2 has the normative data for a large group of his peers, men between 50–59 years old, who were assessed at the Cooper Institute (2013). Based

TABLE 4.2		
	Cardiorespiratory Fitness	Cardiorespiratory Performance
Percentile Ranking	VO_2 max (ml/kg/min)	1.5 Mile Run (time)
99	54.0	9:34
95	49.0	10:38
90	46.7	11:11
85	44.6	11:45
80	43.4	12:07
75	41.9	12:36
70	41.0	12:53
65	39.9	13:17
60	39.2	13:32
55	38.1	13:57
50	37.4	14:16
45	36.7	14:34
40	35.6	15:03
35	35.0	15:20
30	33.8	15:58
25	33.0	16:21
20	32.3	16:46
15	30.9	17:38
10	29.4	18:38
5	27.0	20:53
1	22.8	25:01
n =	11,693	

From Cooper Institute (2013)

on these data, he's at the 99th percentile for cardiorespiratory fitness but at the 45th percentile for performance. The former shows that he is actually quite fit but, if his cardiorespiratory fitness was assessed by his run time, he would be viewed as average at best. If he is so fit, then why is he so slow?

The answer to that question has several components. First, there is specificity to the cardiovascular, respiratory, and muscular adaptations seen with various types of aerobic training. As was likely reviewed in your college exercise physiology course, the exercise training required to evoke the physiologic adaptations needed to run long distances differs from that needed to run a short distance faster. Thus, training to improve cardiorespiratory fitness differs from training to improve performance. The latter requires including "speed work" in the training, such as with interval work, in order to raise the lactate threshold. In other words, this client needs to train at higher intensities. While this *will* also improve his cardiorespiratory fitness, improving cardiorespiratory fitness does not necessarily require high exercise intensities. Specificity can also be seen in the situation where a previously inactive client trained for three months but did so exclusively on a cycle ergometer. The client will probably have a higher VO_2max after training. However, if this client's VO_2max was assessed on a treadmill on one day and a cycle ergometer on another day, they would most likely have the higher VO_2max with the cycle ergometer test (Millet et al. 2009). Why? They just spent three months getting fit, but did so by cycling rather than jogging.

The second part of the answer to the question is that there is a marked genetic component to both a subject's VO_2max and the change in their VO_2max consequent to exercise training (Bouchard et al. 1998; Bouchard et al. 1999). Up to about 50 percent of these responses are heritable. So, if a sedentary client "picked the right parents," they may have a higher-than-expected VO_2max. They may also exhibit greater improvements in their VO_2max compared to another client who is exercising the same way but was not as gifted genetically. In the case of the fit-but-slow 55-year-old man, his dilemma is likely a combination of not doing the type of training needed to improve his running speed and not having the genetics needed to run fast.

"I'm looking for a nine minute mile pace. Ready, and ..."

©Cartoonresource/Shutterstock.com

THE "P" OF CRIPL: PRESCRIBING A CARDIORESPIRATORY EXERCISE PROGRAM

In Chapter 2, you were introduced to the CRIPL rubric. Each component of CRIPL was discussed in detail, including an extensive review of pre-participation screening. Chapter 3 focused on cardiovascular disease risk factor identification and modification. Collectively, Chapters 2 and 3 prepared you to implement the C, R, and I components of CRIPL (i.e., Clinical history, Risk factor assessment, Interpreting the data). In this section, the P of CRIPL will be given considerable attention. However, the focus will be restricted to developing an exercise prescription to improve cardiorespiratory fitness. Developing an exercise prescription for the other components of fitness will be discussed in subsequent chapters of this book.

In Chapter 3 you learned that, from a health perspective, the weekly goal for exercise is to achieve 150 minutes of moderate intensity exercise, or 75 minutes of vigorous intensity exercise, or some combination of the two. When expressed as an absolute intensity, moderate intensity exercise was defined as any activity requiring between 3 to 5.9 METs while vigorous intensity exercise requires 6 METs or more. When expressed as MET-minutes (i.e., METs of exercise × minutes performed), these goals equate to a minimum of 450 MET-minutes weekly (3 METs × 150 minutes or 6 METs × 75 minutes). The goal is 500 to 1,000 MET-minutes, or at least 1,000 kilocalories, weekly in order to achieve a lower risk of dying prematurely (American College of Sports Medicine 2018; USDHHS 2018). Once a client is exercising enough to meet the minimum recommendation of 500 MET-minutes per week (or "Step 2" of Figure 4.1), and if they want to increase their cardiorespiratory fitness ("Step 3"), then these higher values should be the goals to achieve.

As a result, the exercise prescription you develop for a client should be oriented toward achieving 1,000 kcal each week. (Parenthetically, the "calorie" on a food label is technically 1 kilocalorie of energy. From a practical perspective they are the same, so in this book we'll just use "calories.") MET-minutes is an esoteric term and can be challenging to explain to a client. On the other hand, nearly everyone has an intuitive understanding of calories. The resulting exercise prescription will be simpler to explain to your client if you use "calorie" as the guideline. In addition, everything else being equal, higher exercise intensities are associated with greater health benefits than lower intensities. Therefore, within the constraints of the client's capabilities and motivation, the client should strive to exercise at more vigorous intensities rather than either low or moderate intensities.

A summary of the components of an exercise prescription designed to improve cardiorespiratory fitness is below. These four components are often referred to as FITT:

Frequency:	3 to 5 days per week
Intensity: *(see Table 4.2)*	40 (or 50) to 85% Heart Rate Reserve (HRR) 40 (or 50) to 85% VO$_2$ Reserve (VO$_2$R) 12 to 16 on the 6 to 20 Ratings of Perceived Exertion (RPE) scale Average Conditioning Intensity (ACI)
Time:	The American College of Sports Medicine recommends accumulating 30 to 60 min/day of moderate intensity exercise or 20 to 60 min/day of vigorous intensity exercise or some combination. If need be, this accumulation can be done in several bouts of daily exercise of >10 minutes duration. The goal is to achieve an exercise volume equivalent to 1,000 calories/week. The *time* needed to achieve this goal depends on the *frequency* and *intensity* of the exercise bouts.
Type:	Any physical activity that is rhythmic, continuous, and involves large muscle groups.

The exercise prescription needs to be customized to each participant—a "cookbook" approach where the same "recipe" is used for every client is poor professional practice. Consequently, it is important to understand the rationale underlying each of the FITT components so you can intelligently modify them as needed. To that end, each are explained below.

Frequency

It has long been known that training even one day/week can evoke improvements in VO$_2$max in average-fit healthy adults performing vigorous intensity exercise (Gettman et al. 1976). So, why is three days/week the recommended minimum? First, recall from Chapter 2 that the risk of acute cardiac events is markedly elevated in sedentary subjects performing an acute bout of vigorous exercise. This is exactly the situation for subjects who train just one day/week—these "weekend warriors" are at a higher risk for an adverse event. Second, while exercise is only one

©Halfpoint/Shutterstock.com

component of a weight loss program, high volumes of exercise are needed to do so (Swift et al. 2014). One or two days/week is woefully insufficient. Third, it is difficult for exercise to become a habit, or part of a client's lifestyle, if the client does not perform it with regularity. Again, one or two days/week is insufficient to accomplish this goal. On the other hand, if the goal is to increase cardiorespiratory fitness, then training more than five days/week is unnecessary. With vigorous intensity exercise, the improvement in VO$_2$max is not markedly greater with a five day/week program compared to a three day/week program (Gettman et al. 1976) and everything else being equal, four days/week may be optimal (Wenger and Bell 1986). However, the risk of injuries is increased with higher volumes of training (Pollock et al. 1977); cross-training can attenuate this risk but, again, the extra time spent training is largely wasted since the increase in VO$_2$max is minimal. Nevertheless, these extra training days may be justifiable if the client's goals are performance-related (e.g., an athlete) or weight loss-related (e.g., expending calories) such that the desired benefits may outweigh the increased injury risk.

Intensity

Of the FITT components, exercise intensity is the most important determinant of the improvement in cardiorespiratory fitness (Garber et al. 2011; Gormley et al. 2008; Swain and Franklin 2002; Wenger and Bell 1986). Vigorous intensity exercise is more effective at increasing VO$_2$max than moderate intensity exercise, even when the latter is performed for longer durations to elicit the same caloric expenditure (Gormley et al. 2008; Swain and Franklin 2002). On a per-minute basis, more vigorous intensity exercise also burns more calories than less vigorous exercise. Thus, a client can achieve the goal of expending 1,000 calories/week more quickly with the former (e.g., a lower time commitment). Because of this time efficiency and the greater cardiorespiratory benefits of training at high intensities (Wenger and Bell 1986), it makes sense to have clients train at the highest relative intensity they can safely tolerate and are willing to do. To that end, the American College of Sports Medicine recommends a maximal intensity of 90 percent HRR or VO$_2$R rather than the 85 percent suggested here (ACSM 2018).

A major disadvantage of training at high exercise intensities, especially above the ventilatory or lactate thresholds, is that most people find doing so to be quite unpleasant (Ekkekakis et al. 2011). This is also the case if the exercise intensity is imposed upon them, rather than of their own choosing (e.g., the personal trainer dictates the exercise intensity to the client) (Ekkekakis et al. 2011; Vazou-Ekkekakis and Ekkekakis 2009). If a client finds exercising to be unpleasant, then they are more likely to quit. Thus, when communicating the desired exercise prescription to the client, it is important to reinforce to the client that their choice of exercise intensity is ultimately up to them and it should be an intensity they enjoy. Ideally, this choice would be as high an intensity as they can perform without the exercise becoming less enjoyable (Ekkekakis, Parfitt, and Petruzzello 2011).

The exercise should be enjoyable to the client and, in general, lower intensities are more enjoyable than higher intensities. But, if the client wants to increase their cardiorespiratory fitness, it is important that they exercise above the threshold intensity, or the minimum intensity at which the desired physiological adaptations occur. Unfortunately, the evidence supporting specific threshold intensities is not robust, although it is known that the threshold intensity varies by the initial fitness level of the client (Garber et al. 2011; Swain and Franklin 2002). For very unfit clients, there may not be a minimum intensity—*any* exercise may evoke improvements. For relatively unfit individuals, defined as having a VO$_2$max <40 ml·kg^{-1}·min^{-1}, an intensity as low as 30 percent VO$_2$R will likely suffice (see Table 4.3 for how to calculate intensity). For more fit individuals, a minimal exercise intensity of 45 percent VO$_2$R is probably sufficient (Swain and Franklin 2002). For these reasons, ACSM recommends a minimal intensity of 30 percent in deconditioned adults and 40 percent VO$_2$R in most adults (ACSM 2018). To ensure that clients will improve with their training, this textbook recommends using minimum intensities of 40 and 50 percent VO$_2$R in unfit and fit clients, respectively. In *new* exercisers, use a minimum of 30 percent to ensure they have a positive experience when first exercising.

A relatively recent development in exercise training is high-intensity interval training, or HIIT. Here, the client performs short bouts of exercise at or well above the recommended maximum exercise intensities with rest periods between these bursts (Buchheit and Laursen 2013a). HIIT could include bouts of brief all-out, supramaximal exercise or slightly longer bouts of exercise at $\geq$ 85 percent VO$_2$R (Gibala et al. 2018). Several positive adaptations occur with this type of training (Buchheit and Laursen 2013a, 2013b). Many authors tout HIIT as being superior to conventional training in improving cardiorespiratory fitness in less fit or previously sedentary clients (Gibala et al. 2018). In more fit subjects, the improvements in VO$_2$max are not markedly greater than more traditional cardiorespiratory training (Milanović, Sporiš, and Weston 2015; Weston et al. 2014). On the other hand, it can be a very time-efficient way to train with equal fitness benefits occurring with about half the energy expenditure seen with conventional training (2018 Physical Activity Guidelines Committee 2018).

Highly trained endurance athletes, especially those who incorporate HIIT-type interval or speed work into their training, will develop a higher lactate threshold. This helps them to exercise at a higher relative percentage of their VO_2max before they accumulate excessive blood lactate (Joyner and Coyle 2008; Kenney, Wilmore, and Costill 2012). By training to raise their lactate thresholds, clients may be able to run at a higher relative percentage of their VO_2max, and therefore a faster pace. So a client who wished to, say, lower their 5K race time may consider including HIIT into their exercise program.

Because of the relative newness of this training method, there are no set guidelines as to how

"Time for sneakers. Next class is across campus."

© Cartoonresource/Shutterstock.com

to develop HIIT programs. Almost all HIIT programs in the literature use work:rest intervals of predetermined time durations. These intervals often have rest intervals that are shorter than the work interval. The latter is at odds with basic exercise physiology. In general, supramaximal bouts of training require longer recovery times and less intense bouts require shorter recovery times. These work:rest intervals can therefore vary from 1:10 (e.g., 10 sec on: 60 secs off for a supramaximal bout) to 1:1 (60 secs on:60 secs off for a less intense bout). Because of differences in individual responses to exercise, it is actually better to use heart rate responses rather than time as your guide in developing work:rest intervals. Here, heart rate is a surrogate measure of VO_2. For example, rather than using a set time interval of 60 secs on:60 secs off for a HIIT session, a client could exercise at a high workload until their HR exceeded 90 percent HRR, and then exercise at a much lower workload until their HR fell below 50 percent HRR. After the HR fell below this 50 percent HRR they could begin the next interval by going back to that high initial workload. As the client adapted to this training program, the duration of these intervals will inherently change (e.g., faster recovery in the rest interval, changes in programmed workloads to elicit desired HR responses). By monitoring the HR responses, you can be more responsive to their fitness adaptations and modify the program when you know they are ready, rather than based on some arbitrary schedule.

When determining exercise intensity, an additional consideration is how best to calculate the desired exercise intensity. The four methods provided here (Table 4.3) give you enough choices to fit most situations and most clients. All are reasonable methods and, assuming both maximal heart rate and VO_2max are assessed accurately, they overlap sufficiently to be considered interchangeable. For example, moderate intensity exercise can be defined as 40–59 percent HRR, 40–59 percent VO_2R, or an RPE of 12–13 and vigorous intensity exercise is 60–84 percent HRR, 60–84 percent VO_2R, or an RPE of 14–16 (Howley 2001; 2018 Physical Activity Guidelines Advisory Committee 2018). Being skilled at using multiple methods of exercise intensity will give you flexibility when working with a client. Suppose a client is on a medication that attenuates the HR response to exercise. It is no longer appropriate to use %HRR, so what can you do? RPE or %VO_2R would be viable alternatives so you could use those instead.

Unlike these other methods, the ACI yields a specific training intensity rather than a range of intensities within which the client trains. The ACI typically falls within the aforementioned VO_2R. It is important to remember that this is the *average* conditioning intensity and not the *minimal* conditioning intensity. The ACI can best be used to develop an interval workout where the client alternates between training above and below the ACI. As an example, the ACI for the subject in Table 4.3 was 7.7 METs; he could alternate between 1-minute bouts of exercise at 6.7 METs and 8.7 METs to average this 7.7 MET goal. If the client was motivated to do HIIT training, you could use the ACI to determine that the bouts of exercise could alternate between 9.7 (near maximal intensity) and 5.7 METs (recovery intensity).

Finally, while there are a number of scales used to assess the client's perceptions of effort (Borg 1982), the Borg 6 to 20 RPE scale is probably the most commonly used. The lactate threshold can vary considerably among individuals (Joyner and Coyle 2008) but coincides with when most people begin to find exercise unpleasant (Ekkekakis, Parfitt, and Petruzzello 2011). An RPE of ~14 ± 2 corresponds with the lactate threshold for most people (Scherr et al. 2013). Encouraging the client to exercise within the RPE range of 12 to 16 will help to keep the exercise enjoyable and, by extension, increase the likelihood that the client will continue to exercise. For this reason, if the client's perceived effort seems to be disproportionately high relative to the physical demands of the exercise (e.g., client's RPE is 17 even though he is exercising at just 50 percent HRR), then reduce the latter to ensure that the exercise remains enjoyable.

An increasingly common alternative to the 6–20 RPE scale is the 0–10 scale. Here, 0 is the effort associated with seated rest and 10 is maximal effort. Moderate intensity exercise should evoke a 5 or 6 and vigorous intensities should be a 7 or 8 (2018 Physical Activity Guidelines Advisory Committee 2018). The sing-talk test is an acceptable alternative if a client struggles with numeracy. Here, if the client can sing while exercising, then they are a light intensity activity. They should be able to talk but not sing in moderate intensity activities, and would struggle to talk during vigorous activities.

TABLE 4.3
Methods of Calculating Exercise Intensity

---

40 (or 50) to 85% Heart Rate Reserve (HRR) (Swain et al. 1998)

Step 1. Determine maximum heart rate (HR) or, if not known, estimate it based on the client's age.* There are several acceptable formulae; for this book, the formula [208 – 0.7(age)] (Tanaka et al. 2001) is being used.

Step 2. Determine minimum, or resting, HR.

Step 3. Subtract resting HR from maximum HR to determine HR Reserve (HRR). The HRR represents the entire range of the client's possible HR responses—from minimum to maximum.

Step 4. Multiply HRR by 0.40 if the client is unfit, or 0.50 if the client is fit and/or has been exercising. Add resting HR to this number, since resting HR is the subject's "baseline."

Step 5. Multiply HRR by 0.85 for all subjects. Add resting HR to this number.

Example:
55-year-old male client with resting HR of 68 and has not been exercising.
1. Maximum HR is estimated as [208 – (0.7 x 55)] = 170
2. Resting HR = 68
3. HRR = 170 – 68 = 102
4. (102 x 0.40) + 68 = 109
5. (102 x 0.85) + 68 = 155

This client would train at heart rates of 109 to 155 bpm if training at 40–85% HRR.

* Age-predicted estimates of maximal HR are usually within about ± 10 bpm of the true maximal HR for about 2/3 of clients. They will differ by more than 10 bpm for the other 1/3.

(Continued)

40 (or 50) to 85% VO$_2$ Reserve (VO$_2$R) (Swain et al. 1998)

Step 1. Determine maximum VO$_2$ or, if not known, estimate it using a submaximal exercise test.

Step 2. Estimate minimum, or resting, VO$_2$ as 3.5 ml·kg^{-1}·min^{-1}.

Step 3. Subtract resting VO$_2$ from VO$_2$max to determine VO$_2$R. As with HRR, the VO$_2$R represents the entire range of the subject's possible VO$_2$ responses—from minimum to maximum.

Step 4. Multiply VO$_2$R by 0.40 if the subject is unfit, or 0.50 if the client is fit and/or has been exercising. As with HRR, add resting VO$_2$, since this is the client's "baseline."

Step 5. Multiply VO$_2$R by 0.85 for all subjects. Add resting VO$_2$ to this number.

Example:
  55-year-old male client who has not been exercising and with a VO$_2$ max of 38 ml·kg^{-1}·min^{-1}.
  1. VO$_2$max = 38 ml·kg^{-1}·min^{-1}
  2. resting VO$_2$ = 3.5 ml·kg^{-1}·min^{-1}
  3. VO$_2$R = 38 − 3.5 = 34.5
  4. (34.5 x 0.40) + 3.5 = 17.3
  5. (34.5 x 0.85) + 3.5 = 32.8

This client would train at VO$_2$ of between 17.3 and 32.8 ml·kg^{-1}·min^{-1} if training at 40–85% VO$_2$R.

12 to 16 on the 6 to 20 Ratings of Perceived Exertion (RPE) scale (Borg 1982)

6	
7	very, very light
8	
9	very light
10	
11	fairly light
12	
13	***somewhat hard***
14	
15	***hard***
16	
17	very hard
18	
19	very, very hard
20	

This 12–16 range is used for all clients.

Average Conditioning Intensity (ACI) (ACSM 1980)

Step 1. Determine maximum VO$_2$ or, if not known, estimate it using a submaximal exercise test.

Step 2. Convert VO$_2$max to METs to create a METmax.

Step 3. Sum 60 and METmax. Divide this value by 100.

Step 4. Multiply this decimal figure by the METmax to determine the ACI, or the average intensity at which the subject should train.

(Continued)

Example:

    55-year-old client with a VO$_2$max of 38 ml·kg^{-1}·min^{-1}.

1. VO$_2$max = 38 ml·kg^{-1}·min^{-1}
2. METmax = 38/3.5 = 10.85 METs
3. (60 + 10.86)/100 = .7086
4. .7086 x 10.86 = 7.69 METs

This client would train at an average VO$_2$ of 7.69 METs, which could also be expressed as 26.9 ml·kg^{-1}·min^{-1} (7.69 x 3.5 = 26.9). Note that the ACI is within the 40–85% VO$_2$R; this comparison is a handy check of your arithmetic, since this will be the case for virtually all your clients.

Time

In many respects, the issues which affect the Time component of FITT parallel those which affect the Frequency component. Just as a low exercise frequency (i.e., one day/week) can improve cardio-respiratory fitness in previously inactive clients, short bouts of exercise (i.e., ten minutes) can also be effective. Some evidence suggests that even five-minute bouts of exercise can be beneficial in unfit subjects (2018 Physical Activity Guidelines Committee 2018). Moreover, in previously sedentary subjects and in the short-term, multiple short bouts of exercise daily probably improves fitness about as well as one continuous bout (Mcfarlane et al. 2006) and also improves many CVD risk factors (Murphy et al. 2009). In the long-term and everything else being equal, longer durations of exercise training should elicit greater improvements in VO$_2$max than shorter durations (Wenger and Bell 1986). A caveat to this assertion is that the vast majority of research in this area has assessed training durations of no more than forty-five minutes, so "longer" here means durations of about forty-five minutes. Regardless, ACSM recommends that adults accumulate thirty to sixty minutes of moderate intensity exercise daily, twenty to sixty minutes of vigorous intensity exercise daily, or some combination of the two (ACSM 2018).

There are several considerations to be made when developing the Time component of the exercise prescription. First, recall that the risk of injury increases with higher exercise frequencies; this is also true here in that the risk increases with longer durations of training. Second, time constraints pose a major barrier, and a very common excuse, to people beginning an exercise program. Third, as described before, the exercise must be enjoyable, or at least not unpleasant, to increase the likelihood that a new exerciser will not quit.

In addressing these concerns, durations of thirty to thirty-five minutes seem to be the best choice for clients who primarily want to improve their cardiorespiratory fitness. Compared to forty-five minutes of exercise, this shorter duration poses less risk of injury, especially if the client is performing impactful exercises such as jogging (Pollock et al. 1977). The improvement in VO$_2$max by exercising longer is relatively modest (Wenger and Bell 1986) so time-crunched clients need not feel compelled to exercise longer. Finally, recall that the goal of the FITT exercise prescription is to evoke an energy expenditure of at least 1,000 calories per week. Most clients can achieve this without having to exercise at unpleasantly high exercise intensities (e.g., HIIT training). For example, men and women at the median age in the United States (37 and 39 years, respectively; http://worldpopulationreview.com/countries/median-age/), of average weight (197 and 171 lbs., respectively; http://www.cdc.gov/nchs/fastats/body-measurements.htm) and average cardiorespiratory fitness (50th percentile, Cooper Institute 2013) can achieve this desired caloric expenditure by exercising at 50–65 percent VO$_2$R for thirty minutes, three to five times per week. The net effect is that most clients need not exercise longer than thirty or thirty-five minutes unless they have goals that are either performance-related (e.g., an athlete training for a marathon) or weight loss-related (e.g., a client who is focused on expending calories).

Type

Any physical activity that is rhythmic, continuous, and involves large muscle groups will be appropriate for improving cardiorespiratory fitness. As long as the other components of the FITT exercise prescription (i.e., frequency, intensity, time) are followed, then any activity that meets the aforementioned definition would be appropriate. Because of specificity of training, it is recommended that clients perform a variety of exercise types as part of their exercise program.

When working with a client to identify the desired type(s) of exercise, the challenge will likely be educating the client as to the possibilities. Most people think of stereotypical exercise modes (e.g., walking, jogging, bicycling, fitness classes) when they think about exercising. However, activities as diverse as dancing, hunting (e.g., walking through the woods), home and yard work activities (e.g., scrubbing floors, yard mowing, shoveling snow), occupational activities (e.g., walking with a book bag, feeding animals, baling hay, manual labor), recreational activities (e.g, canoeing, ice skating), and volunteer activities (e.g., cooking and cleaning at a local food pantry) could be applicable (Ainsworth et al. 2011). Given this considerable flexibility, the choice of the types of exercise to be performed by the client should be left up to the client. Doing so will help to create a greater sense of autonomy, and therefore "buy-in," by the client when implementing the exercise prescription. And anything you can do that will increase the client's chance for success is something that you should consider!

METABOLIC CALCULATIONS

The focus of the previous section was to help you understand how to develop an exercise prescription that will increase a client's cardiorespiratory fitness, or VO_2max. This section is oriented to helping you understand how to use metabolic calculations to better enable you to optimize the prescription. Metabolic calculations are most helpful in two ways: (1) determining the workloads at which to train and (2) determining the caloric expenditures associated with this training. Determining these workloads beforehand will minimize the trial-and-error often needed when your client is beginning to implement a new exercise prescription. And since energy balance or weight loss is a focus of many people who are beginning an exercise program, it is advantageous to be able to determine the caloric costs of their program.

Determining Workloads

As part of developing an exercise prescription, you will determine the best minimum and maximum exercise intensities, such as between 40–85 percent of their VO_2R, at which your client should train. Take the example client from Table 4.3, with a VO_2max of 38 ml·kg^{-1}·min^{-1}. From applying the "I" of CRIPL to the data from Table 4.2, you know your client is at the 55th percentile of cardiorespiratory fitness compared to other men his age. Put another way, he is about average. From Table 4.3, you know that if he trained between 40–85 percent of his VO_2R, then he would be exercising between

$17.3–32.8$ ml·kg^{-1}·min^{-1}. From your other academic courses, such as an exercise physiology course, you understand what the concept of VO$_2$ or oxygen uptake means. However, how do you explain this esoteric information to your client, who does not have your educational background? How do you "translate" this oxygen consumption data into something your client can act on? This is where metabolic equations can help.

With metabolic equations, you either (1) begin with a VO$_2$ and calculate a workload that elicits that oxygen consumption or (2) begin with a workload and calculate the VO$_2$ that is elicited with that workload. In this case, you can quickly determine that a VO$_2$ of 17.3 could be elicited by walking on a treadmill at 2.5 mph up a 6 percent grade and a VO$_2$ of 32.8 ml·kg^{-1}·min^{-1} could be elicited by walking at 2.5 mph up a 19 percent grade. Consequently, when talking to your client, you can tell them that if they are comfortable walking at 2.5 mph on a treadmill, then if they walk at that speed and up a hill of at least 6 percent, they will be training at the correct intensity. Your client can readily begin exercising using a research-based, scientifically accurate exercise prescription—regardless of how well they understand the esoteric information underlying it.

As you can see, being comfortable with these kinds of calculations will enable you to help a new client begin exercising with a focused, "spot on" exercise prescription and program. In so doing, it may also increase the client's confidence in your expertise. For our purposes here, the metabolic equations which will likely be of most use to you are:

▶ Walking (best for speeds of 50–100 m/min^{-1} or 1.9–3.7 mph)

$$\text{VO}_2 \text{ in ml·kg}^{-1}\text{·min}^{-1} = (0.1 \times \text{Speed}) + (1.8 \times \text{Speed} \times \text{Grade}) + 3.5$$

▶ Running (best for speeds > 134 m/min^{-1} or 5 mph)

$$\text{ml·kg}^{-1}\text{·min}^{-1} = (0.2 \times \text{Speed}) + (0.9 \times \text{Speed} \times \text{Grade}) + 3.5$$

▶ Cycle ergometry (best for workloads of 300–1200 kg·m^{-1}·min^{-1} for legs and 150–750 kg·m^{-1}·min^{-1} for arms)

$$\text{Leg ergometry: ml·kg}^{-1}\text{·min}^{-1} = [(1.8 \times \text{workload})/\text{body weight}] + 3.5 + 3.5$$

$$\text{Arm ergometry: ml·kg}^{-1}\text{·min}^{-1} = [(3.0 \times \text{workload})/\text{body weight}] + 3.5 + 3.5$$

These formulae use metric units. Therefore, you will need to convert the common British units of miles per hour and pounds of body weight to meters per minute (1 mph = 26.8 m·min^{-1}) and kilograms (1 kg = 2.205 lbs), respectively. For the cycle ergometer formulae, the workload is expressed in kg·m^{-1}·min^{-1}. Some cycle ergometers express workloads in Watts; if that is the case, it will need to be converted (1 W = 6.12 kg·m^{-1}·min^{-1}).

How were these formulae derived? Each of the three calculations for determining oxygen consumption can be thought of as consisting of a horizontal component, a vertical component, and a resting component (American College of Sports Medicine 2006). For all the equations, the client's resting VO$_2$ is estimated at 3.5 ml·kg^{-1}·min^{-1}. This is the standard metric for estimating resting VO$_2$. However, it is likely an overestimate for up to 20 or 30 percent of the population, especially for older adults and obese individuals (McMurray et al. 2014). For the horizontal component, walking on level ground requires a VO$_2$ of 0.1 ml·kg^{-1}·min^{-1} to move the body 1 meter. When running, because of the vertical displacement and greater inertia needed to be overcome, the oxygen demand for the horizontal component is twice as high, or 0.2 ml·kg^{-1}·min^{-1}. The work associated with overcoming gravity is greater with walking (1.8 ml·kg^{-1}·min^{-1} to move 1 meter vertically), but because of the afore-mentioned vertical displacement, not quite as costly with running (0.9 ml·kg^{-1}·min^{-1} to move 1 meter vertically). Regardless of whether walking or running, the vertical component must be multiplied by the treadmill grade, since that is the amount of vertical displacement they are actually doing.

With cycle ergometry, there is not a true horizontal component like there is with exercising on a treadmill. The analog is the VO_2 associated with cycling against no resistance. This is estimated as 3.5 ml·kg^{-1}·min^{-1}. Pedaling against a resistance is the analog of the treadmill "vertical component." When cycling with one's legs, this requires a VO_2 of 1.8 ml·kg^{-1}·min^{-1} for each kg·m^{-1}·min^{-1} of resistance. When cycling using arm ergometry, the oxygen cost is considerably higher because of the need to stabilize the torso. Thus, the oxygen cost is 3.0 ml·kg^{-1}·min^{-1} for each kg·m^{-1}·min^{-1} of resistance when pedaling with the arms rather than the legs.

In determining the workloads at which to train, simply follow these steps:

1. *Determine what you already know and what you want to figure out.* In general, you'll either start with some expression of VO_2 and use it to determine the workload or start with a workload and use it to determine VO_2. It is important to remember that there are several ways of expressing VO_2, such as METs, ml·kg^{-1}·min^{-1}, ml·min^{-1}, l·min^{-1}, calories·min^{-1}, and calories per workout. The metabolic equations are designed to use VO_2 expressed in ml·kg^{-1}·min^{-1}. So in order to use the metabolic equations, you may need to convert the VO_2 from one expression to another. The conversions for these are:

$$\text{METs} \times 3.5 = \text{ml·kg}^{-1}\text{·min}^{-1}$$

$$\text{ml·kg}^{-1}\text{·min}^{-1} \times \text{body weight in kg} = \text{ml·min}^{-1}$$

$$\text{ml·min}^{-1} \times 1000 = \text{L·min}^{-1}$$

$$\text{L·min}^{-1} \times 5 = \text{calories·min}^{-1}$$

$$\text{calories·min}^{-1} \times \text{min} = \text{calories per workout}$$

2. *Based on the aforementioned information, determine what metabolic equation to use.* In other words, will your client be walking, running, cycling with their legs or cycling with their arms? Choose the metabolic equation that is most appropriate.

3. *Make sure all the units are in the correct form in the equation.* If your client is on a treadmill, be sure to express the speed as m·min^{-1} rather than miles per hour. If on a cycle ergometer, the workload is in kg·m^{-1}·min^{-1}, not Watts, and the client's body weight is in kilograms, not pounds.

4. *Solve the equation.* See Table 4.4 for examples of how these steps are performed.

TABLE 4.4

Metabolic Equations in Use

---

1. **Your client wants to walk at 3.0 mph up a 5% grade. What VO$_2$ would this require?**

   Step 1.   Determine what you already know and what you want to figure out.

   You know his workload and want to determine the resulting VO$_2$.

   Step 2.   Determine what equation to use.

   You know he wants to walk at 3.0 mph and 5% grade. Therefore, the metabolic equation for walking [(0.1 × Speed) + (1.8 × Speed × Grade) + 3.5] is appropriate.

   Step 3.   Make sure all the units are in the correct form in the equation.

   The speed of 3.0 mph is expressed as 80.4 m·min^{-1} (3.0 mph × 26.8 m·min^{-1})

   Step 4.   Solve the equation.

   $$VO_2 \text{ in ml·kg}^{-1}\text{·min}^{-1} = (0.1 × 80.4) + (1.8 × 80.4 × 0.05) + 3.5$$
   $$= 8.04 + 7.236 + 3.5$$
   $$= 18.776 \text{ ml·kg}^{-1}\text{·min}^{-1}$$

   Your client would be exercising at 18.8 ml·kg^{-1}·min^{-1} when he walks at 3.0 mph up a 5% grade.

2. **Your client wants to exercise on a cycle ergometer at 75 Watts. She weighs 154 pounds.**

   Step 1.   Determine what you already know and what you want to figure out.

   You know her workload and body weight. You want to determine the resulting VO$_2$.

   Step 2.   Determine what equation to use.

   You know she wants to cycle. Therefore, the metabolic equation is the leg cycle ergometer formula: [(1.8 × workload)/body weight] + 3.5 + 3.5.

   Step 3.   Make sure all the units are in the correct form in the equation.

   The workload of 75 Watts should be expressed as 459 kg·m^{-1}·min^{-1} (75 × 6.12 = 459 kg·m^{-1}·min^{-1}). Her body weight of 154 pounds should be expressed as 70 kg (154/2.205 = 70 kg).

   Step 4.   Solve the equation.

   $$VO_2 \text{ in ml·kg}^{-1}\text{·min}^{-1} = [(1.8 × \text{workload})/\text{body weight}] + 3.5 + 3.5$$
   $$= [(1.8 × 459)/70] + 3.5 + 3.5$$
   $$= [826.2/70] + 7$$
   $$= 11.803 + 7$$
   $$= 18.803 \text{ ml·kg}^{-1}\text{·min}^{-1}$$

   Your client would be exercising at 18.8 ml·kg^{-1}·min^{-1} when she biked at 75 Watts.

Determining Caloric Expenditures

Recall that the goal of a cardiorespiratory exercise prescription is to expend at least 1,000 calories weekly. Being able to determine the volume of exercise, or the total time spent exercising weekly, needed to achieve this goal is a useful skill. In addition, many clients begin exercising with the goal of either losing weight or maintaining their weight. They may be less focused on improving their cardiorespiratory fitness. Consequently, your being able to give them insight into their caloric expenditure with exercise is a very useful skill to have. Being comfortable in the use of metabolic calculations will enable you to do so.

©Syda Productions/Shutterstock.com

There are two "schools of thought" about how best to determine exercise-related caloric expenditure. One school supports determining the client's <u>gross</u> energy expenditure and the other supports determining the <u>net</u> energy expenditure (Swain 2000). Gross energy expenditure is the total energy expenditure of exercise, including resting VO_2, which can be thought of as the sum of the exercise energy expenditure + the resting energy expenditure. Net energy expenditure is that expenditure solely associated with the effort of exercising, or just the exercise energy expenditure. Proponents of using net energy expenditure feel that using gross energy expenditure may overestimate the contribution of exercise to potential body weight loss. On the other hand, the client is alive when exercising so including the resting VO_2, and thereby using gross energy expenditure, may be more practical. For our purposes here, gross energy expenditure will be used.

To determine gross energy expenditure, first recall that calories·min^{-1} is simply one way of expressing VO_2. This means that, if you know the client's exercise VO_2 and their body weight, then you can very readily calculate their caloric expenditure. Simply remember the different ways of expressing VO_2 and how to convert from one expression to another:

$$\text{METs} = \text{ml·kg}^{-1}\text{·min}^{-1} = \text{ml·min}^{-1} = \text{L·min}^{-1} = \text{calories·min}^{-1} = \text{calories per workout}$$

Consequently, if you know the client's VO_2, then all you have to do is convert it to either calories·min^{-1} or calories per workout. See Table 4.5 for examples of how to do so. These are continuations of the examples from Tables 4.3 and 4.4.

TABLE 4.5
Determining Caloric (Energy) Expenditures with Exercise

1. **Your client walks at 3.0 mph up a 5% grade for 30 minutes. How many calories does he expend?**

   Step 1.   Determine what you already know and what you want to figure out.

   You previously determined his exercise VO_2 to be 18.8 ml·kg^{-1}·min^{-1}. You want to determine his caloric expenditure, so you also need to know his body weight. For this problem, assume he weighs 175 pounds.

   Step 2.   Determine what equation to use.

   Of the different ways of expressing VO_2 (METs = ml·kg^{-1}·min^{-1} = ml·min^{-1} = L·min^{-1} = calories·min^{-1} = calories per workout), you will start at "ml·kg^{-1}·min^{-1}" since that's how the VO_2 was expressed in Step 1, above. You will need to make the appropriate conversions to determine "calories per workout." This is done in the following steps.

   Step 3.   Make sure all the units are in the correct form in the equation.

   Convert body weight from pounds to kg (175/2.205 = 79.4 kg)

   Step 4.   Solve the equation.

   18.8 ml·kg^{-1}·min^{-1} × 79.4 kg body weight = 1492.7 ml·min^{-1}

   1492.7 ml·min^{-1} ÷ 1000 = 1.4927 L·min^{-1}

   1.4927 L·min^{-1} × 5.0 = 7.464 calories·min^{-1}

   7.464 calories·min^{-1} × 30 minutes = 224 calories per workout

Your client will burn about 224 calories if he walked for 30 minutes at 3.0 mph and 5% grade.

2. **Your client has a VO_2R of between 17.3 and 32.8 ml·kg^{-1}·min^{-1}. She weighs 70 kg. How long would she have to exercise at 17.3 ml·kg^{-1}·min^{-1} to expend 1,000 calories in a week?**

   Step 1.   Determine what you already know and what you want to figure out.

   You know your client's exercise VO_2 (17.3 ml·kg^{-1}·min^{-1}), her body weight, and her goal energy expenditure of 1,000 calories per week. You want to determine how long she'd have to exercise to achieve this.

   Step 2.   Determine what equation to use.

   Of the different ways of expressing VO_2, (METs = ml·kg^{-1}·min^{-1} = ml·min^{-1} = L·min^{-1} = calories·min^{-1} = calories per workout), you will start at "ml·kg^{-1}·min^{-1}" and make the appropriate conversions to determine "calories per minute." You'll then divide this into 1,000 calories to determine minutes per week.

   Step 3.   Make sure all the units are in the correct form in the equation. For this problem, all the data are in metric units so you don't need to make any conversions.

   Step 4.   Solve the equation.

   17.3 ml·kg^{-1}·min^{-1} × 70 kg body weight = 1211 ml·min^{-1}

   1211 ml·min^{-1} ÷ 1000 = 1.211 L·min^{-1}

   1.211 L·min^{-1} × 5.0 = 6.055 calories·min^{-1}

   1000 minutes ÷ 6.055 = 165 minutes per week

Your client would have to exercise for 165 minutes weekly if she trained at 17.3 ml·kg^{-1}·min^{-1}.

While these formulae are the best available tools, there are several limitations that need to be recognized (American College of Sports Medicine 2006). First, at a given workload, an individual's VO_2 is relatively consistent; however, the VO_2 at a given workload can vary quite a bit between subjects. Thus, the estimated VO_2 may be more (or less) accurate for one client compared to another client. Consequently, use multiple methods of prescribing the exercise intensity (HRR, VO_2R, RPE, ACI) to ultimately determine what works best for the client. Second, the estimated VO_2 is most accurate for submaximal steady state exercise. The equations will overestimate VO_2 when applied to non-steady state exercise. Since the methods of prescribing exercise intensities reviewed here evoke submaximal levels of effort, this limitation is likely not a major issue. But they'll be very inaccurate if prescribing high intensity exercise, such as HIIT. Third, differences in mechanical efficiency (e.g., a "smooth" runner versus an ungainly runner) can markedly skew the estimated VO_2 for an individual (Joyner and Coyle 2008). Again, use multiple methods of prescribing the exercise intensity to avoid inadvertently prescribing too-intense workloads. Finally, the gap in speeds between the walking and running formulae (e.g., 3.8–4.9 mph) reflects the speeds at which people typically transition between walking and running. If the client is truly walking or running within this speed range, then use the appropriate equation. Despite these limitations, these equations work quite well for predicting caloric expenditures at moderate exercise intensities and only modestly less so at high exercise intensities (Cunha et al. 2012).

THE "L" OF CRIPL: THE LIFESTYLE CHANGE OF BEGINNING A CARDIORESPIRATORY EXERCISE PROGRAM

In Chapter 2, you were introduced to the CRIPL rubric, including the L, or Lifestyle Changes, component. The two major foci within L are (1) how best to modify the client's risk factors for chronic disease, primarily cardiovascular disease, through lifestyle changes and (2) how best to adopt a program of regular exercise. Methods to accomplish the former were reviewed extensively in Chapter 3. You may recall that research suggests that about half of new exercisers will drop out of their program within the first six months. These are challenging odds and improving these odds is a major research focus of many exercise psychologists. Of course, more definitive discussions on how to increase exercise adherence can be found elsewhere, such as in an exercise psychology textbook (e.g., Lox et al. 2019). The emphasis here is on practical approaches you can take, as a health/fitness professional, to increase the likelihood that a new client who has not exercised in the past will be successful in their efforts to begin and continue exercising.

When working with a new client, it is very important that the client have input into the development of their exercise prescription. This autonomy, or freedom of choice, is critical to success. You are the person with the professional expertise to develop the client's exercise prescription, but it is the client who will be doing the exercise! Consequently, be sure that the prescription is based on the client's desires and make sure that the client feels part of the process. A team-based approach, where you and the client work together, will be far more successful than a hierarchical one, where the expert (you) tells the novice (the client) what to do.

One way to begin this conversation is to ask the client, "What is it that you love to do?" (Church 2019). This is similar to asking them, "What are your goals with an exercise program?" However, the client is now focusing on how exercise can help them have a higher quality of life rather than simply getting more fit. For example, if you ask a new client about their exercise goals, they may say, "I want to feel better." Interpreting what this means can be challenging. But if you asked them, "What is it you love to do?" they may respond by saying, "I used to love to bike outside but, now, I'm not strong enough to put my bike on my cartop bike rack" or "I love to play with my grandkids but I really can't do anything with them on the playground because I can't keep up." You can then work with the client to develop an exercise plan that will focus on helping them improve their ability to do something they *really* want to do.

Another critical aspect to success is that the client believes their prescribed program is realistic for them and achievable. This is also called self-efficacy, where the client believes that they can be successful in a specific situation or when faced with a new task. It is fundamentally critical to succeeding whenever a new behavior, like exercising, is being adopted—there has to be full "buy-in" on the part of the client. For example, if your client says they would love to lose fifty pounds but have not been successful in the past, then their self-efficacy is probably low. In this case, you might re-direct the conversation to "Why is losing weight important to you?" It may be that they are motivated to lose weight in order to have a lower risk of CVD or to be able to go on a hiking trip with their significant other. Weight loss is not critical to achieving either of these goals; consequently, you could steer the conversation to other lifestyle changes such as eating healthier or being consistently physically active. In this case, the client may see these lifestyle behaviors as much more realistic or "doable." These behaviors also will help them achieve their true goals.

"How was aerobics class?"

Finally, the exercise program must be enjoyable. If the client does not like what it is they are doing in your health/fitness facility, then the likelihood that they will do it for any length of time is low. An unpleasant exercise program will eventually be an unsuccessful program.

When beginning to work with a client, an important consideration is to recognize characteristics that may predispose them to quitting. If you see these traits in your client, then you need to address them as best as you can. Some major risk factors for dropping out are:

1. illness,
2. disability,
3. time issues such as schedule conflicts and vacation,
4. work commitments such as travel, shift work, or a new job,
5. family conflicts such as daycare needs,
6. dissatisfaction,
7. embarrassment,
8. boredom, and
9. discomfort or pain.

You have little control over some of these factors, such as an illness or disability, but you *can* do something about the others. For example, if your client has major time conflicts such that it is very challenging to make it to the health/fitness facility to exercise, perhaps you can help them determine how best to incorporate physical activity into their day. This could mean parking farther away from their work and walking a few minutes to and from their office or, if they sit at a desk most of their workday, being mindful about getting up and walking or stretching every hour or so. If the client is self-conscious about exercising in the facility, it may be due to the layout of the exercise equipment. Is the equipment arranged such that clients are staring at themselves in a mirror as they exercise?

Can other clients stand behind them and watch them exercise? New exercisers can be self-conscious about their appearance, especially when compared to "hard body" exercisers, so the equipment should be arranged to attenuate these concerns. If they are easily bored with the exercise program, then you can give them alternative activities to do and devise a plan for when to use them. If they are uncomfortable or in pain when exercising, such as due to arthritis, then you can work with the client to determine how best to mitigate this discomfort. This may mean spending more time doing non-weight bearing activities, such as a NuStep exercise, rather than weight exercises. The keys in all these situations are to, first, focus on determining how best to fit the "exercise needs" of your client within the other constraints of their life and, second, adapting the exercise program in order to do so.

Part of the aforementioned adaptability requires you to be mindful of characteristics of either the exercise program or the health/fitness facility that may need to be altered to improve adherence. An example of this is the aforementioned equipment arrangement. Other common concerns are:

1. The need for a slow start. Many new exercisers want to "jump right in" to their exercise program. But they quickly become disenchanted due to the resultant soreness and fatigue. To mitigate this issue, be sure to adjust the initial exercise prescription—primarily with a lower exercise intensity and shorter exercise time. To that end, you may consider reducing the initial exercise intensity by 10 percent of the HRR or VO_2R or, as an alternative, by 1 MET. You may suggest the client begin with an exercise time of fifteen or twenty minutes and gradually work up to the desired thirty or thirty-five minutes. The important point here is to ensure that the client views their exercise program as achievable and pleasant. They will be more likely to adhere to the program if they do.

2. Provide social support. Social support is critical to success for new exercisers. As alluded to previously, social support from the client's significant others (e.g., family, friends) is a powerful tool to maintain adherence to a new exercise program. Personal training, with its one-on-one attention, is another excellent example of this social support. While personal training is a fee-for-service in most health/fitness facilities, it is important that all new clients receive some positive reinforcement from facility staff when they are exercising. An alternative is to encourage the new exerciser to join a fitness class that is oriented to similarly-fit clients. The class leader can encourage interaction among the participants so they get to know each other; the classmates may then provide some measure of social support.

3. For many participants, the time commitment is a major barrier to success. So clients must become accustomed to "carving out" time in their day to exercise. You may need to work with the client to determine strategies for doing so—perhaps have the client review their weekly schedule and literally enter their time for exercising into that schedule. That way, exercise may be viewed as being as important as everything else. There will be less chance of them scheduling something else into their "exercise time." Enlisting the assistance of the client's significant others may be of help here, too. For example, suppose the client is married with school-age children. Perhaps their spouse can play a larger role in getting the children ready for school in the morning to enable the client to go to an early morning exercise class. This is also an example of social support.

4. Set goals but have realistic expectations. When first working with the client, help them identify reasonable goals for them to achieve. The use of normative data and rank ordering their fitness assessment results, as described in Chapter 2, should facilitate this. These goals should be SMART goals (Specific, Measurable, Attainable, Realistic, Timebound) to be

most effective. For example, "I'll work out regularly" seems like a worthwhile goal but is so nebulous that it is difficult to tell when the goal has been achieved. "I'll do cardiorespiratory exercise for 30 minutes 3 times per week for the next 4 weeks" is a SMART goal. It's specific (cardiorespiratory exercise), measurable (30 min 3x/week for 4 weeks), attainable (depending on the client's fitness level), realistic (if the client genuinely thinks he can achieve it), and timebound (he'll know in 4 weeks if he achieved it).

5. Provide pleasant surroundings. Make sure the exercise environment is conducive to a new exerciser's use. Does the health/fitness facility have a "meat market" atmosphere? Is it clean? Is the music appropriate for the age of the clientele? Is the equipment arranged appropriately? Is the facility accessible for people with mobility challenges, such as those using a cane or wheelchair? The facility should meet the needs of the clients, not the other way around.

6. Be a motivated exercise leader. The key here is for you to focus on maintaining participant motivation to exercise. Besides being knowledgeable, you need to be positive, enthusiastic, and attentive to the client. Remember that you are working in a service industry and, if the client perceives that you are not interested in their being successful, they will find someone who is.

7. Give feedback to the client. Feedback can be in the form of follow-up fitness assessments, workout logs to chart progress, weekly chats with an exercise leader, or the like. As long as the feedback is concrete and specific to the client ("You made it to the facility four times this week!") rather than generic ("Good job!"), then it will be meaningful.

8. Give positive reinforcement. This concern overlaps with the aforementioned need to provide feedback. New exercisers need positive external reinforcement while they are developing their own internal positive reward system for exercising. Otherwise, the "negatives" of exercise may begin to outweigh the "positives." This reinforcement can range from simple verbal rewards from the exercise leader (the aforementioned "You made it to the facility four times this week!") to incentive prizes (e.g., receiving a free T-shirt for achieving a SMART goal).

As you can see, there are a number of ways that you can facilitate your client being successful when they are starting a new exercise program. Nevertheless, the most important aspect of a client being successful is that they have self-efficacy—they believe that they can accomplish what it is they have set out to do. Your most important role is to help them develop this self-efficacy. Giving them autonomy in the development of their exercise program, making sure they enjoy the program, and making sure the program is focused on their achieving the goals they truly have (what it is they love to do) will dramatically increase the likelihood that they will be able to start, *and continue*, their new exercise program.

PUTTING IT ALL TOGETHER

The primary goal of this chapter was to increase your understanding of how to develop a cardiorespiratory exercise prescription and do so in a way that will increase the chances that a new exerciser will adhere to the program. The CRIPL rubric was re-visited so you could better understand how this exercise prescription fit into the larger picture of working with a client.

When developing a FITT exercise prescription, always remember that the prescription becomes irrelevant if the client quits exercising. So, modify the exercise prescription, as needed, to better fit the client rather than forcing the client to follow a scientifically sound (but soon to be ignored) exercise program. The goal is that this new exerciser will become a lifelong exerciser. It is your responsibility, as the health/fitness professional, to maximize the likelihood of this occurring.

REFERENCES

2018 Physical Activity Guidelines Advisory Committee. 2018. *Physical Activity Guidelines Advisory Committee Scientific Report, 2018.* Washington, DC: U.S. Department of Health and Human Services.

Ainsworth, B. E., W. L. Haskell, S. D. Herrmann, N. Meckes, D. R. Bassett Jr, C. Tudor-Locke, J. L. Greer, J. Vazina, M. C. Whitt-Glover, and A. S. Leon. 2011. Compendium of Physical Activities: A Second Update of Codes and MET Values. *Med Sci Sports Exerc.* 43: 1575–81. (Compendium of activities can be found at http://links.lww.com/MSS/A82).

American College of Sports Medicine. 1980. *Guidelines for Graded Exercise Testing and Exercise Prescription.* 2nd ed. Philadelphia: Lea & Febiger.

———. 2006. *ACSM's Guidelines for Exercise Testing and Prescription.* 7th ed. Philadelphia: Lippincott Williams & Wilkins.

———. 2018. *ACSM's Guidelines for Exercise Testing and Prescription.* 10th ed. Philadelphia: Wolters Kluwer.

Borg, G. A. V. 1982. "Psychophysical Bases of Perceived Exertion." *Med Sci Sports Exerc.* 14: 377–81.

Bouchard, C., P. An, T. Rice, J. S. Skinner, J. H. Wilmore, J. Gagnon, L. Pérusse, A. S. Leon, and D. C. Rao. 1999. "Familial Aggregation of VO$_2$max Response to Exercise Training: Results from the HERITAGE Family Study." *J Appl Physiol.* 87: 1003–08.

Bouchard, C., E. W. Daw, T. Rice, L. Pérusse, J. Gagnon, M. A. Province, A. S. Leon, D. C. Rao, J. S. Skinner, and J. H. Wilmore. 1998. "Familial Resemblance for VO2max in the Sedentary State: The HERITAGE Family Study." *Med Sci Sports Exerc.* 30: 252–58.

Buchheit, M., and P. B. Laursen. 2013a. "High-Intensity Interval Training, Solutions to the Programming Puzzle. Part I: Cardiopulmonary Emphasis." *Sports Med.* 43: 313–38.

Buchheit, M, and P. B. Laursen. 2013b. "High-Intensity Interval Training, Solutions to the Programming Puzzle. Part II: Anaerobic Energy, Neuromuscular Load and Practical Applications." *Sports Med.* 43: 927–54.

Church, T. 2019. "The 6 Key Concepts That Will Absolutely Change the Way You Prescribe Exercise!" Keynote address. ACSM Health & Fitness Summit. Chicago, IL.

Cooper Institute. 2013. *Physical Fitness Assessments and Norms for Adults and Law Enforcement.* Dallas: Cooper Institute.

Cunha, F. A., Catalão, A. W. Midgley, J. Gurgel, F. Pirto, and P. T. V. Farinatti. 2012. "Do the Speeds Defined by the American College of Sports Medicine Metabolic Equation for Running Produce Target Energy Expenditures during Isocaloric Exercise Bouts?" *Eur J Appl Physiol.* 112: 3019–26.

Ekkekakis, P., G. Parfitt, and S. J. Petruzzello. 2011. "The Pleasure and Displeasure People Feel When They Exercise at Different Intensities: Decennial Update and Progress Toward a Tripartite Rationale for Exercise Intensity Prescription." *Sports Med.* 41: 641–71.

Garber, C. E., B. Blissmer, M. R. Deschenes, B. A. Franklin, M. J. Lamonte, I. M. Lee, D. C. Nieman, and D. P. Swain. 2011. "American College of Sports Medicine Position Stand. Quantity and Quality of Exercise for Developing and Maintaining Cardiorespiratory, Musculoskeletal, and Neuromotor Fitness in Apparently Healthy Adults: Guidance for Prescribing Exercise." *Med Sci Sports Exerc.* 43: 1334–59.

Gettman, L. R., M. L. Pollock, J. L. Durstine, A. Ward, J. Ayres, and A. C. Linnerud. 1976. "Physiological Responses of Men to 1, 3, and 5 Day per Week Training Programs." *Res Quart.* 47: 638–46.

Gormley, S. E., D. P. Swain, R. High, R. J. Spina, E. A. Dowling, U. S. Kotipalli, and R. Gandrakota. 2008. "Effect of Intensity of Aerobic Training on VO$_2$max." *Med Sci Sports Exerc.* 40: 1336–43.

Hawkins, M. N., P. B. Raven, P. G. Snell, J. Stray-Gundersen, and B. D. Levine. 2007. "Maximal Oxygen Uptake as a Parametric Measure of Cardiorespiratory Capacity." *Med Sci Sports Exerc.* 39: 103–07.

Howley, E. T. 2001. "Type of Activity: Resistance, Aerobic and Leisure versus Occupational Physical Activity." *Med Sci Sports Exerc.* 33: S364–69.

Joyner, M. J., and E. F. Coyle. 2008. "Endurance Exercise Performance: The Physiology of Champions." *J Physiol.* 586.1: 35–44.

Kenney, W. L., J. H. Wilmore, and D. L. Costill. 2012. *Physiology of Sport and Exercise.* Champaign: Human Kinetics.

Levine, B. D. 2008. "VO$_2$max: What Do We Know, and What Do We Still Need to Know?" *J Physiol.* 586: 25–34.

Lox, C. L., K. A. Martin Ginis, H. Gainforth, and S. J. Petruzzello. 2019. The Psychology of Exercise: Integrating Theory and Practice. 5th ed. Scottsdale: Routledge.

Mcfarlane, D. J., L. H. Taylor, and T. F. Cuddihy. 2006. "Very Short Intermittent vs Continuous Bouts of Activity in Sedentary Adults." *Prev Med.* 43: 332–36.

McMurray, R. G., J. Soares, C. J. Caspersen, and T. McCurdy. 2014. "Examining Variations of Resting Metabolic Rate of Adults: A Public Health Perspective." *Med Sci Sports Exerc.* 46:1352–58.

Mello, R. P., M. M. Murphy, and J. A. Vogel. 1988. "Relationship between a Two Mile Run for Time and Maximal Oxygen Uptake." *Journal of Applied Sport Science Research* 2: 9–12.

Milanović, Z, G. Sporiš, and M. Weston. 2015. "Effectiveness of High-Intensity Interval Training (HIT) and Continuous Endurance Training for VO2max Improvements: A Systematic Review and Meta-Analysis of Controlled Trials." *Sports Med.* 45: 1469–81.

Murphy, M. H., S. N. Blair, and E.M . Murtagh. 2009. "Accumulated versus Continuous Exercise for Health Benefit. A Review of Empirical Studies." *Sports Med.* 39: 29-43.

Pollock, M. L., L. R. Gettman, C. A. Milesis, M. D. Bah, L. Durstine, and R. B. Johnson. 1977. "Effects of Frequency and Duration on Training on Attrition and Incidence of Injury." *Med Sci Sports* 9: 31–36.

Scherr, J., B. Wolfarth, J. W. Christle, A. Presler, S. Wagenpfeil, and M. Halle. 2013. "Associations between Borg's Rating of Perceived Exertion and Physiological Measures of Exercise Intensity." *Eur J Appl Physiol.* 113: 147–55.

Swain, D. P. 2000. "Energy Cost Calculations for Exercise Prescription: An Udate." *Sports Med.* 30: 17–22.

———. 2005. "Moderate or Vigorous Intensity Exercise: Which Is Better for Improving Aerobic Fitness?" *Prev Cardiol.* 8: 55–58.

Swain, D. P., and B. A. Franklin. 2002. "VO$_2$reserve and the Minimal Intensity for Improving Cardiorespiratory Fitness." *Med Sci Sports Exerc.* 34: 152–57.

Swain, D. P., B. C. Leutholtz, M. E. King, L. A. Haas, and J. D. Branch. 1998. "Relationship between Percent Heart Rate Reserve and Percent VO$_2$reserve in Treadmill Exercise." *Med Sci Sports Exerc.* 30: 318–21.

Swift, D. L., N. M. Johannsen, C. J. Lavie, C. P. Earnest, and T. S. Church. 2014. "The Role of Exercise and Physical Activity in Weight Loss and Maintenance." *Progress in Cardiovascular Disease* 56: 441–47.

Tanaka, H., K. D. Monahan, and D. R. Seals. 2001. "Age-Predicted Maximal Heart Rate Revisited." *J Am Coll Cardiol.* 37: 153–56.

U.S. Department of Health and Human Services. 2018. *Physical Activity Guidelines for Americans.* 2nd ed. Washington, DC: U.S. Department of Health and Human Services.

Vazou-Ekkekakis, S., and P. Ekkekakis. 2009. "Affective Consequences of Imposing the Intensity of Physical Activity: Does the Loss of Perceived Autonomy Matter?" *Hell J Psychol.* 6: 125–44.

Wenger, H. A., and G. J. Bell. 1986. "The Interactions of Intensity, Frequency and Duration of Exercise Training in Altering Cardiorespiratory Fitness." *Sports Medicine* 3: 346–56.

Weston, M., K. L. Taylor, A. M. Batterham, and W. G. Hopkins. 2014. "Effects of Low-Volume High-Intensity Interval Training (HIT) on Fitness in Adults: A Meta-Analysis of Controlled and Non-Controlled Trials." *Sports Med.* 44: 1005–17.

CHAPTER 5

Exercise Prescription for Developing Muscular Fitness

OVERVIEW

The number of published research studies assessing the health benefits of resistance exercise is far less than the number of studies assessing cardiorespiratory exercise. Nevertheless, it is becoming increasingly clear that resistance exercise should be part of any general fitness program. A growing body of evidence supports the association of increased strength, or resistance exercise training, with reduced premature mortality (Bennie et al. 2018; Cooper, Kuh, and Hardy 2010; Volaklis, Halle, and Meisinger 2015) as well as other health benefits. For example, in one study and in comparison to a measure of cardiorespiratory fitness, the number of push-ups that men could perform was inversely associated with having a cardiovascular event in the next ten years (Yang et al. 2019).

Nevertheless, the strength of this association varies by study. One factor that affects it is how strength was assessed; handgrip strength is a common measurement although some studies assess maximal strength in several large-muscle groups. While the latter is preferred, even an assessment as simple as handgrip strength can be quite informative. For example, in two meta-analyses (where a number of studies are analyzed collectively), subjects in the lowest quartile of grip strength had a risk of dying prematurely that was about 50 percent higher than that of subjects in the highest quartile (Cooper, Kuh, and Hardy 2010; García-Hermoso et al. 2018)!

Another factor that may affect the association of muscular strength and mortality is the overall fitness level of the subjects. In other words, are these findings due to people who lift weights also being people who are likely to do aerobic exercise? Or are these findings truly due to resistance exercise? The short answer is, "Probably a little bit of both but more of the latter." In most high quality studies that assessed mortality as well as directly measured muscular strength and cardiorespiratory fitness, the association between reduced mortality and muscular strength persisted after considering the effects of cardiorespiratory fitness (Artero et al. 2012; FitzGerald et al. 2004; Katzmarzyk and Craig 2002; Ruiz et al. 2008; Volaklis et al. 2015). However, in some studies, the association was weakened after considering cardiorespiratory fitness (Krachnewski et al. 2016). This implies that strength training is important at reducing a client's risk for premature death but completing both strength training and cardiorespiratory exercise needs to be done if your client wants to maximally reduce their risk of dying prematurely. Having said that, resistance training does have substantial health benefits—so if your client *only* wants to lift weights and does not want to do any cardiorespiratory exercise, then they will certainly be healthier than if they did nothing at all.

Of course, there is more to life than not being dead. For many people, quality of life is as important, if not more so, than quantity of life. Developing muscular strength can be enormously beneficial in this regard, too. Some of these effects are summarized in Table 5.1. Given the substantial, robust positive influences that resistance exercise can have on a client's health, the "take home message" is quite clear: everyone should do some form of resistance exercise training (Garber et al. 2011; Ratamess et al. 2009). Because of these health benefits, the recent *Physical Activity Guidelines for Americans* (USDHHS 2018) suggests that "Adults should also do muscle-strengthening activities of moderate or greater intensity and that involve all major muscle groups on 2 or more days a week."

TABLE 5.1
Beneficial Effects of Increased Muscular Strength

- ▸ Improved CVD risk factors (e.g., blood pressure, abdominal adiposity, insulin resistance, lipids, metabolic syndrome)
- ▸ Reduced systemic inflammation
- ▸ Improved muscle function and muscle quality
- ▸ Increased resting metabolic rate
- ▸ Reduced risk of falls
- ▸ Reduced risk for osteoporosis, or loss of bone mineral density and content
- ▸ Reduced pain and disability with osteoarthritis
- ▸ Reduced risk for sarcopenia, or muscle mass loss
- ▸ Improved ability to perform daily living activities and reduced functional limitations
- ▸ Increased endurance time
- ▸ Improved cognitive function
- ▸ Improved symptomology related to depression and anxiety

From Artero et al. (2012); Garber et al. (2011); Volaklis, Halle, and Meisinger (2015)

Unfortunately, even fewer people currently do resistance exercise training than do aerobic exercise. Less than 10 percent of older adults report engaging in strength training at least twice weekly (Kraschnewski et al. 2016) and only about 30 percent of all adults do (Bennie et al. 2018). Even more worrisome, almost 58 percent of adults do not do *any* strength training exercises (Bennie et al. 2018). For perspective, only about 23 percent of adult Americans meet the national guidelines for both aerobic and strength training and 45 percent do not meet either (Blackwell and Clarke 2018).

The rest of this chapter will therefore be devoted to helping you learn how to develop programs for clients.

THE "P" OF CRIPL: PRESCRIBING A RESISTANCE EXERCISE PROGRAM

By now, you should be comfortable working with the components of the CRIPL rubric. Each component of CRIPL has been discussed in detail in the previous chapters of this book. In this section, the P of CRIPL will be extended to include a focus on developing an exercise prescription that includes resistance exercise. To that end, the next sections will provide background information that is needed to understand how best to develop a resistance exercise prescription. This background information will include overviews of the three primary forms of resistance exercise training and six universal principles related to this training (Fleck and Kraemer 2014).

Primary Types of Resistance Exercise Training

When most people think of resistance exercise, they probably think of weight lifting using free weights. This type of resistance exercise is very common, but it is not the only type. Depending on the goals of a client, other forms of training which require different types of muscle actions may be more appropriate. For example, the training program of a fifty-year-old woman who underwent a mastectomy and now wants to return to kayaking will be dramatically different from a twenty-year-old female junior college basketball player who hopes to earn a basketball scholarship at a Division 1 school. Consequently, it is important to understand each of the three types of training so you can develop the most optimal program for your client. The three forms that will be reviewed here are isometric, isokinetic, and isotonic resistance exercise. While each is unique, the most noteworthy differences between them are the velocity of the movement and the resistance encountered. These differences are summarized in Table 5.2.

TABLE 5.2		
Major Differences Between Major Forms of Resistance Exercise		
Form	**Velocity**	**Resistance**
Isometric	Fixed (0°/sec)	Fixed
Isokinetic	Fixed but adjustable (1° – >300°/sec)	Accommodating
Isotonic	Variable (usu. load-dependent)	Fixed
From Davies (1987)		

One form of resistance training is *isometric* exercise ("iso" for "equal" and "metric" for "measure"). Here, there is a muscle contraction but no change in joint angle. Performing a plank or holding a bicep curl with the elbow flexed at a fixed angle are examples (Figure 5.1). The factors which

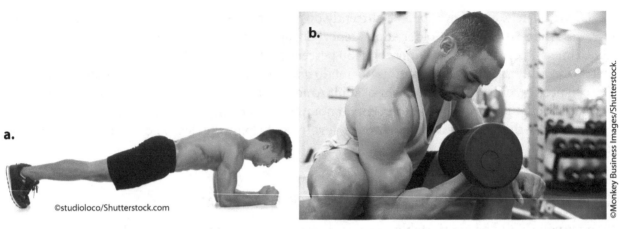

©studioloco/Shutterstock.com

©Monkey Business Images/Shutterstock.com

Figure 5.1 *Isometric* Exercise Examples: (a) Plank and (b) Bicep Curl If Held in This Position

appear to most affect strength gains with isometric training are the intensity of the contractions, the number of contractions performed, the duration of each contraction, and the frequency of training (Fleck and Kraemer 2014). "Intensity" refers to whether the contractions are maximal or submaximal contractions. Both can lead to increases in strength, but maximal effort contractions may be superior for evoking muscle hypertrophy. Many combinations of contraction number and duration have increased strength in research studies. Longer duration contractions may be better for muscle hypertrophy. However, experts feel that, based on their assessment of the research, a minimum of fifteen to twenty contractions held for three to five seconds may be the most time-efficient (Fleck and Kraemer 2014). Performing isometrics daily is most effective for increasing strength, but training three times per week is both effective and more time-efficient. Finally, the gains in strength occur primarily at the joint angles used in the training. This joint-angle specificity can be attenuated following the aforementioned combination of contractions and duration and performed at joint angles throughout the entire range of motion, in increments of 10 to 30°.

The second type of training is *isokinetic* exercise ("iso" for "equal" and "kinetic" for "movement"). As the client performs the desired movement (e.g., knee extension in Figure 5.2), the isokinetic machine provides accommodating resistance, meaning that the resistance is adjusted moment-to-moment so the desired angular velocity is achieved. As long as the client is striving to exceed this velocity, a maximal contraction is achieved throughout almost the entire range of motion. For perspective, a slow velocity (e.g., 60°/sec) is akin to lifting "heavy weights" while a fast velocity (e.g., >300°/sec) is perceived by most people as being almost no resistance at all.

While very effective at increasing strength, isokinetic dynamometers are expensive. For example, systems such as the one shown in Figure 5.2 typically sell for almost $50,000. For this reason, isokinetic dynamometers are far more common in rehabilitative settings rather than in health/fitness facilities. Many, many studies have assessed the effectiveness of various com-

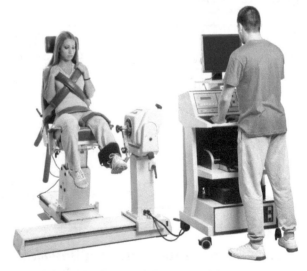

©cirkoglu/Shutterstock.com

Figure 5.2 Example of an *Isokinetic* Dynamometer

binations of sets, repetitions, and angular velocities. A sizable array of combinations haveDbeen found to be effective (Fleck and Kraemer 2014). However, the ideal combination of sets and repetitions remains unclear. Consequently, if you have access to isokinetic equipment when working with a client in a health/fitness setting, a reasonable approach is to use the set-repetition combinations that would be appropriate if using conventional free weights. A final consideration with isokinetic training is that of velocity specificity, wherein the greatest gains in strength are seen when the client is assessed at the velocities at which they trained. While velocity specificity is generally the case, there is carryover to both faster and slower velocities (~20–30°/sec above and below the velocity being trained), albeit more so to slower velocities. For this reason, training either over a range of velocities (e.g., sets at slow, intermediate, and fast velocities) or consistently at intermediate velocities of about 180°/sec are recommended if strength gains over a wide range of velocities are desired (Davies 1987).

The final type of strength training is *isotonic* exercise ("iso" means "equal" and "tonic" means "tension"). Common examples are lifting with free weights and using resistance machines (Figure 5.3). "Isotonics" is a misnomer since the force produced by the muscles, or "muscle tension," is not constant but varies throughout a joint's range of motion. A more appropriate term is *dynamic constant external resistance* (Fleck and Kraemer 2014). Some manufacturers of resistance machines have developed equipment that varies the resistance across the range of motion and, in so doing, purportedly better matches the force curves produced by the muscles across this range. Most research suggests that these efforts have not been very effective (Fleck and Kraemer 2014). The majority of research assessing how to optimize a resistance exercise prescription has used isotonic exercise. Thus, the subsequent sections of this book that detail how best to develop a resistance exercise prescription are primarily based on isotonic training.

Figure 5.3   Examples of Isotonic Exercises Using (a) Free Weights and (b) Machine Weights

Universal Principles of Resistance Exercise

Developing a resistance exercise prescription can be more challenging than developing a cardiovascular exercise prescription. There are more variables to consider with the former and, in the research literature, there is a considerable range of findings as to what constitutes an effective exercise prescription. Part of this variability in findings is simply because most relevant resistance exercise training studies used novice weight lifters, so almost any training program elicits positive results, and have a training duration of just a few weeks or months, which is when the adaptations are the most dramatic in novice lifters. In addition, the goals that motivate individual clients to perform resistance exercise are almost as varied as the clients themselves. Recall the examples of the fifty-year-old woman who underwent a mastectomy and now wants to return to kayaking and the twenty-year-old who hopes to earn a D-1 college basketball scholarship (Figure 5.4). Both have very specific goals and both may be equally motivated to succeed. Yet their resistance exercise programs will be dramatically different.

Some of the principles underlying developing a resistance exercise program are universal, meaning they apply to everyone. These universal principles may not be overtly used in developing the program but they are foundational to doing so. Consequently, they will be used when developing programs for people as diverse as the kayaker and the athlete. Because of their commonality, it is important that you have an appreciation of them.

The first universal principle is that of *specificity* (Fleck and Kraemer 2014; Haff and Triplett 2016). This principle is often discussed in the context of SAID, or "Specific Adaptations to Imposed Demands," which simply means that the adaptations the muscles make will reflect the manner in which they are trained. Examples in this chapter have been joint-angle specificity with isometric exercise and velocity-specificity with isokinetic training. Besides the type of training, specificity also refers to the velocity of the weight lifting movement (e.g., strength versus power), the rest periods used (e.g., the energy system trained), and the muscle groups (e.g., arms versus legs). Training specificity will influence all the components that are considered when developing the actual resistance exercise prescription.

The second principle is that of *progressive overload* (Fleck and Kraemer 2014; Haff and Triplett 2016). The muscles must be stressed, or forced to work harder than they are used to, in order to evoke the desired adaptations. This stress, often referred to as training intensity, must be increased as the muscles adapt. The most common method of overloading the muscles is to increase the resistance. Other methods of increasing the training intensity are to increase the velocity of movement and reduce the rest period between sets. Additional methods of overloading the muscles are to alter the training volume by changing the total number of sets and repetitions or by changing the exercises performed. Because of the SAID principle, however, these different methods of progressive overload will result in different muscle adaptations. In general, increasing the training intensity will increase muscular strength while increasing volume evokes muscle hypertrophy. Thus, the most appropriate overload method(s) for a specific client will likely differ based on the client's goals and may also change over time, as the client adapts to the training stimulus.

Figure 5.4   (a) Fifty-Year-Old Woman Kayaking and (b) Twenty-Year-Old Basketball Player

The third principle is that of having a *balanced program.* This concept refers to the need to train muscle agonists and antagonists equally, and that muscles need to be worked throughout the range of motions of the joints they move. For example, considerable research suggests that a large imbalance in the ratio of hamstring-to-quadriceps concentric muscle strength is associated with an increased risk for hamstring strains (Figure 5.5a; Ahmad et al. 2013), supporting the need to train both the agonist and antagonist muscles. However, what is often neglected is the importance of the hamstrings as hip extensors; other research suggests that most sprint-related hamstring injuries occur as the hamstrings are contracting eccentrically (just before foot strike) and hip extension is beginning. Consequently, eccentric hamstring contractions, with engagement of other hip extensors, may be an effective preventive treatment (Figure 5.5.b; Heiderscheit et al. 2010). Consequently, ensuring that clients have a balanced training program entails considering both the muscle groups and the muscle actions.

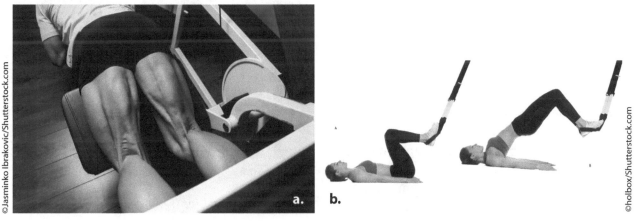

Figure 5.5   Hamstring Muscles as (a) Knee Flexors and (b) Hip Extensors

The fourth principle is the need to have a *varied program.* The components of the resistance exercise prescription should be changed regularly in order to keep the stimulus fresh. The goal is to create an exercise program where the client continues to make positive adaptations but without overtraining. One simple example is to change the choice of exercises such that the types of lifts used varies (e.g., training the chest muscles using barbells, dumbbells, and TRX; varying the inclines used). More sophisticated methods of having a varied program are usually operationalized by using a program of periodization. Periodization is described in Chapter 7.

The fifth principle is that of *rest,* referring to the need for adequate rest between sets of an exercise session, as well as adequate rest between exercise sessions. Careful attention to both will affect the efficacy of the overall exercise program. The duration of time between consecutive rest periods is dictated by the goals of the training program and the energy system to be trained. If muscular endurance is desired, then the rest intervals between sets should be relatively brief. However, if the goal is to increase strength, then longer rest periods are needed (de Salles et al. 2009). Likewise, the recovery period between workouts may vary depending on the intensity of the training sessions (Fleck and Kraemer 2014). High intensity sessions, which typically cause more muscle microdamage than low intensity sessions, require longer recovery times between workouts (e.g., seventy-two hours versus forty-eight hours).

Finally, the sixth principle is recognizing that *adaptations to training are unique to the individual.* Everyone responds differently to exercise training (Timmons 2011). Part of this response parallels the response to cardiorespiratory exercise training in that there is a marked genetic component to the responses to chronic resistance exercise (Costa et al. 2012; Timmons 2011). For example, people with a mesomorphic somatotype (Heath and Carter 1967) will more readily put on muscle mass than ectomorphs performing the same resistance exercise program (Figure 5.6). Another factor which can markedly affect the adaptive response is the current training status of the client (Fleck and Kraemer 2014). Novice weight lifters will have much more robust improvements to a program of resistance exercise than will highly trained lifters. In other words, for a given dose of training, the response will be relatively attenuated in more experienced lifters (Peterson, Rhea, and Alvar 2005). Consequently, it is important to remember that despite the best efforts of both your client and you, some clients will be more successful in their resistance exercise program than others.

These six universal principles underpin the resistance exercise prescription you will develop for your client and serve as the basis for the prescription. However, from your client's perspective, they will not be readily apparent. The components of the resistance exercise prescription your client will see, and which form the overt basis of the prescription, are reviewed in Chapter 6. Recommendations from the American College of Sports Medicine have been developed for individuals focused on general muscular fitness (Garber et al. 2011) or desiring more advanced programs (Ratamess et al. 2009). While these recommendations generally overlap with those of the National Strength and Conditioning Association (Haff and Triplett 2016), the latter are provided in the next two chapters of this textbook.

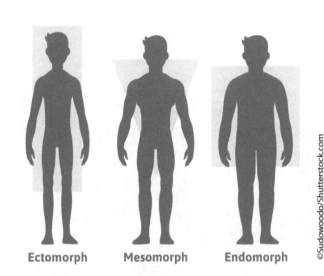

Ectomorph　Mesomorph　Endomorph

©Sudowoodo/Shutterstock.com

Figure 5.6 Three Categories of Body Type

Developing the Resistance Exercise Prescription

The details of how to develop a resistance exercise prescription, with foci on the principles of both day-to-day and long-term variations in the prescription, are covered in Chapters 6 and 7. These chapters are from the current edition of the National Strength and Conditioning Association's *Essentials of Strength Training and Conditioning* (Haff and Triplett 2016). This text is a major component of the recommended study materials for the NSCA Certified Strength and Conditioning Specialist certification. For more information on this certification, an online search using the terms "NSCA CSCS" will take you to the appropriate website (currently at https://www.nsca.com/certification/cscs/). The CSCS is a widely recognized certification for professionals in strength and conditioning fields. Consequently, including these two chapters in this textbook should help prepare you for a career as a health/fitness professional.

PUTTING IT ALL TOGETHER

The primary goal of this chapter was to increase your understanding of how to develop a resistance exercise prescription. To that end, background information on the three primary types of training and six universal principles of resistance exercise training were given. As with developing a cardiorespiratory exercise prescription, it is critical that you develop the resistance exercise program to best fit the client's goals and needs. Integrating the client's expressed goals with the results of the fitness assessment and the needs analysis (which is discussed in the next chapter) will help you identify what the focus of the resistance exercise prescription should be. In the next two chapters of this textbook, you will learn how to develop the exercise prescription. Chapter 6 focuses on the acute program variables of the prescription (exercise selection, frequency, order, load, volume, and rest periods) to fit your client's particular situation. Chapter 7 focuses on how to manipulate these variables over time, or periodization, to ensure that your client will continue to make steady progress toward their goals.

REFERENCES

Ahmad, C. S., L. H. Redler, M. G. Ciccotti, N. Maffulli, U. G. Longo, and J. Bradley. 2013. "Evaluation and Management of Hamstring Injuries." *Am J Sports Med.* 41: 2933–47.

American College of Sports Medicine. 2014. *ACSM's Guidelines for Exercise Testing and Prescription.* 9th ed. Philadelphia: Lippincott Williams & Wilkins.

Artero, E. G., D. C. Lee, C. J. Lavie, V. España-Romero, X. Sui, T. S. Church, and S. N. Blair. 2012. "Effects of Muscular Strength on Cardiovascular Risk Factors and Prognosis." *J Cardiopulm Rehabil Prev.* 32: 351–58.

Bennie, J. A., D-C. Lee, A. Khan, G. H. Wiesner, A. E. Bauman, E. Stamatakis, and S. J. H. Biddle. 2018. "Muscle-Strengthening Exercise among 397,423 U.S. Adults: Prevalence, Correlates, and Associations with Health Conditions." *Am J Prev Med.* 55: 864–74.

Blackwell, D. L., and T. C. Clarke. 2018. State Variation in Meeting the 2008 Federal Guidelines for Both Aerobic and Muscle-Strengthening Activities through Leisure-Time Physical Activity among Adults Aged 18–64: United States 2010–2015. National Health Statistics Reports; no 112. Hyattsville: National Center for Health Statistics.

Cooper, R., D. Kuh, and R. Hardy. 2010. "Mortality Review Group; FALCon and HALCyon Study Teams. Objectively Measured Physical Capability Levels and Mortality: Systematic Review and Meta-Analysis." *BMJ* 341: c4467. doi:10.1136/bmj.c4467

Costa, A. M., L. Breitenfeld, A. J. Silva, A. Pereira, M. Izquierdo, and M. C. Marques. 2012. "Genetic Inheritance Effects on Endurance and Muscle Strength: An Update." *Sports Med.* 42: 449–58.

Davies, G. J. 1987. A Compendium of Isokinetics in Clinical Usage and Rehabilitation Techniques. Onalaska: S&S Publishers.

de Salles, B. F., R. Simão, F. Miranda, S. Novaes Jda, A. Lemos, and J. M. Willardson. 2009. "Rest Interval between Sets in Strength Training." *Sports Med.* 39: 765–77.

FitzGerald, S. J., C. E. Barlow, J. B. Kampert, J. R. Morrow Jr., A. W. Jackson, and S. N. Blair. 2004. "Muscular Fitness and All-Cause Mortality: Prospective Observations." *Journal of Physical Activity and Health* 1: 7–18.

Fleck, S. J., and W. J. Kraemer. 2014. *Designing Resistance Training Programs.* 4th ed. Champaign: Human Kinetics.

Garber, C. E., B. Blissmer, M. R. Deschenes, B. A. Franklin, M. J. Lamonte, I. M. Lee, D. C. Nieman, and D. P. Swain. 2011. "American College of Sports Medicine Position Stand. Quantity and Quality of Exercise for Developing and Maintaining Cardiorespiratory, Musculoskeletal, and Neuromotor Fitness in Apparently Healthy Adults: Guidance for Prescribing Exercise." *Med Sci Sports Exerc.* 43: 1334–59.

García-Hermoso, A., I. Cavero-Redondo, R. Ramírez-Vélez, J. R. Ruiz, F. B. Ortega, D-C. Lee, V. Martínez-Vizcaíno. 2018. "Muscular Strength as a Predictor of All-Cause Mortaility in an Apparently Healthy Population: A Systematic Review and Meta-Analysis of Data from Approximately 2 Million Men and Women." *Arch Phys Med Rehabil.* 99: 2100–13.e5.

Haff, G. G., and T. Triplett, eds. 2016. *Essentials of Strength Training and Conditioning.* 4th ed. Champaign: Human Kinetics.

Heath, B. H., and J. E. L. Carter. 1967. "A Modified Somatotype Method." *American Journal of Physical Anthropology.* 27: 57–74.

Heiderscheit, B. C., M. A. Sherry, A. Silder, E. S. Chumanov, and D. G. Thelen. 2010. "Hamstring Strain Injuries: Recommendations for Diagnosis, Rehabilitation, and Injury Prevention." *J Orthop Sports Phys Ther.* 40: 67–81.

Katzmarzyk P. T., and C. L. Craig. 2002. "Musculoskeletal Fitness and Risk of Mortality." *Med Sci Sports Exerc.* 34: 740–44.

Kraschnewski J. L., C.N. Sciamanna, J. M. Poger, L. S. Rovniak, E. B. Lehman, A. B. Cooper, N. H. Ballentine, and J. T. Ciccolo. 2016. "Is Strength Training Associated with Mortality Benefits? A 15 Year Cohort Study of US Older Adults." *Prev Med.* 87: 121–27.

Peterson, M. D., M. R. Rhea, and B. A. Alvar. 2005. "Applications of the Dose-Response for Muscular Strength Development: A Review of Meta-Analytic Efficacy and Reliability for Designing Training Prescription." *J Strength Cond Res.* 19: 950–58.

Ratamess, N. A., B. A. Alvar, T. K. Evetoch, T. J. Housh, W. B. Kibler, W. J. Kraemer, and N. T. Triplett. 2009. "American College of Sports Medicine Position Stand. Progression Models in Resistance Training for Healthy Adults." *Med Sci Sports Exerc.* 41:687–708.

Ruiz, J. R., X. Sui, F. Lobelo, J. R. Morrow Jr., A. W. Jackson, M. Sjöström, and S. N. Blair. 2008. "Association between Muscular Strength and Mortality in Men: Prospective Cohort Study. *BMI* 337: a439.

Timmons, J. A. 2011. "Variability in Training-Induced Skeletal Muscle Adaptation." *J Appl Physiol* 110: 846–53.

U.S. Department of Health and Human Services. 2018. *Physical Activity Guidelines for Americans.* 2nd ed. Washington, DC: U.S. Department of Health and Human Services.

Volaklis, K. A., M. Halle, C. Meisinger. 2015. "Muscular Strength as a Predictor of Mortality: A Narrative Review. *Eur J Intern Med.* 26: 303–10.

Yang, J., C. A. Christophi, A. Farioli, D. M. Baur, S. Moffat, T. W. Zollinger, and S. N. Kales. 2019. "Association between Push-Up Exercise Capacity and Future Cardiovascular Events among Active Men." *JAMA Network Open* 2:e188341. doi:10.1001/jamanetworkopen.2018.8341

CHAPTER 6

Resistance Training

© Mark McElroy/Shutterstock.com

PRINCIPLES OF ANAEROBIC EXERCISE PRESCRIPTION

Resistance training programs for athletic populations require attention to the principles of specificity, overload, and progression. One of the most basic concepts to incorporate in all training programs is **specificity**. The term, first suggested by DeLorme in 1945 (14), refers to the method whereby an athlete is trained in a specific manner to produce a specific adaptation or training outcome. In the case of resistance training, *specificity* refers to aspects such as the muscles involved, the movement pattern, and the nature of the muscle action (e.g., speed of movement, force application), but does not always reflect the combination of all of these aspects. Importantly, it does not mean that all aspects of the training must mimic that of the sporting skill. For example, a squat movement is relevant to vertical jump because it involves overcoming resistance in the same movement and muscles that are involved in the vertical jump, yet the speed of movement and force application are disparate between the squat and vertical jump. Sometimes used interchangeably with *specificity* is the acronym **SAID,** which stands for *specific adaptation to imposed demands.* The underlying principle is that the type of demand placed on the body dictates the type of adaptation that will occur. For instance, athletes training for power in high-speed movements (e.g., baseball pitch, tennis serve) should attempt to activate or recruit the same motor units required by their sport at the highest velocity possible (8, 86). Specificity also relates to the athlete's sport season. As an athlete progresses through the preseason, in-season, and postseason, all forms of training should gradually progress in an organized manner from generalized to sport specific (1). Although participation in the sport itself provides the greatest opportunity to improve performance in the sport, proper application of the specificity principle certainly increases the likelihood that other training will also positively contribute to performance.

Overload refers to assigning a workout or training regimen of greater intensity than the athlete is accustomed to. Without the stimulus of overload, even an otherwise well-designed program greatly limits an athlete's ability to make improvements. The obvious application of this principle in the design of resistance training programs involves increasing the loads assigned in the exercises. Other more subtle changes include increasing the number of sessions per week (or per day in some instances), adding exercises or sets, emphasizing complex over simple exercises, decreasing the length of the rest periods between sets and exercises, or any combination of these or other changes. The intent is to stress the body at a higher level that it is used to. When the overload principle is properly applied, overtraining is avoided and the desired training adaptation will occur.

If a training program is to continue producing higher levels of performance, the intensity of the training must become progressively greater. **Progression,** when applied properly, promotes long-term training benefits. Although it is customary to focus only on the resistance used, one can progressively increase training intensity by raising the number of weekly training sessions, adding more drills or exercises to each session, changing the type or technical requirements of the drills or exercises, or otherwise increasing the training stimulus. For example, an athlete may progress from the front squat to learning the hang power clean and eventually the power clean as a technical progression. The issue of importance is that progression is based on the athlete's training status and is introduced systematically and gradually.

Designing a resistance training program is a complex process that requires the recognition and manipulation of seven **program design** variables (referred to in this chapter as steps 1 through 7). This chapter discusses each variable, shown in the sidebar, in the context of three scenarios that enable the strength and conditioning professional to see how training principles and program design guidelines can be integrated into an overall program.

The three scenarios include a basketball center (scenario A) in her preseason, an American football offensive lineman (scenario B) during his off-season, and a cross-country runner (scenario C) during his in-season. (See the scenarios on p 141). It is understood that in each scenario, the athlete is well conditioned for his or her sport, has no musculoskeletal dysfunction, and has been cleared for training and competition by the sports medicine staff. The athletes in scenarios A (basketball center) and B (American football lineman) have been resistance training since high school, are accustomed to lifting heavy loads, and are skilled in machine and free weight exercises. The high school cross-country runner in scenario C, in contrast, began a resistance training program in the preseason only four weeks ago, so his training is limited and his exercise technique skills are not well developed.

ATHLETE SCENARIOS					
Scenario A		**Scenario B**		**Scenario C**	
Sex:	Female	Sex:	Male	Sex:	Male
Age:	20 years old	Age:	28 years old	Age:	17 years old
Sport:	Collegiate basketball	Sport:	Professional American football	Sport:	High school cross-country running
Position:	Center	Position:	Offensive lineman	Position:	(Not applicable)
Season:	Beginning of the preseason	Season:	Beginning of the off-season	Season:	Beginning of the in-season

STEP 1: NEEDS ANALYSIS

The strength and conditioning professional's initial task is to perform a **needs analysis,** a two-stage process that includes an evaluation of the requirements and characteristics of the sport and an assessment of the athlete.

Evaluation of the Sport

The first task in a needs analysis is to determine the unique characteristics of the sport, which includes the general physiological and biomechanical profile, common injury sites, and position-specific attributes. This

> ### Resistance Training Program Design Variables
>
> 1. Needs analysis
> 2. Exercise selection
> 3. Training frequency
> 4. Exercise order
> 5. Training load and repetitions
> 6. Volume
> 7. Rest periods

information enables the strength and conditioning professional to design a program specific to those requirements and characteristics. Although this task can be approached in several ways (30), it should at least include consideration of the following attributes of the sport (20, 43):

- ▶ Body and limb movement patterns and muscular involvement (**movement analysis)**
- ▶ Strength, power, hypertrophy, and muscular endurance priorities (**physiological analysis)**
- ▶ Common sites for joint and muscle injury and causative factors (**injury analysis)**

Other characteristics of a sport—such as cardiovascular endurance, speed, agility, and flexibility requirements—should also be evaluated. This chapter, however, focuses only on the physiological outcomes that specifically relate to resistance training program design: strength, power, hypertrophy, and muscular endurance.

For example, a movement analysis of the shot-put field event reveals that it is an all-body movement that begins with the athlete in a semicrouched stance, with many joints flexed and adducted, and culminates in an upright stance with many joints extended and abducted. The most heavily recruited muscles (not in order) are the elbow extensors (triceps brachii), shoulder abductors (deltoids), hip extensors (gluteals, hamstrings), knee extensors (quadriceps), and ankle plantar flexors (soleus, gastrocnemius). Physiologically, shot putting requires high levels of strength and power for a successful performance. Also, enhanced muscular hypertrophy is advantageous since the muscle's ability to produce force increases as its cross-sectional area becomes greater (40). The muscular endurance requirement is minimal, however. Due to the repetitive nature of training and competition, the muscles and tendons surrounding the shoulder and elbow joints tend to be injured due to overuse (98).

Assessment of the Athlete

The second task is to profile the athlete's needs and goals by evaluating training (and injury) status, conducting a variety of tests (e.g., maximum strength testing), evaluating the results, and determining the primary goal of training. The more individualized the assessment process, the more specific the resistance training program for each athlete can be.

Training Status

An athlete's current condition or level of preparedness to begin a new or revised program (**training status**) is an important consideration in the design of training programs. This includes an evaluation by a sports medicine professional of any current or previous injuries that may affect training. Also important is the athlete's **training background** or **exercise history** (training that occurred *before* he or she began a new or revised program), because this information will help the strength and conditioning professional better understand the athlete's training capabilities. An assessment of the athlete's training background should examine the

- ▶ type of training program (sprint, plyometric, resistance, and so on),
- ▶ length of recent regular participation in previous training program(s),
- ▶ level of intensity involved in previous training program(s), and
- ▶ degree of exercise **technique experience** (i.e., the knowledge and skill to perform resistance training exercises properly).

Table 6.1 provides an example of how such information might be used to classify athletes' training status as beginner, intermediate, or advanced. The strength and conditioning professional should realize that the three classifications exist on a continuum and cannot be definitively demarcated.

TABLE 6.1
Example of Classifying Resistance Training Status

RESISTANCE TRAINING BACKGROUND					
Resistance Training Status	**Current Program**	**Training Age**	**Frequency (Per Week)**	**Training Stress***	**Technique Experience and Skill**
Beginner (untrained)	Not training or just began training	<2 months	≤1–2	None or low	None or minimal
Intermediate (moderately resistance trained)	Currently training	2–6 months	≤2–3	Medium	Basic
Advanced (well resistance trained)	Currently training	≥1 year	≥3–4	High	High

*In this example, "training stress" refers to the degree of physical demand or stimulus of the resistance training program.

Physical Testing and Evaluation

Physical evaluation involves conducting assessments of the athlete's strength, flexibility, power, speed, muscular endurance, body composition, cardiovascular endurance, and so on. In this chapter, the needs analysis focuses on assessing maximal muscular strength, but a comprehensive assessment goes beyond that.

To yield pertinent and reliable data that can be used effectively to develop a resistance training program, the tests selected should be related to the athlete's sport, consistent with the athlete's level of skill, and realistically based on the equipment available. The result of the movement analysis discussed previously provides direction in selecting tests. Typically, major upper body exercises (e.g., bench press and shoulder press) and exercises that mimic jumping movements to varying degrees (e.g., power clean, squat, leg press) are used in testing batteries.

After testing is completed, the results should be compared with normative or descriptive data to determine the athlete's strengths and weaknesses. Based on this evaluation and the needs analysis of the sport, a training program can be developed to improve deficiencies, maintain strengths, or further develop physiological qualities that will enable the athlete to better meet the demands of the sport.

Primary Resistance Training Goal

The athlete's test results, the movement and physiological analysis of the sport, and the priorities of the athlete's sport season determine the primary goal or outcome for the resistance training program. Typically, this goal is to improve strength, power, hypertrophy, or muscular endurance. Despite a potential desire or need to make improvements in two different areas (e.g., strength *and* muscular endurance), an effort should be made to concentrate on only one training outcome per season. An example of how the strength and conditioning professional may prioritize the resistance training emphases during the four main sport seasons is shown in Table 6.2.

TABLE 6.2			
Example of General Training Priorities by Sport Season			
PRIORITY GIVEN TO			
Sport Season	**Sport Practice**	**Resistance Training**	**Resistance Training Goal***
Off-season	Low	High	Hypertrophy and muscular endurance (initially); strength and power (later)
Preseason	Medium	Medium	Sport and movement specific (i.e., strength, power, or muscular endurance, depending on the sport)
In-season	High	Low	Maintenance of preseason training goal
Postseason (active rest)	Variable	Variable	Not specific (may include activities other than sport skill or resistance training)
*The actual training goals and priorities are based on the specific sport or activity and may differ from the goals listed here.			

Application of the Needs Analysis		
(Refer to the first scenario table in the chapter for a description of the scenario athletes.)		
SCENARIO A **Female Collegiate Basketball Player** **Preseason**	**SCENARIO B** **Male Professional American Football Lineman** **Off-Season**	**SCENARIO C** **Male High School Cross-Country Runner** **In-Season**
Sport Evaluation **Movement analysis** *Sport:* Running and jumping, ball handling, shooting, blocking, and rebounding *Muscular involvement:* All major muscle areas, especially the hips, thighs, and shoulders **Physiological analysis (primary requirement)** Strength/power	*Sport Evaluation* **Movement analysis** *Sport:* Grabbing, pushing, repelling, and deflecting opponents *Muscular involvement:* All major muscle areas, especially the hips, thighs, chest, arms, and low back **Physiological analysis (primary requirement)** Hypertrophy	*Sport Evaluation* **Movement analysis** *Sport:* Running, repetitive leg and arm movements *Muscular involvement:* All lower body muscle areas, postural muscles, shoulders, and arms **Physiological analysis (primary requirement)** Muscular endurance

Athlete's profile
Training background
• Has resistance trained regularly since high school
• Possesses excellent skill in performing free weight and machine exercises
• Just completed a 4x/week resistance training program in the off-season consisting of:
Upper body exercises (2x/week):
  6 exercises (2 core, 4 assistance), 3 sets of 10RM–12RM loads
Lower body exercises (2x/week):
  6 exercises (2 core, 4 assistance), 3 sets of 10RM–12RM loads
	Athlete's profile
	Training background
	• Has resistance trained regularly throughout high school, college, and his professional career
	• Possesses excellent skill in performing free weight and machine exercises
	• Just completed a 2x/week resistance training program in the postseason[b] consisting of:
	All exercises performed in each session:
	  8 exercises (3 core, 5 assistance; 2 lower body, 6 upper body), 2–3 sets of 12RM–15RM loads
		Athlete's profile
		Training background
		• Just began resistance training in preseason
		• Has only limited skill in performing free weight and machine exercises
		• Just completed a 2x/week resistance training program in the preseason[c] consisting of:
		All exercises performed in each session:
		  7 exercises (3 core, 4 assistance; 3 lower body, 4 upper body), 1–2 sets of 15RM loads

Classification of resistance training status Advanced	*Classification of resistance training status* Advanced	*Classification of resistance training status* Beginner
Primary preseason resistance training goal Strength/power[a]	*Primary off-season resistance training goal* Hypertrophy	*Primary in-season resistance training goal* Muscular endurance
COMMENTS [a]The preseason will address both of these goals through a combination of appropriate exercise selection and volume-load assignments.	**COMMENTS** [b]Due to the extreme physical demands of American football, this athlete's postseason training volume was greater than is often assigned for the active rest phase of a typical program.	**COMMENTS** [c]Because this athlete just began his resistance training program, his frequency was limited to only 2x/week in the preseason rather than the three to four sessions/week typically completed by better-trained individuals.
The information in this table reflects one approach to evaluating the requirements of a sport and profiling an athlete.		

STEP 2: EXERCISE SELECTION

Exercise selection involves choosing exercises for a resistance training program. To make informed exercise selections, the strength and conditioning professional must understand the nature of various types of resistance training exercises, the movement and muscular requirements of the sport, the athlete's exercise technique experience, the equipment available, and the amount of training time available.

Exercise Type

Although there are literally hundreds of resistance training exercises to select from when one is designing a program, most involve primary muscle groups or body areas and fall into categories based on their relative importance to the athlete's sport.

Core and Assistance Exercises

Exercises can be classified as either core or assistance based on the size of the muscle areas involved and their level of contribution to a particular sport movement. **Core exercises** recruit one or more large muscle areas (i.e., chest, shoulder, back, hip, or thigh), involve two or more primary joints **(multijoint exercises),** and receive priority when one is selecting exercises because of their direct application to the sport. **Assistance exercises** usually recruit smaller muscle areas (i.e., upper arm, abdominal muscles, calf, neck, forearm, lower back, or anterior lower leg), involve only one primary joint **(single-joint exercises),** and are considered less important to improving sport performance. Generally, all the joints at the shoulder—the glenohumeral and shoulder girdle articulations—are considered one *primary* joint when resistance training exercises are categorized as core or assistance. The spine is similarly considered a single primary joint (as in the abdominal crunch and back extension exercises).

A common application of assistance exercises is for injury prevention and rehabilitation, as these exercises often isolate a specific muscle or muscle group. The muscles that are predisposed to injury from the unique demands of a sport skill (e.g., the shoulder external rotators for overhand pitching) or those that require reconditioning after an injury (e.g., a quadriceps contusion) can be specifically conditioned by an assistance exercise.

Structural and Power Exercises

A core exercise that emphasizes loading the spine directly (e.g., back squat) or indirectly (e.g., power clean) can be further described as a **structural exercise.** More specifically, a structural exercise involves muscular stabilization of posture during performance of the lifting movement (e.g., maintaining a rigid torso and a neutral spine during the back squat). A structural exercise that is performed very quickly or explosively is considered a **power exercise.** Typically, power exercises are assigned to athletes when they are appropriate for the athlete's sport-specific training priorities (45).

Movement Analysis of the Sport

In the needs analysis (step 1), the strength and conditioning professional has identified the unique requirements and characteristics of the sport. The exercises selected for a resistance training program that focus on conditioning for a particular sport need to be relevant to the activities of that sport in their body and limb movement patterns, joint ranges of motion, and muscular involvement. The exercises should also create muscular balance to reduce risk of injury from disproportionate training.

Sport-Specific Exercises

The more similar the training activity is to the actual sport movement, the greater the likelihood that there will be a positive transfer to that sport (8, 19, 20, 42, 72, 86). This is the specificity concept, also called the specific adaptation to imposed demands (SAID) principle. Table 6.3 provides examples of resistance training exercises that relate in varying degrees to the movement patterns of various sports. The strength and conditioning professional should find this table helpful when trying to identify sport-specific exercises. For example, the primary muscles involved in jumping for basketball are the hip and knee extensors. An athlete can exercise these muscles by performing the leg press or back squat, but which exercise is preferable? Certainly both exercises strengthen the hip and knee extensors, but because jumping is performed from an erect body position with balance and weight-bearing forces as considerations, the back squat is more relevant to jumping and is therefore preferred over the leg press (97). The power clean and snatch are relevant to jumping because of their quick movement characteristics, thereby applying a fast rate of force development and high power.

TABLE 6.3	
Examples of Movement-Related Resistance Training Exercises	
Movement Pattern	**Related Exercises**
Ball dribbling and passing	Close-grip bench press, dumbbell bench press, triceps pushdown, reverse curl, hammer curl
Ball kicking	Unilateral hip adduction and abduction, single-leg squat, forward step lunge, leg (knee) extension, leg raise
Freestyle swimming (including start and turns)	Pull-up, lateral shoulder raise, forward step lunge, upright row, barbell pullover, single-leg squat
Vertical jumping	Snatch, power clean, push jerk, back squat, front squat, standing calf (heel) raise
Racket stroke	Flat dumbbell fly, lunge, bent-over lateral raise, wrist curl, wrist extension
Rowing	Power clean, clean pull, snatch pull, bent-over row, seated row, angled leg press, horizontal leg press, deadlift, stiff-legged deadlift, good morning
Running, sprinting	Snatch, clean, front squat, forward step lunge, step-up, leg (knee) extension, leg (knee) curl, toe raise (dorsiflexion)
Throwing, pitching	Lunge, single-leg squat, barbell pullover, overhead triceps extension, shoulder internal and external rotation

Muscle Balance

Exercises selected for the specific demands of the sport should maintain a balance of muscular strength across joints and between opposing muscle groups (e.g., biceps brachii and triceps brachii). Avoid designing a resistance training program that increases the risk of injury due to a disparity between the strength of the **agonist**, the muscle or muscle group actively causing the movement (e.g., the quadriceps in the leg [knee] extension exercise), and the antagonist, the sometimes passive (i.e., not concentrically involved) muscle or muscle group located on the opposite side of the limb (e.g., the hamstrings in the leg [knee] extension exercise). If an imbalance is created or discovered, exercises to restore an appropriate strength balance need to be selected. For example, if isokinetic testing reveals that the hamstrings are extremely weak compared with the quadriceps, additional hamstring exercises could be included to compensate for the imbalance (20, 72, 86). Note that **muscle balance** does not always mean equal strength, just a proper ratio of strength, power, or muscular endurance of one muscle or muscle group relative to another muscle or muscle group.

Exercises to Promote Recovery

Exercises that do not involve high muscular stress and high stress on the nervous system but promote movement and restoration can be classified as **recovery exercise**. These exercises are generally included at the conclusion of the main resistance training session, or as a separate session within the microcycle, aimed at promoting recovery and restoration. They can take the form of lightly loaded resistance exercises or low-intensity aerobic exercise to assist the body in returning to its preexercise state (8). These exercises assist in the removal of metabolic wastes and by-products and maintain some amount of blood flow to the exercised muscles so the repair processes can be optimized.

Exercise Technique Experience

An important part of the needs analysis described earlier is evaluating the athlete's training status and exercise technique experience. If there is any question whether an athlete can perform an exercise with proper technique, the strength and conditioning professional should ask the athlete to demonstrate the exercise. If the athlete uses incorrect technique, the strength and conditioning professional should provide complete instruction. Often, unskilled individuals are introduced to machines and free weight assistance exercises (20) because these are considered easier to perform than free weight core exercises due to their lower balance and coordination requirements (20, 86). Despite this, one should not assume that the athlete will perform exercises correctly, even those that are relatively easy to perform.

Availability of Resistance Training Equipment

The availability of training equipment must be considered in the selection of exercises. A lack of certain equipment may necessitate selecting exercises that are not as sport specific. For example, the absence of Olympic-type barbells with revolving sleeves would preclude exercises such as the power clean, and an insufficient supply of barbell plates may result in substituting exercises that do not require as much resistance; for example, the back squat could be replaced by the front squat.

Available Training Time per Session

The strength and conditioning professional should weigh the value of certain exercises against the time it takes to perform them. Some exercises take longer to complete than others. If time for a training session is limited, exercises that are more time efficient may need to be given priority over others. For example, the machine leg press could be selected instead of the free weight lunge to train the hips and thighs of a 100 m sprinter. The time required to move the machine pin to the correct slot in a weight stack and perform 10 repetitions of a machine leg press is much less than the time required for the lunge exercise, for which the athlete has to load both ends of a bar, attach the locks, back out of the power rack, establish a stable starting position, perform 10 repetitions of *each* leg, and rerack the bar. Although the machine leg press is less sport specific, the time saved may permit including other exercises or performing more sets. The benefit of including the more sport-specific lunge exercise, on the other hand, may be worth the additional time needed, although this depends on the goals of the training season and time available.

Application of the Exercise Selection Guidelines

(Refer to the first scenario table in the chapter for a description of the scenario athletes. Exercises are not shown in order of execution.)

SCENARIO A **Female Collegiate Basketball Player Preseason**	SCENARIO B **Male Professional American Football Lineman Off-Season**	SCENARIO C **Male High School Cross-Country Runner In-Season**
Core Hang clean (all body, power)[a] Snatch and clean (all body, power)[a] Push press (all body, power)[a] Front squat (hip and thigh) Incline bench press (chest) Pull-up (back, shoulders, arms)	***Core*[b]** Clean (all body, power) Tire flipping (all body, power) Back squat (hip and thigh) Deadlift (hip and thigh) Bench press (chest) Shoulder press (shoulders)	***Core*** Lunge (hip and thigh)[c] Vertical chest press (chest)[d] Rear leg elevated deadlift (hip and thigh)
Assistance Abdominal crunch (abdomen) Seated row (upper back) Stiff-leg deadlift (posterior hip and thigh) Standing calf raise (posterior lower leg)	***Assistance*** Towel-grip pull-up (forearm grip) Abdominal crunch (abdomen) Step-up (hip and thigh) Leg (knee) curl (posterior thigh) Bent-over row (upper back) Shoulder shrug (upper back and neck) Barbell biceps curl (anterior upper arm) Lying triceps extension (posterior upper arm) Seated calf (heel) raise (posterior lower leg)	***Assistance*** Abdominal crunch (abdomen) Leg (knee) curl (posterior thigh) Lateral shoulder raise (shoulders) One-arm dumbbell row (upper back)[e] Toe raise (dorsiflexion) (anterior lower leg) Machine back extension (lower back) Cable hip flexion (hip flexors)
COMMENTS [a]These exercises are included to maximize power and match the jumping movements of basketball.	**COMMENTS** This athlete has extra time available to perform more resistance training exercises because sport skill practice is not the first priority in the off-season. [b]Greater training frequency allows more core exercises to be included (see step 3).	**COMMENTS** [c]Although not always considered a core exercise, the lunge recruits muscles and joints that have direct application to running. [d]This exercise also involves the triceps brachii muscle, so an assistance exercise to isolate the triceps is not needed. This reduces the time devoted to the resistance training portion of the in-season program. [e]This exercise also involves the biceps brachii muscle, so an assistance exercise to isolate the biceps is not needed. This reduces the time devoted to the resistance training portion of the in-season program.

STEP 3: TRAINING FREQUENCY

Training frequency refers to the number of training sessions completed in a given time period. For a resistance training program, a common time period is one week. When determining training frequency, the strength and conditioning professional should consider the athlete's training status, sport season, projected exercise loads, types of exercises, and other concurrent training or activities.

Training Status

The athlete's level of preparedness for training, which was determined during the needs analysis (step 1), is an influential factor in determining training frequency because it affects the number of rest days needed between training sessions. Traditionally, three workouts per week are recommended for many athletes, because the intervening days allow sufficient recovery between sessions (20). As an athlete adapts to training and becomes better conditioned, it is appropriate to consider increasing the number of training days to four and, with additional training, maybe five, six, or seven (see Table 6.4). The general guideline is to schedule training sessions so as to include at least one rest or recovery day—but not more than three—between sessions that stress the same muscle groups (38). For example, if a strength and conditioning professional wants a beginning athlete to perform a total body resistance training program two times per week, the sessions should be spaced out evenly (e.g., Monday and Thursday, or Tuesday and Friday). If the athlete trains only on Monday and Wednesday, the absence of a training stimulus between Wednesday and the following Monday may result in a *decrease* in the athlete's training status (16, 24, 38), although, for a short time in well-trained athletes, one session a week can maintain strength (16, 24).

More highly resistance-trained (intermediate or advanced) athletes can augment their training by using a **split routine** in which different muscle groups are trained on different days. Training nearly every day may seem to violate the recommended guidelines for recovery, but grouping exercises that train a portion of the body (e.g., upper body or lower body) or certain muscle areas (e.g., chest, shoulder, and triceps) gives the trained athlete an opportunity to adequately recover between similar training sessions (see Table 6.5). For instance, a common lower body–upper body regimen includes four training sessions per week: lower body on Monday and Thursday and upper body on Tuesday and Friday (or vice versa). This way, there are two or three days of rest between each upper or lower body training session, even though the athlete trains on two consecutive days twice a week (39). For split routines with three distinct training days, the rest days are not on the same day each week.

TABLE 6.4 Resistance Training Frequency Based on Training Status	
Training Status	**Frequency Guidelines (Sessions Per Week)**
Beginner	2–3
Intermediate	3–4
Advanced	4–7
Data from references 24, 26, 27, 28, 37, and 47.	

Sport Season

Another influence on resistance training frequency is the sport season. For example, the increased emphasis on practicing the sport skill during the in-season necessitates a decrease in the time spent in the weight room and, consequently, reduces the frequency of resistance training (see Tables 6.2 and 6.6). The problem is that there simply is not enough time to fit all the desired modes of training into each day. So, even though a well-trained athlete may be capable of completing four or more resistance training sessions per week, the other time demands of the sport may not permit this.

Training Load and Exercise Type

Athletes who train with maximal or near-maximal loads require more recovery time before their next training session (20, 74, 86). The ability to train more frequently may be enhanced by alternating lighter and heavier training days (20, 86). There is also evidence that upper body muscles can recover more quickly from heavy loading sessions than lower body muscles (37). The same is true regarding an athlete's ability to recover faster from single-joint exercises compared to multijoint exercises (85). These research findings may explain why, for example, powerlifters may schedule only one very heavy deadlift or squat training session per week.

TABLE 6.5
Examples of Common Split Routines

		Sample Training Week							
Training Day	**Body Parts or Muscle Groups Trained**	**Su**	**M**	**Tu**	**W**	**Th**	**F**	**Sa**	**Resulting Training Frequency**
1	Lower body	*Rest*	Lower body	Upper body	*Rest*	Lower body	Upper body	*Rest*	4 times per week
2	Upper body								
1	Chest, shoulders, triceps	*Rest*	Chest, shoulders, triceps	Lower body	Back, trapezius, biceps	*Rest*	Chest, shoulders, triceps	Lower body	5 times per week*
2	Lower body								
3	Back, trapezius, biceps								
1	Chest and back	Chest and back	Lower body	Shoulders and arms	*Rest*	Chest and back	Lower body	Shoulders and arms	6 times per week*
2	Lower body								
3	Shoulders and arms								

*Frequency varies between five times per week and six times per week, depending on the day of the week that is the first training day.

TABLE 6.6 Resistance Training Frequency Based on the Sport Season (for a Trained Athlete)	
Sport Season	**Frequency Guidelines (Sessions Per Week)**
Off-season	4–6
Preseason	3–4
In-season	1–3
Postseason (active rest)	0–3
Data from references 20, 87, and 90.	

Other Training

Exercise frequency is also influenced by the overall amount of physical stress, so the strength and conditioning professional must consider the effects of all forms of exercise. If the athlete's program already includes aerobic or anaerobic (e.g., sprinting, agility, speed-endurance, plyometric) training, sport skill practice, or any combination of these components, the frequency of resistance training may need to be reduced (13). Additionally, the effects of a physically demanding occupation may be relevant. Athletes who work in manual labor jobs, instruct or assist others in physical activities, or are on their feet all day may not be able to withstand the same training frequency as athletes who are less active outside of their sport-related pursuits.

STEP 4: EXERCISE ORDER

Exercise order refers to a sequence of resistance exercises performed during one training session. Although there are many ways to arrange exercises, decisions are invariable based on how one exercise affects the quality of effort or the technique of another exercise. Usually exercises are arranged so that an athlete's maximal force capabilities are available (from a sufficient rest or recovery period) to complete a set with proper exercise technique. Four of the most common methods of ordering resistance exercises are described in the following paragraphs.

Power, Other Core, Then Assistance Exercises

Power exercises such as the snatch, hang clean, power clean, and push jerk should be performed first in a training session, followed by other nonpower core exercises and then assistance exercises (20, 83, 88). The literature also refers to this arrangement as *multijoint exercises and then single-joint exercises or large muscle areas and then small muscle areas* (18, 20, 72, 86, 90). Power exercises require the highest level of skill and concentration of all the exercises and are most affected by fatigue (20). Athletes who become fatigued are prone to using poor technique and consequently are at higher risk of injury. The explosive movements and extensive muscular involvement of power exercises also result in significant energy expenditure (86). This is another reason to have athletes perform such exercises first, while they are still metabolically fresh. If power exercises are not selected in step 2 (exercise selection), then the recommended order of exercises is core exercises and then assistance exercises.

Application of the Training Frequency Guidelines (Refer to the first scenario table in the chapter for a description of the scenario athletes.)		
SCENARIO A **Female Collegiate Basketball Player Preseason**	**SCENARIO B** **Male Professional American Football Lineman Off-Season**	**SCENARIO C** **Male High School Cross-Country Runner In-Season**
Advanced training status allows 4–7x/week	*Advanced training status allows* 4–7x/week	*Beginner training status allows* 2–3x/week
Frequency guideline based on the sport season 3–4x/week	*Frequency guideline based on the sport season* 4–6x/week	*Frequency guideline based on the sport season* 1–3x/week
Assigned resistance training frequency 3x/week[a] • Monday, Wednesday, and Friday • All exercises performed each session	*Assigned resistance training frequency* 4x/week (split routine)[b] • Monday and Thursday (lower body exercises) • Tuesday and Friday (upper body exercises)	*Assigned resistance training frequency* 2x/week[c] • Wednesday and Saturday • All exercises performed each session
COMMENTS [a]Training frequency is decreased from the previous season (off-season) to allow for more time and physical resources to apply to basketball-specific sport skill training.	**COMMENTS** [b]A split routine allows for more overall exercises to be performed without an excessive increase in training time (per session) because the exercises are divided over more training days.	**COMMENTS** [c]The assigned training days need to be planned so they do not affect the athlete's performance on the scheduled days for cross-country meets.

Upper and Lower Body Exercises (Alternated)

One method of providing the opportunity for athletes to recover more fully between exercises is to alternate upper body exercises with lower body exercises. This arrangement is especially helpful for untrained individuals who find that completing several upper or lower body exercises in succession is too strenuous (20, 72). Also, if training time is limited, this method of arranging exercises minimizes the length of the rest periods required between exercises and maximizes the rest between body areas. The result is a decrease in overall training time, because the athlete can perform an upper body exercise and then immediately go to a lower body exercise without having to wait for the upper body to rest. If the exercises are performed with minimal rest periods (20–30 seconds), this method is also referred to as **circuit training**—a method sometimes also used to improve cardiorespiratory endurance (23), although to a lesser extent than conventional aerobic exercise training.

"Push" and "Pull" Exercises (Alternated)

Another method of improving recovery and recruitment between exercises is to alternate pushing exercises (e.g., bench press, shoulder press, and triceps extension) with pulling exercises (e.g., lat pulldown, bent-over row, biceps curl) (2). This push–pull arrangement ensures that the same muscle group will not be used in two exercises (or sets, in some cases) in succession, thus reducing fatigue in the involved muscles. In contrast, arranging several pulling exercises (e.g., pull-up, seated row, hammer curl) one after the other, even with a rest period between each, will compromise the number of repetitions performed because the biceps brachii muscle (involved in all three exercises) will become less responsive due to fatigue. The same result would occur if several pushing exercises (e.g., incline bench press, shoulder press, triceps pushdown) were sequentially arranged (all three engage the triceps brachii)(83). There are also push–pull arrangements for the lower body—for example, leg press and back squat as "push" and stiff-leg deadlift and leg (knee) curl as "pull"—but the classification of some exercises as "push" or "pull" is not as clear (e.g., leg [knee] extension). The alternation of push and pull exercises is also used in circuit training programs and is an ideal arrangement for athletes beginning or returning to a resistance training program (3, 20).

Supersets and Compound Sets

Other methods of arranging exercises involve having athletes perform one set of a pair of exercises with little to no rest between them. Two common examples are supersets and compound sets. A **superset** involves two sequentially performed exercises that stress two opposing muscles or muscle areas (i.e., an agonist and its antagonist) (2). For example, an athlete performs 10 repetitions of the barbell biceps curl exercise, sets the bar down, then goes over to the triceps pushdown station and performs 10 repetitions. A **compound set** involves sequentially performing two different exercises for the same muscle group (2). For instance, an athlete completes a set of the barbell biceps curl exercise, then switches to dumbbells and immediately performs a set of the hammer curl exercise. In this case, the stress on the same muscle is compounded because both exercises recruit the same muscle area. Both methods of arranging and performing pairs of exercises are time efficient and purposely more demanding—and consequently may not be appropriate for unconditioned athletes. Note, however, that sometimes the meanings of *superset* and *compound set* are interchanged (20).

STEP 5: TRAINING LOAD AND REPETITIONS

Load most simply refers to the amount of weight assigned to an exercise set and is often characterized as the most critical aspect of a resistance training program (20, 63, 73, 86).

Terminology Used to Quantify and Qualify Mechanical Work

Mechanical work can be defined as the product of *force* and *displacement* (sometimes referred to as *distance*). An athlete can perform (external) mechanical work via demands made on the body to generate (internal) metabolic energy. Thus, it is important to quantify the amount of mechanical work or degree of metabolic demand in order to plan variation in the training program and to avoid the exhaustion phase of Selye's General Adaptation Syndrome associated with overtraining (8).

Application of the Exercise Order Guidelines
(Refer to the first scenario table in the chapter for a description of the scenario athletes.)

SCENARIO A Female Collegiate Basketball Player Preseason	SCENARIO B Male Professional American Football Lineman Off-Season	SCENARIO C Male High School Cross-Country Runner In-Season
Assigned exercise order strategies • Power, other core, then assistance exercises • "Push" and "pull" exercises (alternated)	**Assigned exercise order strategies** • Core and then assistance exercises • "Push" and "pull" exercises (alternated)	**Assigned exercise order strategies** • Core and then assistance exercises • Upper and lower body exercises (alternated), circuit training
Monday, Wednesday, and Friday Hang clean[a] Push jerk[b] Front squat[a] Incline bench press[b] Seated row Dumbbell alternating curl Triceps pushdown Abdominal crunch	**Lower Body (Monday and Thursday)** Deadlift[c] Back squat[c] Step-up[c] Leg (knee) curl Seated calf (heel) raise **Upper Body (Tuesday and Friday)** Bench press Bent-over row Shoulder press Barbell biceps curl[d] Shoulder shrug Lying triceps extension Abdominal crunch	**Wednesday and Saturday** Lunge Vertical chest press Leg (knee) curl One-arm dumbbell row Toe raise (dorsiflexion) Lateral shoulder raise Machine back extension[e] Abdominal crunch Complete one set of each exercise, then repeat.[f]
COMMENTS [a,b]These exercises are alternated to provide relative rest between their similar movement patterns while still following the "power, other core, then assistance" exercise order strategy.	**COMMENTS** [c]These exercises do not follow the "push" and "pull" (alternated) exercise arrangement and could be performed in a variety of sequences (e.g., back squat, deadlift, step-up). [d]Although the barbell biceps curl exercise is a "pulling" movement and occurs before another "pull" exercise (shoulder shrug), it does not affect the athlete's ability to perform the shoulder shrug exercise.	**COMMENTS** [e]Exercises that concentrically train the lower back muscles should be performed after exercises that require an erect torso or a neutral spine position (e.g., lunge and lateral shoulder raise). Fatigue of the lower back muscles can result in incorrect and potentially injurious exercise technique in structural or standing exercises. [f]The eight exercises are performed one set at a time, one immediately after the other (i.e., in a "circuit").

A quantity measure for resistance training "work" is needed. Traditionally, at least in the sport of Olympic weightlifting, this "work" is called the "load," and one can calculate it by multiplying each weight lifted by the number of times it is lifted and summing all such values over a training session.

However, **volume-load** (48, 77) may be a better term than just *load*. This quantity is highly related to mechanical work (59, 60, 62) and the associated metabolic energy demands and physiological stress, and also is distinguished from **repetition-volume** (rep-volume) (i.e., the total number of repetitions; see "Step 6: Volume" for more explanation).

To explain volume-load further, if a barbell that has 100 "weight units" is lifted 2 vertical "distance units" for 15 repetitions, the total concentric mechanical work is 3,000 "work units" (100 x 2 x 15). However, volume-load (1,500 units) does not include the distance value but is still directly related to the amount of mechanical work performed and the extent of the metabolic demand the athlete experiences to lift the weight for the required repetitions. Volume-load should be considered as *system mass volume-load* in the calculation of resistance training in which the athlete or a mass is moved (e.g., loaded jump squats) (10, 59, 61). For example, an 80 kg athlete with a 40 kg jump squat load for four sets of three is doing 120 kg x 12, or 1,440 kg. Volume-load approaches are also very useful in quantifying the nature of the total resistance training load, by separating the volume-load from core and assistance exercises or delineating between hypertropy, maximal strength, and power training. In this way, the strength and conditioning practitioner can plan or determine not just the total volume-load for the session, but also what stimulus is achieved primarily from the session.

Note that the volume-load is not affected by the rep and set scheme (i.e., 15 sets of 1 repetition, 5 sets of 3 repetitions, 3 sets of 5 repetitions, or 1 set of 15 repetitions). Various repetition and set schemes affect the true **intensity** value for resistance exercise and indicate the *quality* of work performed. Instead of using time to calculate mechanical or metabolic power or intensity, it is more practical to use a value that is proportional to time, namely, rep-volume. The more repetitions performed, the longer the training session (rest period lengths are an additional consideration and are not directly accounted for). Dividing volume-load by rep-volume results in the average weight lifted per repetition per workout session (86). This is a good approximation for mechanical and metabolic power output, which are true intensity or quality of work parameters.

Relationship Between Load and Repetitions

The number of times an exercise can be performed (**repetitions**) is inversely related to the load lifted; the heavier the load, the lower the number of repetitions that can be performed. Therefore, focusing on one training goal automatically implies the use of a certain load and repetition regimen (e.g., training for muscular strength involves lifting heavy loads for few repetitions).

Before assigning training loads, the strength and conditioning professional should understand this relationship between loads and repetitions. Load is commonly described as either a certain percentage of a **1-repetition maximum (1RM)**—the greatest amount of weight that can be lifted with proper technique for only one repetition—or the most weight lifted for a specified number of repetitions, a **repetition maximum (RM)** (19). For instance, if athletes can perform 10 repetitions with 60 kg in the back squat exercise, the 10RM is 60 kg. It is assumed that the athlete provided a *maximal effort;* if he or she had stopped at nine repetitions but could have performed one more, a 10RM would not have been achieved. Likewise, if he or she lifted 55 kg for 10 repetitions (but could have performed more), the true 10RM was not accurately assessed because the athlete possibly would have lifted 60 kg for 10 repetitions.

TABLE 6.7
Percent of the 1RM and Repetitions Allowed
(%1RM–Repetition Relationship)

%1RM	Number of Repetitions Allowed
100	1
95	2
93	3
90	4
87	5
85	6
83	7
80	8
77	9
75	10
70	11
67	12
65	15

Data from references 9, 49, 54, and 65.

Table 6.7 shows the relationship between a submaximal load—calculated as a percentage of the 1RM—and the number of repetitions that can be performed at that load. By definition, 100% of the 1RM allows the athlete to perform one repetition. As the percentage of the 1RM (i.e., the load lifted) decreases, the athlete will be able to successfully complete more repetitions. Other %1RM–repetition tables with slightly different %1RM values can be found in the literature (9, 49, 54, 65), but they vary by only about 0.5 to 2 percentage points from those provided in Table 6.7.

Although %1RM–repetition tables provide helpful guidelines for assigning an athlete's training loads, research to date does not support the widespread use of such tables for establishing training loads for every exercise assigned to athletes, for the following reasons:

▶ Table 6.7 assumes there is a linear association between the loads lifted and the repetitions performed; however, several studies have reported a curvilinear relationship (51, 54, 56).

▶ Resistance-trained athletes may be able to exceed the number of repetitions listed in the table at any given percentage of their 1RM, especially in lower body core exercises (35, 36).

▶ The number of repetitions that can be performed at a certain percent of the 1RM is based on a single set. When an athlete performs multiple sets, the loads may need to be reduced so that the desired number of repetitions can be completed in all of the sets (20.

▶ Despite the prevalence of 1RM research, athletes may not always perform the predicted number of repetitions at a specified percentage of a 1RM (20, 90). For instance, studies conducted by Hoeger and colleagues (35, 36) showed that subjects were able to perform two or three *times* more repetitions than are listed in Table 6.7.

▶ A certain percentage of the 1RM assigned to a machine exercise can result in more repetitions at the same percentage of the 1RM than with a similar free weight exercise (35, 36).

▶ Exercises involving smaller muscle areas may not produce as many repetitions as seen in Table 6.7, and exercises recruiting large muscle areas are likely to result in more repetitions performed (90).

▶ The most accurate relationship between percentages of the 1RM and the maximum repetitions possible is for loads greater than 75% of the 1RM and fewer than 10 repetitions (9, 84, 94). Empirical evidence further suggests that as the percentage of the 1RM decreases, the variability in the number of repetitions that can be completed increases.

Therefore, loads calculated from the %1RM in Table 6.7 should be used only as a guideline for estimating a particular RM load for a resistance training exercise. Even with the inherent weaknesses just explained, it appears that it is still more accurate to assign loads based on a percentage of a test-established 1RM than it is to estimate a 1RM from a submaximal load (34, 35).

1RM and Multiple-RM Testing Options

To gather information needed to assign a training load, the strength and conditioning professional has the option of determining the athlete's

▶ actual 1RM (directly tested),

▶ estimated 1RM from a multiple-RM test (e.g., a 10RM), or

▶ multiple RM based on the number of repetitions planned for that exercise (the "goal" repetitions; e.g., five repetitions per set).

Once the actual 1RM is measured or estimated, the athlete's training load is calculated as a percentage of the 1RM. Alternatively, a multiple-RM test may be performed based on goal repetitions, thereby eliminating computations or estimations. In many cases, the strength and conditioning professional will use a variety of testing options depending on the exercises selected and the athlete's training background. A common strategy for testing sufficiently conditioned athletes is to conduct a 1RM test in several core exercises and use multiple-RM testing for assistance exercises.

Testing the 1RM

To assign training loads based on a percentage of the 1RM, the strength and conditioning professional must first determine the athlete's 1RM. This method of assessment is typically reserved for resistance-trained athletes who are classified as intermediate or advanced and have exercise technique experience in the exercises being tested. Individuals who are untrained, inexperienced, injured, or medically supervised may not be appropriate participants for 1RM testing. One-repetition maximum testing requires an adequate training status and lifting experience, as the assessment of maximal strength places significant stress on the involved muscles, connective tissues, and joints. Thus, it has been suggested that a 3RM test could be used instead of a maximal 1RM test (90). Ignoring an athlete's training status and exercise technique experience diminishes the safety and accuracy of 1RM test results.

When selecting exercises for 1RM testing, the strength and conditioning professional should choose core exercises, because the large muscle groups and multiple joints are better able to handle the heavy loads. Despite this guideline, an exercise should not be selected for 1RM testing if it cannot provide valid and reliable data (i.e., does not accurately and consistently assess maximal muscular strength). For instance, the large upper back musculature and multiple joints involved in the bent-over row exercise can probably tolerate the loads from a 1RM test, but maintaining a correct body position throughout testing would be extremely difficult. The weaker stabilizing muscles of the lower back might become very fatigued after several testing sets, resulting in a loss of proper exercise technique and invalid and potentially unreliable test data.

A variety of procedures can be used to accurately determine a 1–RM; one method is described in Figure 6.1. Despite an orderly testing sequence, variations in training status and exercise type will affect the absolute load increases in sequential testing sets. For example, the gradual load increase for 1RM attempts for an athlete who can back squat 495 pounds (225 kg) may be 20 to 30 pounds (9–14 kg) per testing set. For a weaker athlete with a back squat 1RM of 100 pounds (45 kg), a 20- or 30-pound testing load increment is too aggressive and is not precise enough to yield an accurate 1RM value. To improve the appropriateness and accuracy of the sequential testing sets, Figure 6.1 also includes relative percentages that can be used instead of the absolute load adjustments.

FIGURE 6.1
A 1RM Testing Protocol

---

1. Instruct the athlete to warm up with a light resistance that easily allows 5 to 10 repetitions.

2. Provide a 1-minute rest period.

3. Estimate a warm-up load that will allow the athlete to complete three to five repetitions by adding
   - 10 to 20 pounds (4–9 kg) or 5% to 10% for upper body exercise or
   - 30 to 40 pounds (14–18 kg) or 10% to 20% for lower body exercise.

4. Provide a 2-minute rest period.

5. Estimate a conservative, near-maximal load that will allow the athlete to complete two or three repetitions by adding
   - 10 to 20 pounds (4–9 kg) or 5% to 10% for upper body exercise or
   - 30 to 40 pounds (14–18 kg) or 10% to 20% for lower body exercise.

6. Provide a 2- to 4-minute rest period.

7. Make a load increase:
   - 10 to 20 pounds (4–9 kg) or 5% to 10% for upper body exercise or
   - 30 to 40 pounds (14–18 kg) or 10% to 20% for lower body exercise.

8. Instruct the athlete to attempt a 1RM.

9. If the athlete was successful, provide a 2- to 4-minute rest period and go back to step 7. If the athlete failed, provide a 2- to 4-minute rest period then decrease the load by subtracting
   - 5 to 10 pounds (2–4 kg) or 2.5% to 5% for upper body exercise or
   - 15 to 20 pounds (7–9 kg) or 5% to 10% for lower body exercise.

   AND then go back to step 8.

Continue increasing or decreasing the load until the athlete can complete one repetition with proper exercise technique. Ideally, the athlete's 1RM will be measured within three to five testing sets.

Reprinted, by permission, from Earle, 2006 (18).

Estimating a 1RM

When maximal strength testing is not warranted, testing with a 10RM load (and then estimating or predicting the 1RM) can be a suitable secondary option. This approach is appropriate for nearly all athletes, provided they can demonstrate the proper technique in the exercise tested. Core and assistance exercises can be selected for 10RM testing, but excessive warm-up and testing sets may fatigue the athlete and compromise the accuracy of the test. Additionally, power exercises do not lend themselves well to multiple-RM testing above five repetitions for repeated testing sets because technique can deteriorate rapidly (8, 86). Lower (and more accurate) multiple-RM determinations using heavier loads can be made once the athlete has sufficient training and technique experience.

The protocol for 10RM testing is similar to that for 1RM testing, but each set requires 10 repetitions, not one. After the completion of warm-up sets, the athlete's sequential load changes for the 10RM test are smaller than those listed in Figure 6.1 (approximately one-half). Continue the process of testing until a load allowing only 10 repetitions is determined. An experienced strength and conditioning professional will be able to adjust the loads so that the 10RM can be measured within three to five testing sets.

Using a 1RM Table To estimate the athlete's 1RM, consult Table 6.8. In the "Max reps (RM)" = 10(%1RM = 75) column, first find the tested 10RM load; then read across the row to the "Max reps (RM)" = 1 (%1RM = 100) column to discover the athlete's projected 1RM. For example, if an athlete's 10RM is 300 pounds, the estimated 1RM is 400 pounds. As noted in connection with Table 6.7, the %1RM–repetition associations vary in the literature. This table is intended for use as a guide until the athlete has developed the neuromuscular attributes that will make testing with heavier loads (e.g., 1RM-5RM) safe and effective (20, 86).

TABLE 6.8												
Estimating 1RM and Training Loads												
Max reps (RM)	**1**	**2**	**3**	**4**	**5**	**6**	**7**	**8**	**9**	**10**	**12**	**15**
%1RM	**100**	**95**	**93**	**90**	**87**	**85**	**83**	**80**	**77**	**75**	**67**	**65**
Load (pounds or kg)	10	10	9	9	9	9	8	8	8	8	7	7
	20	19	19	18	17	17	17	16	15	15	13	13
	30	29	28	27	26	26	25	24	23	23	20	20
	40	38	37	36	35	34	33	32	31	30	27	26
	50	48	47	45	44	43	42	40	39	38	34	33
	60	57	56	54	52	51	50	48	48	45	40	39
	70	67	65	63	61	60	58	56	54	53	47	46
	80	76	74	72	70	68	66	64	62	60	54	52
	90	86	84	81	78	77	75	72	69	68	60	59
	100	95	93	90	87	85	83	80	77	75	67	65
	110	105	102	99	96	94	91	88	85	83	74	72
	120	114	112	108	104	102	100	96	92	90	80	78
	130	124	121	117	113	111	108	104	100	98	87	85
	140	133	130	126	122	119	116	112	108	105	94	91
	150	143	140	135	131	128	125	120	116	113	101	98
	160	152	149	144	139	136	133	128	123	120	107	104
	170	162	158	153	148	145	141	136	131	128	114	111

Max reps (RM)	1	2	3	4	5	6	7	8	9	10	12	15
%1RM	100	95	93	90	87	85	83	80	77	75	67	65
	180	171	167	162	157	153	149	144	139	135	121	117
	190	181	177	171	165	162	158	152	146	143	127	124
	200	190	186	180	174	170	166	160	154	150	134	130
	210	200	195	189	183	179	174	168	162	158	141	137
	220	209	205	198	191	187	183	176	169	165	147	143
	230	219	214	207	200	196	191	184	177	173	154	150
	240	228	223	216	209	204	199	192	185	180	161	156
	250	238	233	225	218	213	208	200	193	188	168	163
	260	247	242	234	226	221	206	208	200	195	174	169
	270	257	251	243	235	230	224	216	208	203	181	176
	280	266	260	252	244	238	232	224	216	210	188	182
	290	276	270	261	252	247	241	232	223	218	194	189
	300	285	279	270	261	255	249	240	231	225	201	195
	310	295	288	279	270	264	257	248	239	233	208	202
	320	304	298	288	278	272	266	256	246	240	214	208
	330	314	307	297	287	281	274	264	254	248	221	215
	340	323	316	306	296	289	282	272	262	255	228	221
	350	333	326	315	305	298	291	280	270	263	235	228
	360	342	335	324	313	306	299	288	277	270	241	234
	370	352	344	333	322	315	307	296	285	278	248	241
	380	361	353	342	331	323	315	304	293	285	255	247
	390	371	363	351	339	332	324	312	300	293	261	254
	400	380	372	360	348	340	332	320	308	300	268	260
	410	390	381	369	357	349	340	328	316	308	274	267
	420	399	391	378	365	357	349	336	323	315	281	273
	430	409	400	387	374	366	357	344	331	323	288	280
	440	418	409	396	383	374	365	352	339	330	295	286
	450	428	419	405	392	383	374	360	347	338	302	293
	460	437	428	414	400	391	382	368	354	345	308	299
	470	447	437	423	409	400	390	376	362	353	315	306
	480	456	446	432	418	408	398	384	370	360	322	312
	490	466	456	441	426	417	407	392	377	368	328	319
	500	475	465	450	435	425	415	400	385	375	335	325
	510	485	474	459	444	434	423	408	393	383	342	332
	520	494	484	468	452	442	432	416	400	390	348	338
	530	504	493	477	461	451	440	424	408	398	355	345
	540	513	502	486	470	459	448	432	416	405	362	351
	550	523	512	495	479	468	457	440	424	413	369	358
	560	532	521	504	487	476	465	448	431	420	375	364
	570	542	530	513	496	485	473	456	439	428	382	371
	580	551	539	522	505	493	481	464	447	435	389	377
	590	561	549	531	513	502	490	472	454	443	395	384
	600	570	558	540	522	510	498	480	462	450	402	390

Using Prediction Equations Equations are also available to predict the 1RM from multiple-RM loads (9, 54). Researchers who have reviewed such equations report that as the loads used in multiple-RM testing become heavier (i.e., bringing the loads closer to the actual 1RM), the accuracy of the 1RM estimation increases. Likewise, predictions are more accurate when the equations are based on loads equal to or less than a 10RM (9, 55, 84, 86, 94). Furthermore, the results obtained from lower multiple-RM testing (and subsequent predictions of the 1RM) are generally more accurate when an athlete has been consistently training with low multiple-RM resistances (i.e., heavy loads) for a few months before testing (8).

Multiple-RM Testing Based on Goal Repetitions

A third option for determining training loads requires the strength and conditioning professional to first decide on the number of repetitions (i.e., the **goal repetitions**) the athlete will perform in the actual program for the exercise being tested. For example, if the strength and conditioning professional decides that the athlete should perform six repetitions for the bench press exercise in the training program, the multiple-RM testing protocol should have the athlete perform the exercise with a load that will result in six repetitions (6RM). Core and assistance exercises can be selected for multiple-RM testing, but, as previously mentioned, high-repetition testing sets can create significant fatigue and may compromise the accuracy of the tested multiple RM. This effect seems to be more problematic for exercises that involve multiple joints and large muscle areas due to their high metabolic demand (86). Further, multiple-RM testing (and subsequent load assignments) for assistance exercises should be at or above an 8RM to minimize the isolative stress on the involved joint and connective tissue (2, 18). In other words, even if an athlete is following a muscular strength training program that involves 2RM loads for the core exercises, the heaviest load the assistance exercises should be assigned is an 8RM.

Assigning Load and Repetitions Based on the Training Goal

During the needs analysis, the strength and conditioning professional is challenged to choose the primary goal of the resistance training program based on the athlete's testing results, the movement and physiological analysis of the sport, and the priorities of the athlete's sport season. Once decided on, the training goal can be applied to determine specific load and repetition assignments via the RM continuum, a percentage of the 1RM (either directly tested or estimated), or the results of multiple-RM testing. As explained previously, the testing methods determine how the loads and repetitions are assigned for each exercise (i.e., loads are calculated as a percentage of a tested or estimated 1RM, or training loads are specifically determined from multiple-RM testing). The options for testing and assigning training loads and repetitions are summarized in Figure 6.2.

Repetition Maximum Continuum

Figure 6.3 shows how RM ranges are associated with training goals; relatively heavy loads should be used if the goal is strength or power, moderate loads for hypertrophy, and light loads for muscular endurance (as indicated by the larger font sizes). To state this another way, low-multiple RMs appear to have the greatest effect on strength and maximum power training, and high-multiple RMs seem to result in better muscular endurance improvements (1, 20, 63, 90). The continuum concept effectively illustrates that a certain RM *emphasizes* a specific outcome, but the training benefits are blended at any given RM.

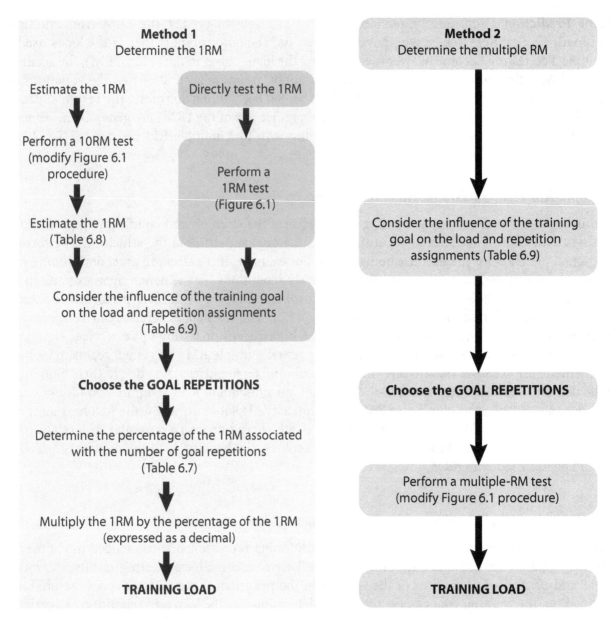

FIGURE 6.2 Summary of Testing and Assigning Training Loads and Repetitions
Reprinted, by permission, from Earle, 2006 (18).

Percentage of the 1RM

Despite the physiological blend of training effects, the specificity principle still dictates the dominant outcome that is attained and enhanced with a particular training load. The relationship between the percentage of the 1RM and the estimated number of repetitions that can be performed at that load (Table 6.7) allows the strength and conditioning professional to assign a specific resistance to be used for an exercise in a training session. In other words, the training goal is attained when the athlete lifts a load of a certain percentage of the 1RM for a specific number of repetitions (Table 6.9).

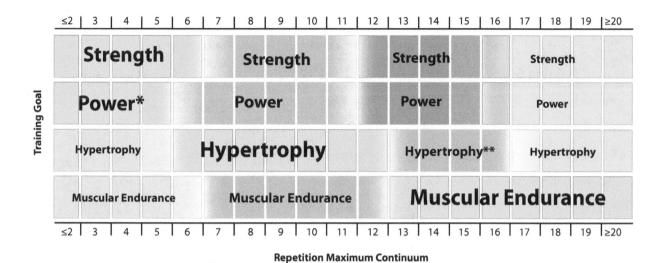

FIGURE 6.3 This continuum shows how RM ranges are associated with various training goals.
*The repetition ranges shown for power in this figure are not consistent with the %1RM-repetition rela-
tionship. Refer to the discussion of assigning percentages for power training for further explanation.
**While the existing repetition range for hypertrophy appears most efficacious, there is emerging
evidence that some fiber types, depending on training status, may experience significant hypertrophy
outside this range. It is too early to tell if these results would be experienced by the larger population.
Adapted from references 20 and 87.

How to Calculate a Training Load   For example, suppose an athlete's training goal is muscular
strength and the tested 1RM in the bench press exercise is 220 pounds (100 kg). To increase strength,
the athlete needs to handle loads of at least 85% of the 1RM (after warm-up) that typically allow
performance of up to six repetitions per set (Table 6.9). More specifically, if the strength and conditioning professional assigns four repetitions per set for this exercise, the corresponding load will
be approximately 90% of the 1RM (Table 6.7), or approximately 200 pounds (90 kg). Note that the
strength and conditioning professional should make adjustments to assigned loads based on observation of the ease or difficulty an athlete experiences in lifting the load for the required repetitions.

Assigning Percentages for Power Training   The force–velocity curve illustrates that the greater the
amount of concentric muscular force generated, the slower the muscle shortening and corresponding movement velocity (and vice versa). Maximal power, in contrast, is produced at intermediate
velocities with the lifting of light to moderate, not maximal, loads (11, 12, 57, 61, 67, 68). Performing
a 1RM involves slower movement velocities; maximum force is generated, but with reduced power
output (20, 21, 100). Seldom is an athlete required to demonstrate a singular, maximal, slow-speed
muscular strength effort in a sport (except in powerlifting, for example). Most sport movements are
faster (66) and involve higher power outputs (41) than those produced during a 1RM test. This does
not mean that an athlete's power capabilities are unaffected by maximal muscular strength training,
however. Because speed- or power-related sport movements often begin from zero or near-zero
velocities, slow-velocity strength gains have direct application to power production (20). For these
reasons, the load and repetition assignments for power training overlap the guidelines for strength
training (Table 6.9).

<table>
<tr><td colspan="3" align="center">**TABLE 6.9**
Load and Repetition Assignments Based on the Training Goal</td></tr>
<tr><td>**Training Goal**</td><td align="center">**Load (%1RM)**</td><td align="center">**Goal Repetitions**</td></tr>
<tr><td>Strength*</td><td align="center">≥85</td><td align="center">≤6</td></tr>
<tr><td>Power**:</td><td></td><td></td></tr>
<tr><td>   Single-effort event</td><td align="center">80–90</td><td align="center">1–2</td></tr>
<tr><td>   Multiple-effort event</td><td align="center">75–85</td><td align="center">3–5</td></tr>
<tr><td>Hypertrophy</td><td align="center">67–85</td><td align="center">6–12</td></tr>
<tr><td>Muscular endurance</td><td align="center">≤67</td><td align="center">≥12</td></tr>
</table>

*These RM loading assignments for muscular strength training apply only to core exercises; assistance exercises should be limited to loads not heavier than an 8RM (2).

**Based on weightlifting-derived movements (clean, snatch, and so on). The load and repetition assignments shown for power in the table are *not consistent* with the %1RM-repetition relationship. In nonexplosive movements, loads equaling about 80% of the 1RM apply to the two- to five-repetition range. Refer to the discussion of assigning percentages of the 1RM for power training for further explanation.

Data from references 7, 20, 32, 33, 45, 86, 91, and 92.

Non-weightlifting multijoint power exercise (jump squat, bench press throw, overhead press throw) and single-joint muscle action data reveal that peak power is generally reached with the lifting of very light loads—from body weight (0%) to 30% of the 1RM (11, 12, 21, 57, 61, 68). With such a light weight, however, these exercises are difficult to execute properly with typical resistance training equipment because the athlete cannot sufficiently overload the muscles without needing to decelerate at the end of the exercise range of motion. Performing some of these exercises (bench press throw, overhead press throw) in a Smith machine, for example, can help to address the safety issues. The jump squat is one exception and is best performed in a power rack (11, 12, 57, 59, 61, 68). On the other end of the load continuum, data from multiple national- and world-level weightlifting and powerlifting championships clearly indicate that power output increases as the weight lifted decreases from 100% of the 1RM (i.e., the 1RM) to 90% of the 1RM (21, 22, 81). In fact, for the back squat and deadlift exercises, power output for a load at 90% of the 1RM may be *twice* as high as with the 1RM load due to a large decrease in the time required to complete the exercise with the lighter load (22). Even for the already "fast" power exercises (weightlifting-based movements), there is still a 5% to 10% increase in power output as the load decreases from the 1RM to 90% of the 1RM (22). Considering these issues, the most effective and practical application is to assign loads that are about 75% to 90% of the 1RM for resistance training exercises that can be heavily loaded such as the snatch and clean and other weightlifting-derived movements (11, 21, 45, 57, 61).

To promote program specificity, particular load and repetition assignments are indicated for athletes training for *single-effort power events* (e.g., shot put, high jump, weightlifting) and for *multiple-effort power events* (e.g., basketball, volleyball). For example, single-effort event athletes may be assigned sets of one or two repetitions using loads that equal 80% to 90% of the 1RM, especially on heavy training days. For sports with multiple maximum-power efforts (e.g., the frequent maximum vertical jumping motions of a volleyball blocker), three to five repetitions per set with loads at 75% to 85% of the 1RM may be most appropriate (8, 11).

On the basis of the %1RM-repetition relationships shown in Table 6.7, the strength and conditioning professional may question the load assignments for power training in Table 6.9. The %1RM loads may appear to be too low compared to the goal number of repetitions. For example, according to Table 6.7, three to five repetitions are typically associated with loads 93% to 87% of the 1RM, not 75% to 85% of the 1RM or less as Table 6.9 indicates. Power exercises cannot be maximally loaded at any repetition scheme, because the quality of the movement technique will decline before momentary muscle fatigue defines a true multiple-RM set (20). Therefore, lighter loads allow the athlete to complete repetitions with maximum speed to promote maximum power development. For example, power exercises are usually limited to five repetitions per set, but with loads up to and equal to a 10RM (i.e., approximately 75% of the 1RM) (45). This load adjustment to promote peak power output also applies to the RM continuum (Figure 6.3). Power training can be emphasized across the range of five repetitions or fewer, but the strength and conditioning professional should realize that these loads are not true repetition *maximums*.

Variation of the Training Load

Training for muscular strength and power places a high physiological stress on an athlete's body. Intermediate and advanced resistance-trained athletes are accustomed to lifting heavy loads and possess the experience and motivation to exert to near failure on every set, but this should not always be the goal. Despite the high training status, this degree of training demand typically cannot be tolerated very long without contributing to an over-trained state. For example, an athlete may resistance train three days a week with muscular strength as the goal (e.g., Mondays, Wednesdays, and Fridays). It would be difficult for the athlete to perform the same high-load, low-volume regimen—especially in the power and other core exercises—with only one or two days of rest between sessions.

One strategy to counterbalance the overtraining associated with the heavy loads is to alter the loads (%1RMs) for the power and other core exercises to that only one training day each week (e.g., Monday) is a heavy day. These "heavy day" loads are designed so be full repetition maximums, the greatest resistance that can be successfully lifted for the goal number of repetitions. The loads for the other training days are reduced (intentionally) to provide recovery after the heavy day while still maintaining sufficient training frequency and volume. In the example of the three-days-a-week program, Wednesdays and Fridays are "light" and "medium" training days (respectively). For the light day, calculate 80% of the loads lifted in the power and other core exercises on the heavy day (Monday) and instruct the athlete to complete the same number of goal repetitions. Even if the athlete is able to perform more repetitions than the designated goal number, he or she should not do so. Similarly, calculate 90% of the loads lifted in the power and other core exercises from Monday's training session for the "medium" day, and instruct the athlete to perform only the assigned number of goal repetitions (2, 8, 86). This approach can be used for any training frequency. For instance, a two-days-a-week program could have a heavy day and a light day, or an upper body–lower body split routine could consist of two heavy days (one upper body day and one lower body day) followed by two light days. Varying the training loads also works well with an athlete's other training, in that heavy lifting days can fall on light sport conditioning days, and light lifting days on heavy sport conditioning days (8). The strength and conditioning professional needs to monitor this schedule so that it does not lead to heavy training *every* day (86).

Progression of the Training Load

As the athlete adapts to the training stimulus, the strength and conditioning professional needs to have a strategy for advancing exercise loads so that improvements will continue over time (progression). Monitoring each athlete's training and charting his or her response to the prescribed workouts enable the strength and conditioning professional to know when and to what extent the loads should be increased.

Application of the Training Load and Repetition Guidelines
(Refer to the first scenario table in the chapter for a description of the scenario athletes.)

SCENARIO A Female Collegiate Basketball Player Preseason	SCENARIO B Male Professional American Football Lineman Off-Season	SCENARIO C Male High School Cross-Country Runner In-Season
Primary preseason resistance training goal Strength/power	*Primary off-season resistance training goal* Hypertrophy	*Primary in-season resistance training goal* Muscular endurance
Testing and assigning loads and repetitions **Influence of the training goals** *Power exercises:* 75–85% of the 1RM: 3–5 repetitions[a] *Other core exercises:* > 85% of the 1RM; <6 repetitions *Assistance exercises:* limited to loads not heavier than an 8RM	*Testing and assigning loads and repetitions* **Influence of the training goals** 67–85% of the 1RM; 6–12 repetitions	*Testing and assigning loads and repetitions* **Influence of the training goals** <67% of the 1RM; <12 repetitions
Number of goal repetitions *Power exercises:* 5 *Core exercises:* 6 *Assistance exercises:* 10	**Number of goal repetitions** *Core exercises:* 10 *Assistance exercises:* 10	**Number of goal repetitions** *Core exercises:* 12 *Assistance exercises:* 15
Testing methods *3RM testing for power exercises*[b] • Hang clean • Push jerk *1RM testing for other core exercises*[c] • Front squat • Incline bench press *10RM testing for assistance exercises*[d] • Seated row • Dumbbell alternating curl • Triceps pushdown	**Testing methods** *1RM testing for core exercises* • Deadlift • Back squat[i] • Bench press[i] • Shoulder press[i] *10RM testing for new assistance exercises*[j] • Step-up • Seated calf (heel) raise • Bent-over row • Shoulder shrug	**Testing methods** *12RM testing for core exercises*[k] • Lunge • Vertical chest press *15RM testing for new assistance exercises*[k] • One-arm dumbbell row • Lateral shoulder raise

Testing results
3RM hang clean   115 lb (53 kg)
  Estimated 1RM[a]   *124 lb (58 kg)*
3RM push jerk   110 lb (50 kg)
  Estimated 1RM[a]   *118 lb (54 kg)*
1RM front squat   185 lb (84 kg)
1RM incline bench press 100 lb (45 kg)
10RM seated row   90 lb (41 kg)
10RM dumbbell
  alternating curl   20 lb (9 kg)
10RM triceps pushdown 40 lb (18 kg)
	Testing results
	1RM deadlift 650 lb (295 kg)
	1RM back squat 675 lb (307 kg)
	1 RM bench press 425 lb (193 kg)
	1 RM shoulder press 255 lb (116 kg)
	10RM step-up 205 lb (93 kg)
	10RM seated calf
	  (heel) raise 155 lb (70 kg)
	10RM bent-over row 215 lb (98 kg)
	10RM shoulder shrug 405 lb (184 kg)
		Testing results
		12RM lunge 45 lb (20 kg)
		12RM vertical chest press 70 lb (32 kg)
		15RM one-arm dumbbell
		  row 25 lb (11 kg)
		15RM lateral shoulder
		  raise 10 lb (5 kg)

Training loads
For power exercises:
• Assign 75% of the estimated 1RM
  Hang clean   95 lb (43 kg)
  Push jerk   90 lb (41 kg)
(All loads are rounded off to the nearest 5 lb.)
	Training loads
	For core exercises:
	• Assign 75% of the tested 1RM
	  Deadlift 490 lb (223 kg)
	  Back squat 505 lb (230 kg)
	  Bench press 320 lb (145 kg)
	  Shoulder press 190 lb (86 kg)
	(All loads are rounded off to the nearest 5 lb.)
		Training loads
		For all exercises:
		• Equal to the loads from 12RM (or 15RM) testing or
		• Equal to the loads used in the preseason
		Leg (knee) curl 65 lb (30 kg)
		Toe raise (dorsiflexion) 20 lb (9 kg)
		Machine back extension 50 lb (23 kg)

(Continued)

Training loads (continued) *For other core exercises:* • Assign 85% of the tested 1RM Front squat 155 lb (70 kg) Incline bench press 85 lb (39 kg) (All loads are rounded off to the nearest 5 lb.) *For assistance exercises:* • Assign loads equal to the loads from 10RM testing	**Training loads (continued)** *For assistance exercises:* • Assign loads equal to the loads from the 10RM testing or • Equal to the loads used in the postseason Leg (knee) curl 190 lb (86 kg) Barbell biceps curl 115 lb (52 kg) Lying triceps extension 125 lb (57 kg)	
Weekly loading regime (power/core exercises)[f] *Mondays ("heavy" day)* • Assign the full load assignments (calculated under "Training loads") *Wednesdays ("light" day)* • Assign only 80% of Mondays' "heavy day" loads[g] *Fridays ("medium" day)* • Assign only 90% of Monday's "heavy day" loads[h]		

COMMENTS

[a]The load and repetition assignments shown for power exercises are based on basketball, a multiple-effort event, and are not consistent with the %1RM repetition relationship.

[b]To test for power, a multiple-RM (3RM) protocol is used. From the result, the 1RM is estimated and load assignments are made by calculating a percent of the estimated 1RM.

[c]The athlete did perform these exercises in the off-season, but to raise the accuracy of the load assignments for the preseason, the athlete will be tested to determine the current 1RM.

[d]Even though some of these exercises were part of the off-season program, they all require multiple-RM testing because the preseason goal repetitions for these exercises is 10, rather than 12 from the previous season.

[e]Estimate the 1RM using Table 6.8, pages 134–135.

[f]The loads for the assistance exercises remain constant throughout the week; only the loads for the power and other core exercises change.

[g]Calculate 80% of the loads lifted in Monday's training session and perform the same number of goal repetitions. Even if the athlete is able to, do not allow more repetitions than the designated goal number (power, 5; other core, 6).

[h]Calculate 90% of the loads lifted in Monday's training session and perform the same number of goal repetitions. Even if the athlete is able to, do not allow more repetitions than the designated goal number (power, 5; other core, 6).

COMMENTS

[i]The athlete did not perform these exercises in the postseason, but to raise the accuracy of the load assignments for the off-season, the athlete will be tested to determine the current 1RM.

[j]The exercises shown here were selected as new exercises for the off-season program and therefore require 10RM testing. The other assistance exercises were carried over from the postseason and do not require testing because the load and repetition assignments will be identical.

COMMENTS

[k]The exercises shown here were selected as new exercises for the in-season program and therefore require 12RM or 15RM testing. The other assistance exercises were carried over from the preseason and do not require testing because the load and repetition assignments will be identical.

Timing Load Increases

A conservative method that can be used to increase an athlete's training loads is called the **2-for-2 rule** (2). If the athlete can perform two or more repetitions over his or her assigned repetition goal for a given exercise in the last set in two consecutive workouts, weight should be added to that exercise for the next training session. For example, a strength and conditioning professional assigns three sets of 10 repetitions in the bench press exercise, and the athlete performs all 10 repetitions in all sets. After several workout sessions (the specific number depends on many factors), the athlete is able to complete 12 repetitions in the third (last) set for two consecutive workouts. In the following training session, the load for that exercise should be increased.

Quantity of Load Increases

The decision as to the size of the load increase can be difficult to make, but Table 6.10 provides general recommendations based on the athlete's condition (stronger or weaker) and body area (upper or lower body). Despite these guidelines, the significant variation in training status, volume-loads, and exercises (type and muscular involvement) greatly influences the appropriate load increases. To contend with this variability, relative load increases of 2.5% to 10% can be used instead of the absolute values shown in Table 6.10.

STEP 6: VOLUME

Volume relates to the total amount of weight lifted in a training session (20, 58, 69), and a **set** is a group of repetitions sequentially performed before the athlete stops to rest (20). Repetition-volume is the total number of repetitions performed during a workout session (4, 20,75, 86), and volume-load is the total number of sets multiplied by the number of repetitions per set, then multiplied by the weight lifted per repetition. For example, the volume-load for two sets of 10 repetitions with 50 pounds (23 kg) would be expressed as $2 \times 10 \times 50$ pounds or 1,000 pounds (454 kg). (If different sets are performed with different amounts of weight, the volumes per set are calculated and then added to obtain the total training session volume.)

TABLE 6.10 Examples of Load Increases		
Description of the Athlete*	**Body Area Exercise**	**Estimated Load Increase****
Smaller, weaker, less trained	Upper body	2.5–5 pounds (1–2 kg)
	Lower body	5–10 pounds (2–4 kg)
Larger, stronger, more trained	Upper body	5–10+ pounds (2–4+ kg)
	Lower body	10–15+ pounds (4–7+ kg)

*The strength and conditioning professional will need to determine which of these two subjective categories applies to a specific athlete.

**These load increases are appropriate for training programs using approximately three sets of 5 to 10 repetitions. Note that the goal repetitions per set remain constant as the loads are increased.

In the example just given (a volume-load of 1,000 pounds), multiplying each repetition by the additional factor of vertical displacement of the weight during that repetition would yield the concentric work performed. The displacement factor is fairly constant for a given athlete, so it is not used, but the resulting volume-load is still directly proportional to concentric work. As previously stated, volume-load divided by repetition-volume results in the average weight lifted per repetition, which is related to intensity or the quality of work. In running exercise, the common (rep) volume measure is distance. If an intensity value is known or measured (such as running pace, which relates to percent VO_2max), then total metabolic energy cost (which is proportional to mechanical work done) can be calculated. This value is comparable to volume-load in resistance exercise. The same concepts are applicable to the number of foot or hand contacts (volume) in plyometric exercise, the number of strokes (volume) in swimming or rowing, or the number of throws or jumps (volume) for various sport activities.

Multiple Versus Single Sets

Some have advocated that one set of 8 to 12 repetitions (after warm-up) performed to volitional muscular failure is sufficient to maximize gains in muscular strength and hypertrophy. Additionally, others have reported increases in maximum strength after the performance of only one set per exercise per session (24, 52, 53).

Single-set training may be appropriate for untrained individuals (20) or during the first several months of training (24), but many studies indicate that higher volumes are necessary to promote further gains in strength, especially for intermediate and advanced resistance-trained athletes (44, 64, 89, 99). Further, the musculoskeletal system will eventually adapt to the stimulus of one set to failure and require the added stimulus of multiple sets for continued strength gains (20). Moreover, performing three sets of 10 repetitions *without going to failure* enhances strength better than one set to failure in 8 to 12 repetitions (46, 48), although the higher training volume with use of three sets is a contributing factor (4, 20, 86). Therefore, an athlete who performs multiple sets from the initiation of his or her resistance training program will increase muscular strength faster than with single-set training (48, 63). The strength and conditioning professional cannot expect, however, that an athlete will be able to successfully complete multiple sets with full RM loads at fixed repetition schemes for every exercise in each training session. Fatigue will affect the number of repetitions that can be performed in later sets.

Training Status

The training status of athletes affects the volume they will be able to safely tolerate. It is appropriate for an athlete to perform only one or two sets as a beginner and to add sets as he or she becomes better trained. As the athlete adapts to a consistent and well-designed program, more sets can gradually be added to match the guidelines associated with the given training goal.

Primary Resistance Training Goal

Training volume is directly based on the athlete's resistance training goal. Table 6.11 provides a summary of the guidelines for the number of repetitions and sets commonly associated with strength, power, hypertrophy, and muscular endurance training programs.

TABLE 6.11
Volume Assignments Based on the Training Goal

Training Goal	Goal Repetitions	Sets*
Strength	<6	2–6
**Power:		
Single-effort event	1–2	3–5
Multiple-effort event	3–5	3–5
Hypertrophy	6–12	3–6
Muscular endurance	≥12	2–3

*These assignments do not include warm-up sets and typically apply to core exercises only (2, 45).

**Based on weightlifting-derived movements (clean, snatch, and so on). The load and repetition assignments shown for power in this table are *not consistent* with the %1RM–repetition relationship. In nonexplosive movements, loads equaling about 80% of the 1RM apply to the two- to five-repetition range. Refer to the discussion of assigning percentages of the 1RM for power training for further explanation.
Data from references 20, 32, 86, 91, and 92.

Strength and Power

In classic research, DeLorme (14) and DeLorme and Watkins (15) recommended sets of 10 repetitions as ideal to increase muscular strength, although the regimen was originally developed for injury rehabilitation. Later, Berger (6, 7) determined that three sets of six repetitions created maximal strength gains, at least in the bench press and back squat exercises. Although Berger's work seemed to be conclusive, his subsequent research (5) showed no significant difference among six sets of a 2RM load, three sets of a 6RM load, and three sets of a 10RM load, despite the differences in volume. Since then, many other studies have also been unable to support an exact set and repetition scheme to promote maximal increases in strength (17, 24, 25, 70, 80, 85). An important qualifier regarding these inconclusive reports is that most involved relatively untrained subjects, thus implying that nearly *any* type of program will cause improvements in strength for these individuals.

When training an athlete for strength, assigning volume begins with an examination of the optimal number of repetitions for maximal strength gains. As discussed earlier (and shown in Figure 6.3 and Table 6.9), this appears to be sets of six or fewer repetitions (at the corresponding RM load) for core exercises (20, 32, 33, 45, 86, 87, 91, 92). Comprehensive reviews of the literature by Fleck and Kraemer (20) and Tan (90) conclude that a range of two to five sets or three to six sets (respectively) promotes the greatest increases in strength. Specific set guidelines based on exercise type suggest that only one to three sets may be appropriate or necessary for assistance exercises (2, 45).

Volume assignments for power training are typically lower than those for strength training in order to maximize the quality of exercise. This reduction in volume results from fewer goal repetitions and lighter loads (Figure 6.3 and Table 6.9) rather than the recommended number of sets (11, 12, 45, 57, 61, 68). The common guideline is three to five sets (after warm-up) for power exercises included in a trained athlete's program (33, 86, 87).

Hypertrophy

It is generally accepted that higher training volumes are associated with increases in muscular size (31, 63). This is the result of both a moderate to higher number of repetitions per set (6 to 12; see Figure 6.3 and Table 6.9) and the commonly recommended three to six sets per exercise (20, 32, 33, 71, 91). Additionally, although research studies usually focus on only one or two exercises (total or per muscle group), empirical observations and interviews with elite bodybuilders, as well as more exhaustive prescriptive guidelines (20, 45), suggest that performing three or more exercises per muscle group is the most effective strategy for increasing muscle size (32). The effect on training volume from these assignments can be quite substantial.

Muscular Endurance

Resistance training programs that emphasize muscular endurance involve performing many repetitions—12 or more—per set (20, 45, 87, 91, 92). Despite this relatively high repetition assignment, the overall volume-load is not necessarily overly inflated since the loads lifted are lighter and fewer sets are performed, commonly two or three per exercise (45).

STEP 7: REST PERIODS

The time dedicated to recovery between sets and exercises is called the **rest period** or **interset rest.** The length of the rest period between sets and exercises is highly dependent on the goal of training, the relative load lifted, and the athlete's training status (if the athlete is not in good physical condition, rest periods initially may need to be longer than typically assigned).

The amount of rest between sets is strongly related to load; the heavier the loads lifted, the longer the rest periods the athlete will need between sets in order to safely and successfully complete the prescribed subsequent sets. For example, training for muscular strength with 4RM loads requires significantly longer rest periods between sets than training for muscular endurance in which lighter 15RM loads are lifted (20, 74, 86). Despite the relationship between training goals and the length of rest periods (e.g., long rest periods for muscular strength training programs), not all exercises in a resistance training program should be assigned the same rest periods. It is important that the strength and conditioning professional allocate rest periods based on the relative load lifted and the amount of muscle mass involved in each exercise. An example of this specificity is for an assistance exercise as part of a muscular strength training program. Whereas a core exercise such as the bench press may involve a 4RM load and a 4-minute rest period, an assistance exercise such as the lateral shoulder raise may be performed with a 12RM load and therefore require only a 1-minute rest period (even though 1-minute rest periods generally apply to a hypertrophy training program). The recommended rest period lengths for strength, power, hypertrophy, and muscular endurance programs are shown in Table 6.12.

Strength and Power

Training may enhance an athlete's ability to exercise with less rest (20, 86), but athletes who seek to perform maximal or near-maximal repetitions with a heavy load usually need long rest periods, especially for lower body or all-body structural exercises (95). For example, Robinson and colleagues (77) observed that, in the back squat exercise, 3 minutes of interset rest resulted in greater strength gains than a 30-second rest period. Common guidelines for rest period length are at least 2 minutes (45, 82, 96) or a range of 2 to 5 minutes (47, 50) or 3 to 5 minutes (20, 86, 96). These recovery intervals appear to apply equally to resistance training programs designed to improve maximal strength and those that focus on muscular power (45).

Application of the Volume Guidelines

(Refer to the first scenario table in the chapter for a description of the scenario athletes.)

SCENARIO A Female Collegiate Basketball Player Preseason	SCENARIO B Male Professional American Football Lineman Off-Season	SCENARIO C Male High School Cross-Country Runner In-Season
Power exercises — 4 sets of 5 repetitions Other core exercises — 3 sets of 6 repetitions Assistance exercises — 2 sets of 10 repetitions (The number of sets does not include warm-ups.)	Core exercises — 4 sets of 10 repetitions Assistance exercises — 3 sets of 10 repetitions (The number of sets does not include warm-ups.)	Core exercises — 3 sets of 12 repetitions Assistance exercises — 2 sets of 15 repetitions (The number of sets does not include warm-ups.)
Monday, Wednesday, and Friday Hang clean — 4 x 5[a] Push jerk — 4 x 5 Front squat — 3 x 6 Incline bench press — 3 x 6 Seated row — 2 x 10 Dumbbell alternating curl — 2 x 10 Triceps pushdown — 2 x 10 Abdominal crunch — 3 x 20	***Lower Body (Monday and Thursday)*** Deadlift — 4 x 10 Back squat — 4 x 10 Step-up — 3 x 10 Leg (knee) curl — 3 x 10 Seated calf (heel) raise — 3 x 10 ***Upper Body (Tuesday and Friday)*** Bench press — 4 x 10 Bent-over row — 3 x 10 Shoulder press — 4 x 10 Barbell biceps curl — 3 x 10 Shoulder shrug — 3 x 10 Lying triceps extension — 3 x 10 Abdominal crunch — 3 x 20	***Wednesday and Saturday*** Lunge — 3 x 12 Vertical chest press — 3 x 12 Leg (knee) curl — 2 x 15 One-arm dumbbell row — 2 x 15 Toe raise (dorsiflexion) — 2 x 15 Machine back extension — 2 x 15 Abdominal crunch — 3 x 20 Complete one set of each exercise, then repeat.[b]
COMMENTS [a]Represented as sets x repetitions here and in scenarios B and C.		**COMMENTS** [b]The eight exercises are performed one set at a time, one immediately after the other (i.e., in a "circuit"). Once two sets (circuits) are completed, the athlete performs the final sets of the lunge, vertical chest press, and abdominal crunch exercises in that order.

TABLE 6.12	
Rest Period Length Assignments Based on the Training Goal	
Training goal*	**Rest period length**
Strength	2–5 minutes
Power:	
Single-effort event	2–5 minutes
Multiple-effort event	
Hypertrophy	30 seconds–1.5 minutes
Muscular endurance	≤30 seconds

*Because there are occasions when the prescribed percentage of the 1RM for assistance exercises falls outside the range associated with the training goal (e.g., >8RM loads are recommended for assistance exercises as part of a muscular strength training program [21]), the strength and conditioning professional should examine the loads used for each exercise when assigning rest periods rather than generally applying the guidelines for a training goal.
Data from references 7, 20, 50, 86, and 96.

Hypertrophy

Athletes who are interested in gaining muscular size often use a short to moderate interset rest period (20, 45, 47, 74, 86). Some reviews of hypertrophy training programs support a limited rest period because they recommend that the athlete begin the next set before full recovery has been achieved (32, 91). Despite this, the high metabolic demand of exercises involving large muscle groups merits consideration (i.e., extra recovery time) when rest period lengths are being assigned (86). Typical strategies for the length of rest periods are less than 1.5 minutes (45) or a span of 30 seconds to 1 minute (47, 50, 92) or 30 seconds to 1.5 minutes (32, 91).

Muscular Endurance

A muscular endurance training program has very short rest periods, often less than 30 seconds. This restriction of the recovery time is purposeful; only a minimal amount of rest is allowed when light loads are being lifted for many repetitions. This type of program is designed to meet the guideline of the specificity principle for muscular endurance (2). Short rest periods are characteristic of circuit training programs (23, 29) in which it is common to alternate exercises and limit rest period lengths to 30 seconds or less (76, 78, 79).

CONCLUSION

Well-designed programs are based on the application of sound principles during each step of a process referred to as *program design*. The process begins with a needs analysis to determine the specific demands of the sport and the training status of the athlete. With this knowledge, appropriate exercises are selected and training frequency is established. The order of exercises in the workout is considered next, followed by load assignments and training volume choices based on desired training outcomes. Deciding on the length of the rest periods is the last step leading to the design of a sport-specific resistance training program. A composite view that includes all of the program design variables (steps 1–7) for the three scenarios is shown in the scenario table.

Application of the Rest Period Guidelines
(Refer to the first scenario table in the chapter for a description of the scenario athletes.)

SCENARIO A Female Collegiate Basketball Player Preseason	SCENARIO B Male Professional American Football Lineman Off-Season	SCENARIO C Male High School Cross-Country Runner In-Season
Power and core exercises 3 minutes Assistance exercises 60 seconds–1.5 minutes	Core exercises 1.5 minutes Assistance exercises 60 seconds	Core exercises 30 seconds[e] Assistance exercises 20 seconds[e]
Monday, Wednesday, and Friday Hang clean 3 minutes Push jerk 3 minutes Front squat 3 minutes Incline bench press 3 minutes Seated row 1.5 minutes[a] Dumbbell alternating curl 60 seconds[a] Triceps pushdown 60 seconds[a] Abdominal crunch 20 seconds[b]	**_Lower body (Monday and Thursday)_** Deadlift 1.5 minutes Back squat 1.5 minutes Step-up 1.5 minutes[c] Leg (knee) curl 60 seconds Seated calf (heel) raise 60 seconds **_Upper body (Tuesday and Friday)_** Bench press 1.5 minutes Bent-over row 60 seconds Shoulder press 1.5 minutes Barbell biceps curl 60 seconds Shoulder shrug 60 seconds Lying triceps extension 60 seconds Abdominal crunch 20 seconds[d]	**_Wednesday and Saturday_** Lunge 30 seconds Vertical chest press 30 seconds Leg (knee) curl 20 seconds One-arm dumbbell row 20 seconds Toe raise (dorsiflexion) 20 seconds Lateral shoulder raise 20 seconds Machine back extension 20 seconds Abdominal crunch 20 seconds Complete one set of each exercise, then repeat.[f]
COMMENTS [a]Despite following a muscular strength training program, the athlete is performing sets of 10 repetitions in this exercise, a volume assignment for hypertrophy training. Therefore, the length of the rest period should be 30 seconds to 1.5 minutes. The rest period for the single-joint exercises is slightly shorter because fewer muscles are involved. [b]Again, although this athlete is training for muscular strength, she is performing sets of 20 repetitions in this exercise, a volume assignment for muscular endurance. Therefore, the length of the rest period should be <30 seconds.	**COMMENTS** [c]This exercises is classified as an assistance exercise and, like the others, could be assigned a 60-second rest period. Despite this, the step-up is a unilateral exercise that requires more time for completion of each set. Therefore, a longer rest period is provided. [d]Although this athlete is training for hypertrophy, he is performing sets of 20 repetitions in this exercise, a volume assignment for muscular endurance. Therefore, the length of the rest period should be <30 seconds.	**COMMENTS** [e]Both of these rest period assignments fall within the guidelines for muscular endurance training. Due to the higher goal repetitions and lighter loads for assistance exercises, the rest period length was slightly shortened. [f]The eight exercises are performed one set at a time, one immediately after the other (i.e., in a "circuit"). Once two sets (circuits) are completed, the athlete performs the final sets of the lunge, vertical chest press, and abdominal crunch exercises in that order.

Application of All Program Design Variables (Steps 1–7)
(Refer to the first scenario table in the chapter for a description of the scenario athletes.)

SCENARIO A Female Collegiate Basketball Player Preseason	SCENARIO B Male Professional American Football Lineman Off-season	SCENARIO C Male High School Cross-Country Runner In-Season

SCENARIO A — Female Collegiate Basketball Player Preseason

Monday ("heavy" day)

Hang clean[a]	4 x 5 @ 95 lb (43 kg)
Push jerk[a]	4 x 5 @ 90 lb (41 kg)
Front squat[a]	3 x 6 @ 155 lb (70 kg)
Incline bench press[a]	3 x 6 @ 85 lb (39 kg)
Seated row[b]	2 x 10 @ 90 lb (41 kg)
Dumbbell alternating curl[d]	2 x 10 @ 20 lb (9 kg)
Triceps pushdown[d]	2 x 10 @ 40 lb (18 kg)
Abdominal crunch[d]	3 x 20

Wednesday ("light" day)

80% of Monday's load in power/core exercises

Hang clean[a]	4 x 5 @ 75 lb (34 kg)
Push jerk[a]	4 x 5 @ 70 lb (32 kg)
Front squat[a]	3 x 6 @ 125 lb (57 kg)
Incline bench press[a]	3 x 6 @ 70 lb (32 kg)
Seated row	2 x 10 @ 90 lb (41 kg)
Dumbbell alternating curl[d]	2 x 10 @ 20 lb (9 kg)
Triceps pushdown[d]	2 x 10 @ 40 lb (18 kg)
Abdominal crunch 3 x 20	

Friday ("medium" day)

90% of Monday's load in power/core exercises

Hang clean[a]	4 x 5 @ 85 lb (39 kg)
Push jerk[a]	4 x 5 @ 80 lb (36 kg)
Front squat[a]	3 x 6 @ 140 lb (64 kg)
Incline bench press[a]	3 x 6 @ 75 lb (34 kg)
Seated row[b]	2 x 10 @ 90 lb (41 kg)
Dumbbell alternating curl[d]	2 x 10 @ 20 lb (9 kg)
Triceps pushdown[d]	2 x 10 @ 40 lb (18 kg)
Abdominal crunch 3 x 20	

SCENARIO B — Male Professional American Football Lineman Off-season

Lower body (Monday and Thursday[g])

Deadlift[b]	4 x 10 @ 490 lb (223 kg)
Back squat[b]	4 x 10 @ 505 lb (230 kg)
Step-up[b]	3 x 10 @ 205 lb (93 kg)
Leg (knee) curl[d]	3 x 10 @ 190 lb (86 kg)
Seated calf raise[d]	3 x 10 @ 155 lb (70 kg)

Upper body (Tuesday and Friday)[g]

Bench press[b]	4 x 10 @ 320 lb (145 kg)
Bent-over row[d]	3 x 10 @ 215 lb (98 kg)
Shoulder press[b]	4 x 10 @ 190 lb (86 kg)
Barbell biceps curl[d]	3 x 10 @ 115 lb (52 kg)
Shoulder shrug[d]	3 x 10 @ 405 lb (184 kg)
Lying triceps extension[d]	3 x 10 @ 125 lb (57 kg)
Abdominal crunch[c]	3 x 20

SCENARIO C — Male High School Cross-Country Runner In-Season

Wednesday and Saturday

Lunge[a]	3 x 12 @ 45 lb (20 kg)
Vertical chest press[b]	3 x 12 @ 70 lb (32 kg)
Leg (knee) curl[c]	2 x 15 @ 65 lb (30 kg)
One-arm dumbbell row[c]	2 x 15 @ 25 lb (11 kg)
Toe raise[e]	2 x 15 @ 20 lb (9kg)
Lateral shoulder raise[e]	2 x 15 @ 10 lb (5 kg)
Machine back extension[c]	2 x 15 @ 50 lb (23 kg)
Abdominal crunch[c]	3 x 20

Complete one set of each exercise, then repeat.[f]

COMMENTS

Rest period lengths:

[a]3 minutes   [b]1.5 minutes   [c]20 seconds   [d]60 seconds   [e]30 seconds

[f]The eight exercises are performed one set at a time, one immediately after the other (i.e., in a "circuit"). Once two sets (circuits) are completed, the athlete performs the final sets of the lunge, vertical chest press, and abdominal crunch exercises in that order.

[g]Reduce the loads on Thursday and Friday by 5% to 10%.

CHAPTER 7

Periodization

©Mark McElroy/Shutterstock.com

The ability of strength and conditioning programs to stimulate the physiological adaptations necessary to enhance performance is largely related to modulating training stressors to enhance adaptive responses while reducing the potential for performance plateaus or overtraining. When training loads are mismanaged, there is an increased risk of injury and the potential for overtraining (46). Ultimately, as athletes become more trained or have a greater training age, it becomes more difficult to stimulate performance gains. Thus increased variation is often required in the training program of more advanced athletes in order to facilitate long-term training and performance gains (3, 59). To meet this requirement, training programs need to be logically designed so that they are structured in a systematic and preplanned manner, allowing variation of training volume, intensity, frequency, density, foci, mode, and exercise selection in accordance with the athlete's needs and the sport's requirements. Central to the effective programming of training interventions is the concept of **periodization** (28). Periodization is often attributed to Leonid Matveyev (43), who proposed the basic theories that underpin periodization in the 1960s. Although Matveyev is often considered the father of periodization, several other individuals were exploring the concept at the same time, including László Nádori (48), Tudor Bompa (2), and Yuri Verkoshansky (64). Later on, American sport scientists Michael H. Stone, Harold O'Bryant, and John Garhammer adapted the concepts of the early periodization theorists with special application to strength and power athletes (57, 58). Ultimately, periodization is a theoretical and practical construct that allows for the systematic, sequential, and integrative programming of training interventions into mutually dependent periods of time in order to induce specific physiological adaptations that underpin performance outcomes.

This chapter discusses the concept of periodization and its application within a strength and conditioning program. In order to understand periodization theories and how they are applied to training program design, it is essential to develop an understanding of how the body responds to training (i.e., stressors) (24, 28); this topic is discussed first. Second, the basic hierarchal structure of a periodized training program is discussed in order to demonstrate how the training year is broken into smaller blocks of training, each with its own training goals and priorities. It is important to note that this overall schedule of training encompasses all aspects of the athletes' training program, including general conditioning, sport-specific activities, and resistance training. Finally, the second half of this chapter presents detailed examples of a yearlong periodized strength and conditioning program.

CENTRAL CONCEPTS RELATED TO PERIODIZATION

A successful training program allows for management of the adaptive and **recovery** responses to specific interventions that are delivered in a structured way (28). The ultimate success of any training program centers on its ability to induce specific physiological adaptations and translate those adaptations into increases in performance. At the center of this process is the ability to manage the adaptive response, handle accumulated fatigue, and capitalize on the aftereffects established from the various training factors encountered. The strength of a periodized training plan lies in its ability to sequence and structure the training interventions in order to manage all of these factors and peak performance at appropriate time points (4-6, 51, 59, 63). Ultimately, peak performance can be optimized only for short periods of time (7–14 days), and the average time it can be maintained is inversely related to the average intensity of the training plan (17, 33, 59). In order to elucidate how periodized training models can manage these factors, three basic mechanistic theories have been established: the **General Adaptation Syndrome (GAS), stimulus-fatigue-recovery-adaptation theory**, and the **fitness–fatigue paradigm** (22, 28, 59, 65).

> Periodization is the logical and systematic process of sequencing and integrating training interventions in order to achieve peak performance at appropriate time points.

The General Adaptation Syndrome

In 1956, Hans Selye, a pioneering researcher on the biological effects of exposure to stressful stimuli, presented the basic concepts of the GAS in which a three-stage response to stress (alarm, resistance, and exhaustion) was defined (54, 55). While not originally conceptualized in the context of physical training, over time the GAS has become one of the foundational concepts from which periodization theories have been developed (21, 59). Any time the body experiences a novel, new, or more intense stress than previously applied (e.g., lifting a heavier training load or a greater volume-load; see chapter 6), the initial response, or alarm phase, is an accumulation of fatigue, soreness, stiffness, or reduction in energetic stores that results in a reduction in performance capacity (59). Depending on the magnitude of the stress encountered by the athlete, this response may last several hours, days, or weeks. After this initial response, the body moves into the resistance phase, in which it adapts to the stimulus and returns to a normal functional capacity. If the training stress is appropriately structured and not excessive, these adaptive responses can result in specific biochemical, structural, and

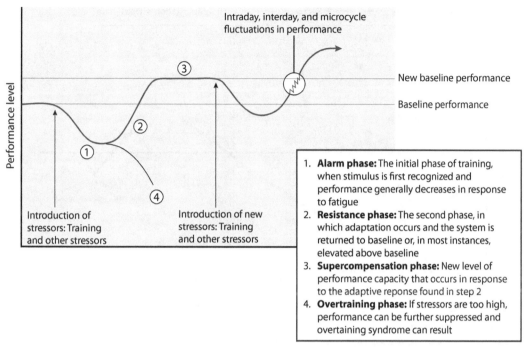

Figure 7.1   The General Adaptation Syndrome (GAS) and application to periodization. Adapted, by permission, from Haff and Haff, 2012 (28).

mechanical adjustments that further elevate the athlete's performance capacity, resulting in what is termed **supercompensation** (58).

If, however, the stress persists for an extended period of time, the athlete can move into the exhaustion phase. If this occurs, the athlete is demonstrating an inability to adapt to the imposed stressors and will present some of the same symptoms noted in the alarm phase. Ultimately, when athletes reach the exhaustion phase they are most likely experiencing overreaching or overtraining responses (20). From a training perspective, excessive loading, monotonous training, and overly varied training can all result in the occurrence of the exhaustion phase. Additionally, the responses to training can be affected by other nontraining-related stress (e.g., occupational issues, insufficient sleep, relationship, poor diet) that can contribute to the overall stress level experienced by the athlete. Ultimately, the strength and conditioning professional should strive to avoid the occurrence of this phase of the GAS through the proper planning and management (periodization) of training stressors. Although the actual dimensions (i.e., slope, magnitude, and timing) of the curve shown in Figure 7.1 are highly individualized, the figure represents the basic application of the GAS to training responses.

Stimulus-Fatigue-Recovery-Adaptation Theory

The stimulus-fatigue-recovery-adaptation theory is an extension of the GAS and suggests that training stimuli produce a general response (Figure 7.2) that is influenced by the overall magnitude of the training stressor (59). Specifically, the greater the overall magnitude of the workload encountered, the more fatigue accumulates and the longer the delay before complete recovery and adaptation can occur. As the athlete recovers from and adapts to the training stimuli, fatigue will dissipate, and preparedness and performance increase. If no new training stimulus is introduced, a state of involution or detraining (i.e., a reduced overall capacity, to below the current baseline) is observed. In contrast,

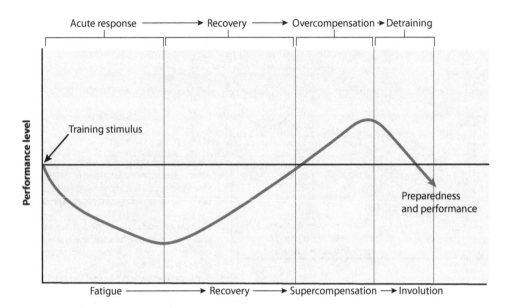

Figure 7.2 The stimulus-fatigue-recovery-adaptation theory, with interchangeable terminology.

Adapted, by permission, from Haff and Haff, 2012 (28).

if a new training stimulus is introduced, the process is repeated. This basic pattern is present whenever an athlete is exposed to a training exercise, session, day, or cycle within a periodized training plan. It should be noted that while recovery is an important part of the training process, it is not always necessary to reach a state of complete recovery before engaging in a new bout or session of training (49). The manipulation of workloads and training intensities through use of light and heavy sessions or days of training can be used to modulate fatigue and recovery responses (9, 19) while allowing for fitness to be either increased or maintained. Conceptually, this theory serves as the foundation for sequential periodization models in that these models allow for the manipulation of various training factors to modulate the athlete's overall fatigue levels, rate of recovery, and adaptive response to the training stimuli.

Fitness–Fatigue Paradigm

Generally, there is a summation of the two primary training aftereffects (i.e., fitness and fatigue) in response to training interventions that influence the athlete's level of preparedness (3, 14, 66). Zatsiorsky (65) presents the classic explanation of these relationships as the fitness-fatigue paradigm (Figure 7.3). Ultimately, every training bout, session, or cycle creates both fatigue and fitness aftereffects, which summate to create a state of preparedness (14, 65). When training loads are the highest, fitness becomes elevated; but because of the high training loads, a concomitant increase in fatigue occurs. When fitness and fatigue are summed in this case, the level of fatigue results in a reduction in preparedness. On the other hand, when training workloads are low, little fatigue occurs and minimal fitness is developed, resulting in a low level of preparedness. Thus the sequencing of training loads becomes important in that it allows for training workloads to be varied in a systematic manner. An important thing to remember is that fatigue dissipates at a faster rate than fitness, thus allowing preparedness to become elevated if appropriate training strategies are used to retain fitness while reducing fatigue (25, 28). While the fitness–fatigue paradigm is classically represented as one fatigue, fitness, and preparedness curve, it is likely that each training factor stimulates its own individual fitness, fatigue, and preparedness aftereffect response (14, 59). These aftereffects are often considered

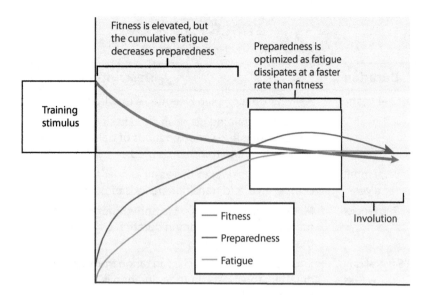

Figure 7.3   The fitness–fatigue paradigm.
Adapted, by permission, from Haff and Haff, 2012 (28).

to be residual training effects and serve as a fundamental concept underlying the use of sequential periodization models (25, 28). Ultimately, the residual training effects of one training period have the potential to affect the level of preparedness in subsequent training periods, depending on the overall structure of the periodized training plan (28).

PERIODIZATION HIERARCHY

Ultimately periodization is simply a means of organizing the planning of a training intervention so that the program is partitioned into specific time periods (Table 7.1) (22, 24). The multiyear training plan covers the most time but is the least detailed plan within a periodized training structure. For example, it may involve the basic progression of a collegiate football player from his freshman to senior year and contain key developmental goals that are targeted within each year of training. This multiyear training structure is then subdivided into more detailed individual **annual training plans** that are developed based on the athlete's progression through the various stages or benchmarks associated with the multiyear training plan. In sports that have only one competitive season such as American football, an annual training plan would be represented as a **macrocycle**. However, in a sport like college track and field, the annual plan would be divided into two macrocycles because of the indoor and outdoor seasons typical of this college sport. Typically the macrocycle lasts several months up to a year, depending on the sport. Within each macrocycle are **mesocycles**, each lasting several weeks to months; two to six weeks is the most typical duration. The number of mesocycles within each macrocycle is dependent on the training targets and the length of the macrocycle within the annual training plan. Each mesocycle is then broken down into individual microcycles that last from several days to weeks; the most common duration is four weeks (22, 28). Within each **microcycle** are training days that are further subdivided into training sessions.

> Periodization of training begins with general global training targets set forth in the multiyear or annual training plan and becomes more specific as the program is developed for the macro-, meso-, and microcycles. For example, annual training plans set the general pathway for a training year, while the other cycles set the means, methods, and modes used to get to the primary competitive targets.

TABLE 7.1		
Periodization Cycles		
Period	**Duration**	**Description**
Multiyear plan	2–4 years	A 4-year training plan is termed a quadrennial plan.
Annual training plan	1 year	The overall training plan can contain single or multiple macrocycles. Is subdivided into various periods of training including preparatory, competitive, and transition periods.
Macrocycle	Several months to a year	Some authors refer to this as an annual plan. Is divided into preparatory, competitive, and transition periods of training.
Mesocycle	2–6 weeks	Medium-sized training cycle, sometimes referred to as a block of training. The most common duration is 4 weeks. Consists of microcycles that are linked together.
Microcycle	Several days to 2 weeks	Small-sized training cycle; can range from several days to 2 weeks in duration; the most common duration is 1 week (7 days). Composed of multiple workouts.
Training day	1 day	One training day that can include multiple training sessions is designed in the context of the particular microcycle it is in.
Training session	Several hours	Generally consists of several hours of training. If the workout includes >30 min of rest between bouts of training, it would comprise multiple sessions.
Adapted, by permission, from G.G. Haff and E.E. Haff, 2012, Training integration and periodization. In *NSCA guide to program design*, edited by J. Hoffman (Champaign, IL: Human Kinetics), 220.		

PERIODIZATION PERIODS

The overall variation and structure of the program design variables within each individual meso- and microcycle are constructed based on the periods included in the macrocycle or annual training plan (22, 25). Across these periods of the training plan, the volume and intensity of the training and conditioning program generally receive the greatest attention; but the time spent acquiring and perfecting sport-specific technique must also be considered when one is constructing the overall periodized training plan (57). Ultimately, periodized training plans systematically shift training foci from general nonspecific activities of high volume and low intensity toward activities of lower volume and higher intensities over a period of many weeks or months to help reduce the potential for overtraining while optimizing performance capacities.

The basic sequencing of periodized training programs and how training progresses through the various phases for specified training targets are very similar to the sequencing and evolution of learning academic concepts. For example, in academics we start with simple concepts and skills that progress to more complex concepts. Ultimately we are building on the simple skills in order to provide a sound foundation for the more complex items. Ultimately, the periods within a periodized training plan serve as the pathway for developing simple skills into more complex sport-specific targets.

In the classic periodization literature, the major divisions of training are classified as the preparatory, competitive, and transition periods (24, 43). Stone, O'Bryant, and Garhammer (57) modified this classic model to include a "first transition" between the preparatory and competitive periods of training. Based on this structure, contemporary periodization models often contain four distinct but interrelated training periods: preparatory, first transition, competitive, and second transition. Figure 7.4 presents the basic periodization model described by Stone, O'Bryant, and Garhammer

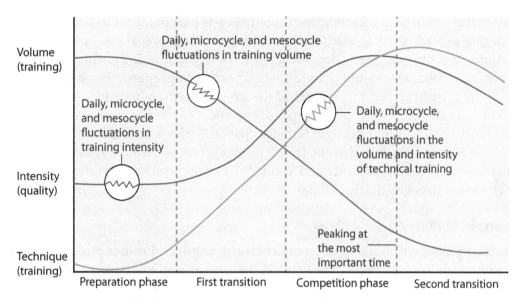

Figure 7.4   Matveyev's model of periodization (appropriate for novices).

Adapted, by permission, from G.G. Haff and E.E. Haff, 2012. Training integration and periodization. In *NSCA guide to program design,* edited by J. Hoffman (Champaign, IL: Human Kinetics), 223; adapted from figure 11.7, p. 2239. Reprinted from *Weight training: A scientific approach,* 2nd edition, by Michael H. Stone and Harold St. O'Bryant, copyright © 1987 by Burgess.

(57). This model is often applied for novice athletes with a lower training status. Generally, in this application, intensity begins lower and gradually increases, while volume starts higher and slowly decreases as the athlete becomes more conditioned. It is important to note that not all novice athletes are able to tolerate large changes in these variables and that smaller fluctuations may be required (58, 61, 62). It is also important to note that even though these fluctuations are often represented graphically as straight lines, the volume and intensity progressions are in fact nonlinear because of the fluctuations in the loadings that occur at the micro- and mesocycle levels (22, 24, 25, 51). This basic misunderstanding of the classic models of periodization has resulted in these types of models being falsely termed *linear periodization models* (25, 51).

Advanced athletes tend to train closer to their abilities and have smaller adaptation windows. Therefore, these athletes require greater training variation as well as higher volumes and intensities in order to allow them to continue to experience appropriate training stimuli (51). For example, Zatsiorsky and Kraemer (66) demonstrate that a stimulating load for a novice athlete would be a maintenance load at best for advanced athletes. To address this issue, the shift from higher-volume to higher-intensity training can occur earlier in the preparatory phase, with higher overall training volumes as compared to those in the base model presented in Figure 7.4.

Preparatory Period

In outlining a periodized training plan, the starting point is usually the **preparatory period.** This period occurs when there are no competitions, and technical, tactical, or sport-specific work is limited. This period often corresponds to what is termed the off-season. The central goal of this period of training is to develop a base level of conditioning in order to increase the athlete's ability to tolerate more intense training. Based on the model presented in Figure 7.4, the conditioning activities would begin with relatively low intensities and high volumes: long, slow distance running or swimming; low-intensity plyometrics; and high-repetition resistance training with light to moderate resistances. Traditionally, the preparatory period is subdivided into general and specific phases. The

general preparatory phase typically occurs during the early part of the period and often targets the development of a general physical base (3). This early part of the preparatory period includes high training volumes, low training intensities, and a larger variety of training means that are structured to develop general motor abilities and skills (36, 44). The **specific preparatory phase** occurs after the completion of the general preparatory phase and involves a shift in training focus. From the training base that has been established, this phase expands the athlete's training base through an increased emphasis on sport-specific training activities that prepare the athlete for the competitive period (15). During the preparatory period, resistance training phases can be created in order to depict more refined differences in training intensity and volume. In order, these are the hypertrophy/strength endurance and basic strength phases (57, 58).

Hypertropohy/Strength Endurance Phase

The **hypertrophy phase,** which is also referred to as the **strength endurance phase,** generally occurs during the early portion of the preparatory period (i.e., the general preparatory phase) (18, 27, 28). During this phase, the training intensity is low to moderate and the overall volume is high. The primary goals during this phase are (a) to increase lean body mass, (b) to develop an endurance (muscular and metabolic) base, or (c) to do both. This development will serve as the foundation for the higher-intensity training in subsequent phases and periods (29, 30). With strength/power athletes, the primary target might be to stimulate hypertrophic effects while increasing strength endurance. With endurance athletes, the primary goal would be to increase strength endurance without significantly increasing hypertrophy. Regardless of the sport or athlete bring trained, it is generally accepted that during the general preparatory phase, sport conditioning activities may not be specific to the athlete's sport. However, as the athlete moves into the specific preparatory phase, over several weeks the training activities will become more sport specific. For example, sprinters may begin the general preparatory phase with longer-distance runs (longer than their competitive distance, not traditional distance running; for example, a 100 m sprinter may do 400 m runs to establish a foundation) at slower speeds in conjunction with lower-intensity plyometrics such as double-leg bounding and hopping, as well as more basic resistance exercises that are not necessarily biomechanically or structurally similar to running (back squat, leg curl, and so on). Generally, the athlete performs resistance training with low to moderate intensities for high volumes (Table 7.2).

However, it is important to note that throughout this phase, daily variations in training intensity and workload will facilitate recovery (27). Additionally, recovery weeks or microcycles may be placed throughout the phase and most often at the end of the phase before the next phase of training begins.

> The hypertrophy/strength endurance phase involves low to moderate intensity (50–75% of the 1-repetition maximum [1RM]) and high volumes (three to six sets of 8–20 repetitions).

Basic Strength Phase

In the later portion of the preparatory period, during the specific preparatory phase, the primary aim of the **basic strength phase** is to increase the strength of the muscles that are essential to the primary sport movements (11–13). For example, the sprinter's running program would progress to include interval sprints of a moderate distance and more complex and specialized plyometric drills. The resistance training program also becomes more specific to the sport (e.g., squats, power cleans, one-leg squats) and involves heavier loads performed at lower volumes than in the hypertrophy/strength endurance phase (Table 7.2). As with the hypertrophy/ strength endurance phase, daily variations in training load facilitate recovery (27, 28).

TABLE 7.2
A Periodization Model for Resistance Training

Period	Preparatory		First Transition	Competition			Second Transition
Subperiod	General Preparatory	Specific Preparatory	Precompetitive	Main Competitive			Postcompetitive
Season	Off-season		Preseason	In-season			Postseason
Phase	Hypertrophy/ Strength Endurance	Basic Strength	Strength/Power	Peaking	Or	Maintenance	Active Rest
Intensity	Low to Moderate 50–75% of 1RM	High 80–95% of 1RM	Low to Very High 87–95% of 1RM* 30–85% of 1RM**	Very High to Very Low 50% to ≥93% of 1RM		Moderate to High 85–93% of 1RM	Recreational Activities (may not involve resistance training)
Volume	High 3–6 sets*** 8–20 repetitions	Moderate to High 2–6 sets*** 2–6 repetitions	Low 2–5 sets*** 2–5 repetitions	Very Low 1–3 sets*** 1–3 repetitions		Low to Moderate ~2–5 sets*** 3–6 repetitions	

*These percentages of 1RM apply to nonpower core exercises.

**These percentages of 1RM apply to power exercises. The actual percentage used to elicit power development depends on the exercise that is used. For more information see Kawamori and Haff (39).

***These recommendations do not include warm-up sets and represent only target sets for core exercises (2); they also do not include lower-intensity recovery days that are often part of a periodized training plan (27).

Adapted from 27, 56, 57, 58, 59.

> The basic strength phase involves higher intensity (80–95% of 1RM) and moderate to high volumes (two to six sets of two to six repetitions).

FIRST TRANSITION PERIOD

As originally described by Stone and colleagues (56–58), the **first transition period** is a link between the preparatory and competitive periods. Classically the resistance training in this period focuses on the development of strength and power as noted in Stone, O'Bryant, and Garhammer's (57) seminal paper on the periodization of strength training. The central aim of this period is to shift training focus toward the elevation of strength and its translation into power development (56, 57). In order to maximize this process and facilitate recovery, there are variations in training intensity and workload at the microcycle level (27, 28). Additionally, the last week of the period is marked by reduced volume, intensity, or both in order to achieve recovery before the beginning of the competition period.

Strength/Power Phase

The main phase within the first transition period is the **strength/power phase**. In this phase, the sprinter's interval and speed training intensifies to near competitive pace; speed drills are performed (e.g., sled towing, sprints against resistance, and uphill sprints); plyometric drills mimic sprinting; and the resistance training program involves programing power/explosive exercises at low to very high loads with low volumes. The load assignments for power exercises do not follow the typical %RM–repetition relationship, but their relative intensities are elevated during this phase (Table 7.2). Specifically, the exercises selected in this phase can dictate the loading that is used (39). For example, the development of power may be facilitated with a load of 80% of 1RM with hang power cleans (38), while a load of 50% to 70% of 1RM may be used with the bench press throw when the aim is to maximize power development (39). Ultimately, in order to address both strength and power development, a mixed training approach is warranted in which heavy- and low-load training is used to optimize both attributes (31).

> The strength/power phase involves low to very high loads (30–95% of 1RM, depending on the exercise) and low volumes (two to five sets for two to five repetitions).

COMPETITIVE PERIOD

The central training target during the **competitive period** is preparing the athlete for competition by further increasing strength and power via additional increases in training intensity while decreasing volume. This process can be a delicate balancing act, as adequate volume and intensity of training are needed in order to maintain competitive preparedness, and reductions in volume, intensity, or both are needed to optimize performance. To understand this conundrum, consider the fitness–fatigue paradigm presented earlier. If training workloads (volume or intensity) are reduced too much, fatigue will be reduced, but there will be a concomitant decrease in overall fitness that results in a reduction in competitive preparedness. Also during this period, time spent practicing sport-specific skills and tactics increases dramatically, and a proportional decrease occurs in time spent performing physical conditioning activities such as resistance training. For example, a sprinter places even more emphasis on speed, reaction time, sprint-specific plyometric drills, and technique training. The competition period may last for one or two weeks for some sports in which a peaking program is employed (7, 23). **Peaking** programs attempt to place the athlete in peak condition for about one or two weeks. Trying to extend this to longer durations ultimately results in reduced performance capacity as a result of reduction in fitness or potential overtraining (3, 23). Depending on the load reduction strategy employed, peaking programs result in a progressive shift from higher-intensity training toward lower-intensity work designed to reduce fatigue as the athlete moves through the taper before competition (23). As shown in Table 7.2, resistance training may range between 50% and ≥93% of 1RM, depending on where athletes are in the peaking program.

For team sports, this period spans an entire season and may last for many months, requiring the use of a **maintenance** program (3). Because of the prolonged duration of the competitive period in this situation, the intensity and volume of training must be manipulated on a microcycle basis in order to maintain strength and power while managing the fatigue associated with a frequent-competition schedule. Generally, a maintenance program is marked by moderate- to high-intensity training (e.g., 85–93% of 1RM) at low to moderate volumes. At the microcycle level, the training loads are modulated based on the training, travel, and competitive schedule. Careful monitoring of the athlete's performance capacity and recovery is critical during the team sport athlete's competitive period.

> The competitive period includes peaking and maintenance. For peaking, athletes use very high to low intensities (50% to ≥93% of the 1RM) and very low volume (one to three sets of one to three repetitions) for one to two weeks. For maintenance, athletes modulate training between moderate and high intensities (85 to 93% of 1RM) with moderate volumes about two to five sets of three to six repetitions).

SECOND TRANSITION PERIOD (ACTIVE REST)

Between the competitive season and the next annual training plan or the preparatory period of a macrocycle, a **second transition period** is often used to create a linkage (57). This period is sometimes referred to as an **active rest** or **restoration** period and generally lasts for one to four weeks (3). It is important to note that if active rest is extended for a prolonged duration, athletes will require a much longer preparatory period in order to regain their performance capacities (26). Therefore, it is generally recommended that the second transition period last no longer than four weeks unless an athlete requires additional time to recover from an injury. During this period, aggressive training immediately after the peak performance or end of the maintenance phase should be avoided so athletes can rehabilitate injuries and rest physically and mentally (11–13). For example, a sprinter may engage in recreational activities such as volleyball, racket sports, and swimming in a leisurely manner and perform very low-volume, nonsport-specific resistance training with very low loads. A secondary use of the active rest concept is to structure one-week breaks between long phases (three weeks) or periods of training. The purpose is to create an unloading week in order to prepare the body for the subsequent phase or period of training. The practice of reducing the training load via the reduction of training intensity and volume is believed by many strength and conditioning professionals to reduce overtraining potential.

> **The second transition (active rest) provides a period of time in which athletes can rehabilitate injuries and refresh both physically and mentally before beginning a new annual training plan or macrocycle. This period should not last longer than four weeks, because long periods with reduced training will require the athlete to engage in a longer preparatory period in order to regain sporting form.**

APPLYING SPORT SEASONS TO THE PERIODIZATION PERIODS

In practical terms, periodization involves a logical, systematic variation and integration of training in order to direct the training responses while managing fatigue and optimizing performance in accordance with the seasonal demands of the sport and athletes. Based on the competitive season, the overall annual plan or macrocycle is structured in order to sequentially develop specific attributes required by the athlete. In order to avoid monotony, staleness, and overtraining potential, the training program must involve structured variation of key training variables (e.g., volume, intensity, training frequency, training foci, exercise selection) (28). Classically, most intercollegiate and professional sports have an annual schedule that includes an off-season, preseason, in-season, and postseason. These seasons are easy to relate to the periods in a periodized training model (see Figure 7.5).

Off-Season

The off-season should be considered the preparatory period; it typically lasts from the end of the postseason to the beginning of the preseason, which can be about six weeks before the first major competition (although this varies greatly). This preparatory period is subdivided into general and specific preparatory phases that are broken down into mesocycles; these interlink to prepare the athlete for the subsequent competitive season. For example, the athlete may complete several rotations of mesocycles that focus on hypertrophy/strength endurance and basic strength (see Figure 7.5). Ultimately, these cyclical rotations are selected based on the sport and the athlete's needs. For example, if an American football player needs to gain muscle mass, more mesocycles that target the hypertrophy phase will be prescribed.

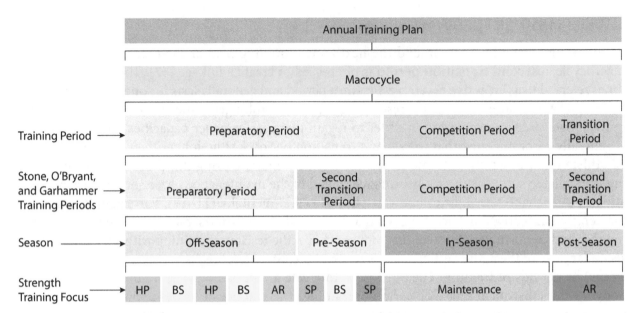

Figure 7.5 Relationship of Periodization Periods to Seasons and Strengh Training Focus.
HP = Hypertrophy/Strenght Endurance; BS = Basic Strength; AR = Active Rest; SP = Strength/Power.

Preseason

After the completion of the off-season, the preseason is used to lead into the first major competition. The first transition period is often undertaken at this time with a focus on the strength/power phase of resistance training. This time is used to prepare the athlete for the subsequent competitive period. It is very important to note that the preseason is not the time to build the foundational physical capacities needed for the sport; this should occur primarily in the off-season. The preseason is designed to capitalize on the off-season and elevate the athlete's performance capacity during the competitive period.

In-Season

The competition, or in-season, period contains all the contests scheduled for the given year, including any tournament games. Most sports have a long season that requires multiple mesocycles arranged around key contests. Thus, a long competition season (12–16+ weeks) presents unique programming challenges. One solution is to structure three- or four-week mesocycle blocks that unload the athlete in the last microcycle in order to allow for fatigue reduction and performance supercompensation before critical contests (28). This does not mean that the athlete is in poor condition for the other contests, as varying training intensities and volumes across the mesocycle can modulate preparedness. Specifically, training intensity and volume are increased or decreased in order to maintain physical capacities while reducing fatigue and peaking preparedness before the competitive engagements. The other approach is to design a maintenance program that modulates moderate intensities with low to moderate volumes.

Postseason

After the final contest, the postseason or a second transition period provides the athlete with a relative or active rest before the beginning of the next year's off-season or preparatory period. It is important to remember that the longer the postseason, the greater the chance for detraining, which results in an increased need for a longer general preparatory phase during the next off-season (3).

UNDULATING VERSUS LINEAR PERIODIZATION MODELS

For better or worse, contemporary periodization literature has adopted the terms *linear* and *nonlinear* when referring to periodization models. However, it should be noted that a central tenet of periodization is the removal of linearity from training (25, 32, 37, 43, 49, 51). Often the traditional resistance training model is falsely referred to as linear due to the gradual and progressive mesocycle increases in intensity over time (8, 37, 51). However, a closer look at the traditional model as described by Stone, O'Bryant, and Garhammer (57, 58) and within the literature (37) shows that the traditional model contains nonlinear variation in training intensity and volume-load at the microcycle level and throughout the mesocycle. Regardless of this, an alternative model termed the **nonlinear periodization** model has been introduced in the strength and conditioning industry (42, 53). This model is probably better described as an undulating or **daily undulating periodization** model, because it involves large daily (i.e., within the microcycle) fluctuations in the load and volume (e.g., repetitions and volume-load) of assigned core resistance training exercises. For example, using this model you might perform four sets with a 6RM load (strength focus) on the first day of the week (e.g., Tuesday), three sets with a 10RM (hypertrophic focus) on the next training day (e.g., Thursday), and five sets with a 3RM load (power focus) on the last training day (e.g., Saturday). In this case the load, volume (e.g., repetitions and volume-load), and training focus are all modified within the microcycle. These modifications are in contrast to what occurs with the **traditional periodization** model, falsely referred to as the **linear periodization** model, according to which the athlete performs the same number of sets and repetitions across the training days and varies the training load. For example, the athlete may perform four sets of six at 85% of 1RM on the first day of training, at 75% of 1RM on the second day, and at 65% of 1RM on the third day to basically train using a heavy-to-light training structure. While the traditional model appears to vary only intensity because the repetitions do not change, one must remember that the volume-load changes in this model result in undulations in workload and training volume, supporting the idea that the traditional model is in fact nonlinear and should not be classified as linear (37).

Some research studies suggest that the undulating model is more effective than the traditional model (16, 41, 45, 47, 53), although other evidence suggests that there is no difference between the models (1, 10, 52) or that the traditional model is superior (34, 35, 50). Proponents of the undulating model suggest that one of its strengths is the absence of accumulated neural fatigue caused by extended, ever-increasing training intensities common to the traditional model (40). Conversely, proponents of the traditional model suggest that the overall high volume-loads of training in the undulating model result in greater peripheral fatigue and increased risk of injury because of the high levels of metabolic fatigue this type of programming can stimulate (50). Additionally, examination of the fatigue–fitness paradigm (Figure 7.3) and the stimulus-fatigue-recovery-adaptation theory (Figure 7.2) indicates that the undulating model has the potential to decrease athlete preparedness because of accumulated fatigue that occurs with higher volume-load training sessions. Some authors suggest that, based upon the GAS, this response may actually increase the potential for overtraining with higher-level athletes (25, 60) and result in an increased injury risk for athletes using this model in conjunction with their sport-based training.

EXAMPLE OF AN ANNUAL TRAINING PLAN

An example of one approach to designing a full annual training plan (i.e., macrocycle for sports with one competitive season) spanning all four sport seasons is presented in the four application tables near the end of this chapter. The program is based on the preseason resistance training program for scenario A from Chapter 6, "Program Design for Resistance Training," which concerns a female collegiate basketball center. Background information and initial testing information about this athlete are provided in Chapter 6.

The annual plan example provided in this chapter begins where the preseason program from Chapter 6 left off and shows a continuation of the training program through the in-season, the postseason, and the following year's off-season. The primary focus of the annual training plan example is the resistance training component of scenario A. Although other modes of training are described briefly (e.g., plyometrics, anaerobic conditioning, aerobic endurance), this example is not intended to illustrate every aspect of variation for a strength and conditioning program for basketball. Also, although this example is divided into four sport seasons that are made up of two- to four-week mesocycles, an alternative approach is to structure each season as an individual macrocycle.

Preseason

After undertaking one or two unloading weeks following the cessation of the off-season training period, the athlete begins the preseason period of training. For this example, the period covers about 3.5 months (mid-August until the first game, possibly mid-November). The goals of the preseason are to increase the intensity of sport-specific training and the attention given to basketball drills and skills. The resistance training portion is planned for three days per week and focuses primarily on strength and power outcomes. Other training modes (e.g., plyometrics and anaerobic conditioning) hold high priority, especially if they directly contribute to basketball training. Although chapter 6 does not show microcycle progressions, it describes the resistance training portion of this season in detail; therefore, please refer to the table titled "Application of All Program Design Variables" (p. 175) in that chapter for the preseason program example. The same method of applying the periodization concepts described in this chapter can be used to design the remainder of the preseason period.

In-Season

After an unloading week following the preseason, the athlete is ready to begin the competition period of training. The in-season period lasts approximately 20 weeks, spanning a time period from November until April (including a four-week tournament period, although it could last longer). The goals for the in-season are to maintain and possibly improve strength, power, flexibility, and anaerobic conditioning. The time constraints of games, skill and strategy practice, and travel result in a lower volume of off-court training activities. Due to multiple games each week, resistance training may be limited to 30 minutes, one to three times per week, consisting of an undulating regimen of varying volume-loads and relative intensities. Power and basketball-specific nonpower core exercises predominate, with assistance exercises added for balance. See the sample in-season program near the end of this chapter. Plyometric sessions should be alternated with resistance training and conducted once or twice weekly, depending on the number of games.

On days when no resistance training is scheduled, 15 to 20 minutes of various short spring intervals could be performed once or twice weekly during practice. Speed, agility, and other running conditioning can be incorporated into practice time, and flexibility training can be part of the practice and game warm-up and cool-down. Two or three days of rest should be afforded between resistance training, plyometrics, and sprint interval sessions, depending on the game schedule. This period is similar to the previous training period in that the majority of the athlete's time is spent on skill and strategy development, with the remainder devoted to conditioning.

The athlete is in good condition from the previous mesocycles, so she should be able not only to maintain that condition but also to peak again if the team continues in the conference tournament. In that case, she would revert back to mesocycle 2 and progress to mesocycle 3 if the team qualifies for a tournament to be held after the conference tournament. If the tournament game schedule does not allow for more than one resistance training session per week, the athlete should perform all the week's power and core exercises (if time allows) and omit the assistance exercises. Two examples of specific weekly tournament schedules are presented near the end of this chapter.

Postseason (Active Rest Period)

Following the completion of the competitive season is a (second) transition period of active rest with no formal or structured workouts. For this example, the transition period lasts a month (from April 4 until May 1). The goal of the period is for the athlete to recuperate physically and psychologically from the long in-season. Recreational games and fitness activities include swimming, jogging, circuit weight training, volleyball, racquetball, and informal basketball. *All activities are performed at low intensities with low volumes.*

Off-Season

Following the postseason active rest period, the athlete should be rested and ready to begin off-season (preparatory period) training. For this example, this preparatory period lasts about 14 weeks, from the beginning of May to the beginning of August. The goal of this period is to establish a base level of conditioning to increase the athlete's tolerance for more intense training in later phases and periods. During the first week, testing should be performed so the strength and conditioning professional can determine initial training loads for the exercises in the first mesocycle. In later mesocycles, when more or other exercises are added, the training loads can be estimated from loads used in similar exercises or can be determined from RM testing. For example, the strength and conditioning professional can reasonably predict training load for the hang clean from the tested power clean maximum, or the actual RM load could be measured. Other monitoring tests related to basketball are shoulder and hip flexibility tests, 12-minute run, 300-yard (274 m) shuttle, line drill, T-test, vertical jump, and skinfold measurements.

The resistance training component holds higher priority in the off-season, and an athlete may follow a split routine of four or more training days per week. In this example, the basketball player begins the off-season with an all-body, three times per week regimen but soon progresses to four training days per week with variations in training intensity across the microcycle to allow fatigue to be managed. These advancements also involve a gradual increase in loading, with associated decreases in training volume. Other training includes aerobic endurance exercises to maintain or improve body composition and cardiovascular fitness. These conditioning workouts are scheduled on nonresistance training days, and flexibility training can be emphasized in the warm-up and cool-down portions of each training session.

Reviewing the Annual Plan Example

For any periodization model to function optimally, the sport coach and the strength and conditioning professional must plan the program together in order to share goals and strategies. This is a critical issue in that working together allows all the training factors that the athlete will engage in to be integrated so as to better manage the training stress and modulate fatigue and recovery. Without the cooperation of all involved professionals, optimal performance cannot be fully achieved.

The example in this chapter is a representation of only one periodization model that could be used to structure training for a sample athlete. Other athletes or sports may require subtle to radical variations in the structure presented here. It is important to remember that a multitude of periodization models can be adapted to meet the needs of the various athletes and sports.

CONCLUSION

Periodization is a process through which the athlete's training is logically and systematically organized in order to promote peak condition (preparedness) for the most important competitions. The annual training plan (year of training) is divided into macrocycles that contain preparatory, competition, and transition periods. Each period is subdivided into mesocycles that target specific phases of development: hypertrophy/strength endurance, basic strength, or strength/power. Transitions are used to link mesocycles or macrocycles and provide the athlete with an unloading period that enhances recovery. The overall structure of the macrocycle, mesocycle, and individual microcycles is dictated by the individual sport's competitive season and demands.

In-Season (Competitive Period)
Female college basketball center
5 months (20 weeks): November 21–April 3 (including tournament play)
(Beginning after an unloading week; November 15–21)

MESOCYCLE 1									
4 Weeks: November 22–December 19; Unload Week December 20–26									
				TRAINING LOADS					
Session	**Exercises**	**Sets**	**Reps**	**Week 1**	**Week 2**	**Week 3**	**Week 4**	**Week 5**	
1	High pull	1	4	75% 1RM	80% 1RM	85% 1RM	90% 1RM	60% 1RM	
	Back squat	1	6	80% 6RM	85% 6RM	90% 6RM	95% 6RM	65% 6RM	
	Incline bench press	1	6	80% 6RM	85% 6RM	90% 6RM	95% 6RM	65% 6RM	
	Lateral shoulder raise	1	10	75% 10RM	80% 10RM	85% 10RM	90% 10RM	70% 10RM	
	Abdominal crunch	Max in 60 s							
2	Push Press	1	6	70% 6RM	75% 6RM	80% 6RM	85% 6RM	60% 6RM	
	Hip sled	1	6	70% 6RM	75% 6RM	80% 6RM	85% 6RM	60% 6RM	
	Closed-grip bench press	1	6	70% 6RM	75% 6RM	80% 6RM	85% 6RM	60% 6RM	
	Seated low pulley row	1	6	70% 6RM	75% 6RM	80% 6RM	85% 6RM	60% 6RM	
	Supine leg raise	Max in 60 s							

MESOCYCLE 2									
4 Weeks: December 27–January 23; Unload Week January 24–30									
				TRAINING LOADS					
Session	**Exercises**	**Sets**	**Reps**	**Week 1**	**Week 2**	**Week 3**	**Week 4**	**Week 5**	
1	Hang clean	1	3	70% 1RM	75% 1RM	80% 1RM	85% 1RM	65% 1RM	
	Front squat	1	5	75% 5RM	80% 5RM	85% 5RM	90% 5RM	60% 5RM	
	Standing shoulder press	1	5	75% 5RM	80% 5RM	85% 5RM	90% 5RM	60% 5RM	
	Lying triceps extension	1	10	75% 10RM	80% 10RM	85% 10RM	90% 10RM	70% 10RM	
	Abdominal crunch	Max in 60 s							
2	Push jerk	1	3	65% 1RM	70% 1RM	75% 1RM	80% 1RM	60% 1RM	
	Step-up	1	5	70% 5RM	75% 5RM	80% 5RM	85% 1RM	60% 5RM	
	Closed-grip bench press	1	10	65% 10RM	70% 10RM	75% 10RM	80% 10RM	60% 10RM	
	Lat pull-down	1	10	65% 10RM	70% 10RM	75% 10RM	80% 10RM	60% 10RM	
	Supine leg raise	Max in 60 s							

MESOCYCLE 3								
4 Weeks: January 31–February 27; Unload Week February 28–March 6								
				TRAINING LOADS				
Session	**Exercises**	**Sets**	**Reps**	**Week 1**	**Week 2**	**Week 3**	**Week 4**	**Week 5**
1	Power clean	1	2	75% 1RM	80% 1RM	85% 1RM	90% 1RM	70% 1RM
	Back squat	1	4	75% 4RM	80% 4RM	85% 4RM	90% 4RM	65% 4RM
	Bench press	1	4	75% 4RM	80% 4RM	85% 4RM	90% 4RM	65% 4RM
	Barbell biceps curl	1	8	75% 8RM	80% 8RM	85% 8RM	90% 8RM	65% 8 RM
	Abdominal crunch	Max in 60 s						
2	Hang snatch	1	3	65% 1RM	70% 1RM	75% 1RM	80% 1RM	60% 1RM
	Forward step lunge	1	4	65% 4RM	70% 4RM	75% 4RM	80% 4RM	60% 4RM
	Closed-grip decline bench press	1	8	65% 8RM	70% 8RM	75% 8RM	80% 8RM	60% 8RM
	Upright row	1	8	65% 8RM	70% 8RM	75% 8RM	80% 8RM	60% 8RM
	Supine leg raise	Max in 60 s						

Tournament Mesocycle
4 Weeks: March 7–April 3

Go back to mesocycle 2; progress again to mesocycle 3 if tournament play extends beyond four weeks.

Comments:

▶ Each mesocycle is considered a block of training and contains five individual microcycles, with the fifth microcycle constituting an unloading microcycle.

▶ This in-season program incorporates a nonlinear approach with variations in volume-load, training intensity (kg), and targeted training exercises.

▶ Repetition maximum loads are not used, as training to failure has been shown to reduce power output and increase the risk of overtraining. Therefore, percentages of RM loads are used to deal with the accumulated fatigue associated with in-season training and competitions.

▶ It is important to note that these are the target sets and that three to five warm-up sets should be performed in order to provide an appropriate specific warm-up for the targeted loadings.

▶ Refer to Table 6.7 for the relationship between the %RM and the number of repetitions allowed and Table 6.8 for the estimation of 1RM.

▶ Refer to Table 6.12 for rest period length assignment based on repetition goal.

Tournament Week A (Two Games)						
Sunday	Monday	Tuesday	Wednesday	Thursday	Friday	Saturday
Practice (or rest)	Practice	Practice	Practice	Game	Practice	Game
	Resistance training		Plyometric session		Interval sprints	

Tournament Week B (Three Games)						
Sunday	Monday	Tuesday	Wednesday	Thursday	Friday	Saturday
Game	Practice (or rest)	Practice	Practice	Game	Practice	Game
		Resistance training			Interval sprints	

Off-Season (Preparation Period)
Female college basketball center
3 1/2 months (14 weeks): May 2–August 7

Initial Pretesting		
(For Mesocycle 1) Microcycle 1: May 2–8		
5RM Power Exercise	**10RM for Assistance Exercises**	**Other Testing**
1. Power clean	1. Leg (knee) curl	1. Sit and reach
	2. Lat pull-down	2. Shoulder elevation
	3. Biceps curl	3. 1.5-mile (2.4 km) run
	4. Lying triceps extension	4. 200-yard (274 m) shuttle run
	5. Upright row	5. Line drill
		6. T-test
		7. Vertical jump
		8. Body composition (skinfolds)
10RM FOR NONPOWER CORE EXERCISES		
1. Back squat 2. Bench press		

Mesocycle 1							
2 Weeks: May 9–22: Hypertrophy/Strength Endurance Phase 1							
		Week 1			**Week 2**		
Day	**Exercise**	**Sets**	**Reps**	**Intensity**	**Sets**	**Reps**	**Intensity**
Mon/Fri	Power clean	2	10/2*	65% 5RM	3	10/2*	70% 5RM
	Back squat	2	10	65% 10RM	3	10	70% 10RM
	Leg (knee) curl	2	10	65% 10RM	3	10	70% 10RM
	Bench press	2	10	65% 10RM	3	10	70% 10RM
	Lying triceps extension	2	10	65% 10RM	3	10	70% 10RM
	Upright row	2	10	65% 10RM	3	10	70% 10RM
	Abdominal crunch	2	20		3	20	
	Note: Friday workout should use a load 10% less than Monday's.						
Wed	Clean pull (floor)**	2	10	60% 5RM	3	10	65% 10RM
	Romanian deadlift**	2	10	60% 5RM	3	10	65% 10RM
	Lat pulldown	2	10	60% 10RM	3	10	65% 10RM
	Biceps curl	2	10	60% 10RM	3	10	65% 10RM
	Abdominal crunch	2	10		3	20	
*Performed as cluster sets with a 20-second rest between clusters of two repetitions. **Training loads are based on the 5RM power clean test.							

		Week 1			Week 2		
Day	**Exercise**	**Sets**	**Reps**	**Intensity**	**Sets**	**Reps**	**Intensity**
Mon/Fri	Power clean	3	5	80% 5RM	3	5	85% 5RM
	Back squat	3	5	80% 5RM	3	5	85% 5RM
	Leg (knee)curl	3	5	80% 5RM	3	5	85% 5RM
	Bench press	3	5	80% 5RM	3	5	85% 5RM
	Lying triceps extension	2	10	70% 10RM	3	10	75% 10RM
	Upright row	2	10	70% 10RM	2	10	75% 10RM
	Abdominal crunch	2	25		3	25	
	Note: Friday workout should use a load 10% less than Monday's.						
Wed	Clean pull (floor)**	3	5	85% 5RM	3	5	90% 5RM
	Romanian deadlift**	3	5	75% 5RM	3	5	80% 5RM
	Lat pulldown	2	10	70% 10RM	3	5	75% 10RM
	Barbell biceps curl	2	10	70% 10RM	3	5	75% 10RM
	Abdominal crunch	2	25		2	10	

Mesocycle 2
2 Weeks: May 23–June 5; Basic Strength Phase 1

**Training loads are based on the 5RM power clean test.

Day	**Exercise**	**Sets**	**Reps**	**Intensity**
Mon/Fri	Power clean	3	5	70% 5RM
	Back squat	3	5	70% 5RM
	Bench press	3	5	70% 5RM
	Abdominal crunch	3	20	
Wed	Clean pull (floor)**	3	5	70% 5RM
	Romanian deadlift	3	5	70% 5RM
	Lat pulldown	2	10	60% 10RM
	Abdominal crunch	3	20	

Unloading Week
1 Week: June 6-12

**Training loads are based on the 5RM power clean test.

Mesocycle 3 2 Weeks: June 13–26; Hypertrophy/Strength Endurance Phase 1							
		Week 1			**Week 2**		
Day	**Exercise**	**Sets**	**Reps**	**Intensity**	**Sets**	**Reps**	**Intensity**
Mon/Thurs	Hang snatch	3	10	55% 10RM	3	10	60% 10RM
	Back squat	3	10	70% 10RM	3	10	75% 10RM
	Incline bench press	3	10	70% 10RM	3	10	75% 10RM
	Lunge	3	10	70% 10RM	3	10	75% 10RM
	Leg (knee) curl	3	10	70% 10RM	3	10	75% 10RM
	Seated calf raise	3	10	70% 10RM	3	10	75% 10RM
	Note: Thursday workout should use a load 15% less than Monday's.						
Tues/Fri	Push jerk	3	10	60% 10RM	3	10	65% 10RM
	Clean pull (floor)**	3	10	65% 10RM	3	10	70% 10RM
	Bent-over row	3	10	65% 10RM	3	10	70% 10RM
	Shoulder press	3	10	65% 10RM	3	10	70% 10RM
	Barbell biceps curl	3	10	65% 10RM	3	10	70% 10RM
	Triceps pushdown	3	10	65% 10RM	3	10	70% 10RM
	Abdominal muscles	3	20		3	20	
	Note: Friday workout should use a load 10% less than Tuesday's.						
**Training loads are based on the power clean test.							

Mesocycle 4 2 Weeks: June 27–July 10: Basic Strength Phase 2							
		Week 1			**Week 2**		
Day	**Exercise**	**Sets**	**Reps**	**Intensity**	**Sets**	**Reps**	**Intensity**
Mon/Thurs	Hang snatch	4	5	80% 5RM	4	5	85% 5RM
	Back squat	3	5	80% 5RM	3	5	85% 5RM
	Incline bench press	3	5	80% 5RM	3	5	85% 5RM
	Lunge	3	6	80% 6RM	3	6	85% 6RM
	Leg (knee) curl	3	6	80% 6RM	3	6	85% 6RM
	Seated calf raise	3	6	80% 6RM	3	6	85% 6RM
	Note: Thursday workout should use a load 15% less than Monday's.						
Tues/Fri	Push jerk	4	5	75% 5RM	4	5	80% 5RM
	Clean pull (floor)**	3	5	75% 5RM	3	5	80% 5RM
	Bent-over row	3	6	75% 6RM	3	6	80% 6RM
	Shoulder press	3	6	75% 6RM	3	6	80% 6RM
	Barbell biceps curl	3	6	75% 6RM	3	6	80% 6RM
	Triceps pushdown	3	6	75% 6RM	3	6	80% 6RM
	Abdominal muscles	3	20		3	20	
	Note: Friday workout should use a load 10% less than Tuesday's.						
**Training loads are based on the power clean test.							

Unloading Week 1 Week: July 11–17				
Day	**Exercise**	**Sets**	**Reps**	**Intensity**
Mon/Tues	Hang snatch	4	5	70% 5RM
	Back squat	3	5	70% 5RM
	Abdominal muscles	3	20	
	Note: Tuesday workout should use a load 15% less than Monday's.			
Thurs/Fri	Push jerk	4	5	70% 5RM
	Clean pull (floor)**	3	5	70% 5RM
	Incline bench press	3	5	70% 5RM
	Shoulder press	3	5	70% 5RM
	Note: Friday workout should use a load 10% less than Thursday.			
**Training loads are based on the 5RM power clean test.				

Mesocycle 5 2 Weeks: July 18–31: Strength/Power Phase 1							
		Week 1			**Week 2**		
Day	**Exercise**	**Sets**	**Reps**	**Intensity**	**Sets**	**Reps**	**Intensity**
Mon/Thurs	Power clean	4	3	90% 3RM	4	3	95% 3RM
	Front squat	5	3	85% 3RM	5	3	90% 3RM
	Push jerk	4	3	85% 3RM	4	3	90% 3RM
	Bench press	5	3	85% 3RM	5	3	90% 3RM
	Hammer curl	2	6	80% 6RM	2	6	85% 6RM
	Lying triceps extension	2	6	80% 6RM	2	6	85% 6RM
	Standing calf (heel) raise	2	6	80% 6RM	2	6	85% 6RM
	Note: Thursday workout should use a load 15% less than Monday's.						
Tues/Fri	Hang snatch	4	3	80% 3RM	4	3	85% 3RM
	Clean pull (floor)	5	3	80% 3RM	5	3	85% 3RM
	Bent-over row	3	6	75% 6RM	3	6	80% 6RM
	Lat pull-down	3	6	85% 6RM	3	6	80% 6RM
	Romanian deadlift	3	6	75% 6RM	3	5	80% 6RM
	Abdominal muscles	3	20		3	20	
	Note: Friday workout should use a load 10% less than Tuesday's.						
**Training loads are based on the power clean test.							

Unloading Week 1 Week: August 1–7				
Day	**Exercise**	**Sets**	**Reps**	**Intensity**
Mon/Tues	Hang snatch	4	3	70% 3RM
	Back squat	5	3	70% 3RM
	Abdominal muscles	3	20	
	Note: Tuesday workout should use a load 15% less than Monday's.			
Thurs/Fri	Push jerk	4	3	70% 3RM
	Clean pull (floor)**	5	3	70% 3RM
	Incline bench press	5	3	70% 3RM
	Note: Friday workout should use a load 10% less than Thursday's.			
**Training loads are based on the 5RM power clean test.				

Posttesting (Before In-Season) Microcycle: August 8–14		
1RM Power Exercise	**1RM for Nonpower Core Exercises**	**Other Testing**
1. Power clean 2. Hang snatch 3. Push jerk 4. Push press	1. Back squat 2. Front squat 3. Bench press	1. Sit and reach 2. Shoulder elevation 3. 1.5-mile (2.4 km) run 4. 200-yard (274 m) shuttle run 5. Line drill 6. T-test 7. Vertical jump 8. Body composition (skinfolds)
Other exercises to test based on in-season program		

Comments:

▶ This in-season program incorporates a nonlinear approach with variations in volume-load, training intensity (kg), and targeted training exercises.

▶ Repetition maximum loads are not used, as training to failure has been shown to reduce power output and increase the risk of overtraining. Therefore percentages of RM loads are used to deal with the accumulated fatigue associated with in-season training and competitions.

▶ It is important to note that these are the target sets and that three to five warm-up sets should be performed in order to provide an appropriate specific warm-up for the targeted loadings.

▶ Refer to Table 6.7 for the relationship between the %RM and the number of repetitions allowed and Table 6.8 for the estimation of 1RM.

▶ Refer to Table 6.12 for rest period length assignment based on repetition goal.

CHAPTER 8

Exercise Prescription for Improving Body Composition

©Luis Louro/Shutterstock.com

OVERVIEW

What Is the Definition of "Obesity"?

When considering obesity, a good starting point is to re-visit the relevant information given in Chapter 3. The Centers for Disease Control and Prevention (CDC) define obesity as "weight that is higher than what is considered as a healthy weight for a given height" (http://www.cdc.gov/obesity/adult/defining.html). This commonsense definition is operationalized as a body mass index (BMI) $\geq$ 30 kg·m^2 where "normal" is defined as a BMI between 18.5 and 24.9 kg/m^2. People in-between these values are considered "overweight." This definition is based on numerous large-scale studies finding an increased risk of premature death in people with a BMI above 25 kg/m^2 (Aune et al. 2016; Cohen et al. 2014; de Gonzalez et al. 2010).

With rare exception (Flegal et al. 2013), virtually all studies suggest a BMI above 30 or 35 kg·m^2 is associated with an increased risk of dying prematurely. But not all research suggests that everyone with a BMI >25 kg/m^2 is at an unhealthy weight. For example, a finding in other studies of large groups of people is that "overweight," or having a BMI of 25 to 29.9 kg·m^2, is not associated with an increased risk of premature death (Finkelstein et al. 2010; Flegal et al. 2013; McGee et al. 2005;

Yi et al. 2015). Moreover, being overweight is associated with *better* health outcomes in some clinical populations, such as survivors of an acute cardiac event (Lamelas et al. 2017). Consequently, defining a healthy weight as a BMI of 18.5 to 24.9 kg·m² may be unrealistically conservative.

The Academy of Nutrition and Dietetics makes it clear that the key issue is the extent to which this excess weight is due to excess body fat (http://www.eatright.org/resource/health/weight-loss/overweight-and-obesity/obesity). In other words, body *weight* is not the concern, but body *fatness* is. Consequently, the CDC clarifies their statement by adding, "At an individual level, BMI can be used as a screening tool but is not diagnostic of the body fatness or the health of an individual. A trained health-care provider should perform appropriate health assessments in order to evaluate an individual's health status and risks."

This statement, and probably the contradictory findings from the aforementioned studies, emanates from the fact that BMI is an imperfect measure of body composition. For example, when 8,550 men were classified as obese based on either a BMI $\geq$ 30 kg·m² or a body fat > 25 percent, the BMI criteria incorrectly classified 2,105 of the men as either normal weight when they were actually obese or obese when they were actually normal weight (Romero-Corral et al. 2008). The comparison of BMI to body fat percentage was especially problematic for men with a BMI of 25 of 29.9, who would be classified as overweight by BMI. However, almost everyone who was classified as obese based on a BMI $\geq$ 35 kg·m² were also classified as obese based on their body composition. Elsewhere, in a study of almost 12,000 adults, the correlation between BMI and body fat cutoffs for obesity was 0.71 and 0.87 for men and women, respectively (Flegal and Graubard 2009). The body fat percentage that was associated with a BMI $\geq$ 30 kg·m² was 26.5% and 37.9% for men and women, respectively, in this study.

These values support the common body composition-oriented definitions of obesity as being >25% body fat in men and >35% in women (Bray, Bouchard, and James 1998; Romero-Corral et al. 2008). These criteria are typically viewed as representing 10% more body fat than is desired in men and women. In other words, a reasonable desired body fatness for adult men and women is 15% and 25%, respectively.

For an additional perspective of how BMI relates to percent body fatness, one study compared BMI to dual energy X-ray absorptiometry (a gold standard measure of body composition) in over 2,500 adults (Pasco et al. 2012). They found that BMI was best related to body fat mass (kg of body fat) and imperfectly related to body composition (percent body fat). This was mostly due to differences in muscularity and bone mineral content among the subjects. The male subjects tended to be more muscular so BMI overestimated their "fatness" compared to the female subjects. Compared to the younger subjects, the older subjects were both less muscular and had less bone mineral so BMI underestimated their "fatness." However, the combination of BMI, gender, and age explained over 82 percent of the variability in percent body fat.

Clearly, a very high BMI likely means a high body fatness but the association is less certain when a client is in the overweight category. Unfortunately, accurately assessing body composition can be quite challenging (Cornier et al. 2011). So how should you proceed in assessing whether your client has an unhealthy amount of body fat? In a typical health/fitness facility, some people will be heavier because they are muscular rather than being overfat. In this setting, using a BMI of 25 or even 30 as the cutoff for identifying obese individuals may not be accurate enough. Nevertheless, except for very dedicated bodybuilders or weight lifters, rarely will a client be more than thirty or forty pounds "overmuscled." Recall that a five unit difference in BMI reflects a difference of thirty to thirty-five pounds for average height people. Consequently, someone with a BMI $\geq$ 35 kg·m² is almost certainly obese since they will likely weigh at least sixty pounds more than they would at a BMI of 25. In this case, there is no need to assess their body composition since BMI is sufficient to categorize them as obese. However, if their BMI is less than 35, then it may be unclear as to whether they have a healthy body composition. This is due to uncertainty regarding how much of this excess weight is muscle and how much is fat. In this case, assessing the client's body composition rather than just BMI would be desired. This will help guide you in determining if the client had an unhealthy amount of body fat. If the client was >25% body fat (if male) or >35% body fat (if female), then they could be considered obese. These recommendations are summarized in Table 8.1.

TABLE 8.1
How to Identify If a Client Is Obese and Estimate a Goal Weight

Step 1: Determine the client's BMI. This is calculated as the quotient of weight in kilograms and height in meters squared (kg/m^2). The conversion for pounds to kilograms is 1 lb = 0.4536 kg and for inches to meters is 1 in = 0.0254 m.

Step 2: If the BMI is $\geq$ 35 kg·m², then you do not need to do anything else—the client very likely has an unhealthy amount of body fat. However, you can estimate an intermediate goal body weight for the client using a goal BMI of 30 (goal weight ~ 30 × ht²) or 25 (25 × ht²). Once they achieve this goal BMI, then you can proceed to the next step, if desired. Regardless, using BMI to estimate goal weight is less accurate than that described in Step 3.

Step 3: If the client's BMI is >25 but <35 kg·m², then consider determining the client's body composition. (Note: You need not determine BMI if your client's body composition has been assessed.) If the client's body fat percentage is >15% or >25%, if male or female, respectively, then you can estimate a desired body weight using these percentages as goals. You could use a different percentage if the client has a different goal in mind.

Example: A 45-year-old male client is 5'10" (70") tall and weighs 220 pounds.

    1.   Determine the client's BMI.

$$70'' \times 0.0254 = 1.778 \text{ m and } 220 \text{ lbs} \times 0.4536 = 99.79 \text{ kg}$$
$$\text{BMI} = 99.79/1.778^2 = 99.79/3.1612 = 31.6 \text{ kg·m}^2$$

    2.   The client's BMI is $\geq$30 kg·m² so determine an intermediate goal weight.

$$\text{BMI of 30} = 30 \times \text{ht}^2 = 30 \times 3.1612 = 94.8 \text{ kg}$$

[You can also use this method to estimate the client's goal weight. At a BMI of 25, this client would weigh 79.0 kg (25 × 3.1612 = 79.0 kg)].

    3.   Suppose this client's body composition was determined to be 28% body fat*. What would he weigh if he achieved 15% body fat?

Fat Weight	=	percent body fat × total body weight
	=	0.28 × 99.79 kg
	=	27.94 kg
Fat-Free Weight	=	total body weight – fat weight
	=	99.79 – 27.94
	=	71.85 kg
Goal weight	=	Fat-Free Weight/(1-goal body fat)
	=	71.85/(1 – .15)
	=	71.85/0.85
	=	84.5 kg

* Again, if you know your client's body composition, then you do not need to determine BMI. Body composition is a more accurate estimate of fatness than is BMI.

What Are the Concerns with Having Too Much Body Fat?

Physical Costs

The number of people who are obese, defined as a BMI $\geq$ 30 kg·m², in the United States is staggering. Almost 40 percent of adults are in this category (Hales et al. 2017). About 12 percent of adults have a BMI $\geq$35 (Nichols et al. 2017), which you now know equates to being about 60 or 70 pounds heavier than if their BMI was 25. Over 7 percent of adults have a BMI $\geq$40 (Hales et al. 2018; Nichols et al. 2017) which equates to about 100 pounds overweight. Obesity has significant health implications (Table 8.2). In two very large studies (one assessed 900,000 people and the other 1.46 million), each 5 unit increase in BMI was associated with at least a 30 percent higher overall mortality over the next ten to thirteen years (de Gonzalez et al. 2010; Prospective Studies Collaboration 2009). This increased risk begins in one's youth in that teenagers who are overweight or obese have as much as a fourfold higher risk of dying from cardiovascular disease as middle-age adults (Twig et al. 2016)! While the criterion of what is considered a healthy weight (i.e., BMI <25 versus BMI < 30 kg·m²) is debatable, a consistent finding is that a BMI >35 kg·m² is associated with negative health effects. At eighteen years of age, a white person with a BMI above 35 will likely die about four to five years earlier than someone with a BMI in the normal range (Finkelstein et al. 2010). A black person this age will likely die one to three years earlier.

There are a number of mechanisms by which excess body fatness contributes to an increased risk for dying. It appears to be a major contributor to a variety of noncommunicable diseases with cardiovascular diseases (CVD) being the most common cause of death. Recall from Chapter 3 that obesity directly contributes to CVD risk via an increased pro-inflammatory vascular environment. It also contributes indirectly by increasing the risk for developing several multiple risk factors for CVD, such as hypertension, dyslipidemia, and hypertension, as well as increasing the negative impact of these other risk factors. In general, the prevalence of risk factors is relatively high in normal weight

---

TABLE 8.2
Medical Complications Associated with Obesity

Asthma/reactive airway disease
Cardiovascular disease and cardiovascular disease mortality
Depression
Diabetes risk, metabolic syndrome, and prediabetes
Dyslipidemia
Female infertility
Gastroesophageal reflux disease (GERD)
Hypertension
Male hypogonadism
Metabolic syndrome
Nonalcoholic fatty liver disease/nonalcoholic steatohepatitis
Obstructive sleep apnea
Osteoarthritis
Polycystic ovary syndrome (PCOS)
Type 2 diabetes, prediabetes
Urinary stress incontinence

From Garvey et al (2016).

populations but increases in a stepwise manner in overweight and obese populations (Saydah et al. 2014). At least three times as many obese adults have three or more CVD risk factors than do normal weight adults.

Besides the health concerns of CVD, obesity raises the risk for other diseases such as gallbladder disease, osteoarthritis, sleep apnea, and some cancers (Jensen et al. 2014; U.S. Department of Health and Human Services 2013). The incidence of some of these health concerns is increasing; for example, the risk of developing a number of obesity-related cancers is increasing in younger adults and the increase is steeper in younger generations (Sung et al. 2019). The net effect is that, regardless of the mechanisms, obesity is associated with an increased risk of dying from any cause. Because so many Americans are obese, it contributes substantially to the relatively low life expectancy seen in the US compared to other high-income countries (Preston and Stokes 2011).

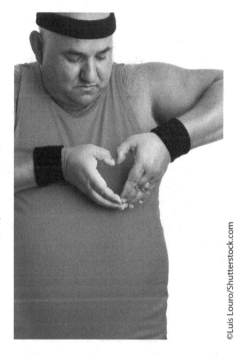

©Luis Louro/Shutterstock.com

Of course, there is more to life than simply not being dead, meaning quality of life rather than quantity of live. For a number of reasons, living with excess body fat can be challenging. First, obesity can affect a person's health-related quality of life with the most pronounced negative impacts being related to physical functioning and overall general health (Fontaine and Barofsky 2001; Kolotkin and Anderson 2017; Slagter et al. 2015). This negative effect becomes more pronounced as people become heavier and may (Pan et al. 2014) or may not (Kolotkin and Anderson 2017) improve with weight loss. Second, when an obese individual becomes ill, health care costs will likely be higher. Compared to normal weight individuals, ill obese patients typically have 46 percent greater inpatient costs, 27 percent more outpatient costs and physician visits, and 80 percent more prescription costs (Finkelstein et al. 2009). These researchers estimated that the medical care costs of obesity in the United States were over $145 billion. Others suggest that the costs associated with being obese range from $28,000 to $36,000 over the lifetime of the person (Fallah-Fini et al. 2017).

Third, besides these increased health care and "life costs," some evidence suggests that being excessively heavy may be associated with a lower income. For women, obesity is associated with living closer to the poverty level in the United States (Ogden et al. 2010). This may be partly due to differences in education, in that women with college degrees are less likely to be obese than women without. This trend was not seen in men. However, some evidence suggests that the social "penalty" incurred in an obese teenage boy may affect his income when he becomes an adult. One study found that adults who were obese as teenagers earned 17 percent less compared to their normal weight peers, partly by having developed fewer "non-cognitive" skills such as motivation, self-confidence, and persistence and partly by more likely working in lower-paid occupations (Lundborg, Nystedt, and Rooth 2014). Fourth, assessment of genetic markers of aging suggests that being obese is associated with accelerated aging (Kim et al. 2009). Finally, excessive weight gain is associated with an increased risk for developing Alzheimer's disease (Beydoun et al. 2008). Collectively, the take-home message from all these studies is that obesity increases the risk of dying prematurely, but can also make living one's life more challenging than it need be.

Psychological Costs

An important, and often overlooked, challenge of being considered too heavy is the mental stress associated with it. While varying in magnitude, the prejudices, discrimination, negative attitudes, and unconscious bias associated with fat stigmas can be found around the world (Brewis et al. 2011). It is more socially acceptable, severe, and in some cases more prevalent than racism and sexism (Puhl and Heuer 2009). The microaggressions associated with weight, such as microinsults ("You don't look fat in that outfit"), microinvalidations ("They didn't mean it that way"), or microassaults ("Fat people have no willpower") are very real (Munro 2017).

Discrimination and biases may partially explain the lower salaries and differences in educational attainment often seen in people with obesity (Puhl and Heuer 2009). Negative stereotypes also affect interpersonal relationships with family, friends, and romantic partners (Puhl and Heuer 2009). This stereotyping extends even into health care. Health-care providers may view heavy patients as being less likely to adhere to the recommended treatment, may be treated with less respect, may be given less time by the provider, and the provider may over-attribute symptoms and problems to obesity rather than pursuing more diagnostic testing (Phelan et al. 2015). One obesity specialist summarized this by saying, "There is not a single patient with significant obesity who has not experienced weight bias, whether it's comments from doctors or nurses, the way waiting rooms are set up, or privacy issues. . . . Weight bias is ubiquitous in society as a whole. Doctors are part of society" (Rubin 2019).

The stresses associated with being perceived as "fat" can negatively affect a heavy person, both biologically and psychologically. The physiological responses to the chronic stress of this stigmatization can include an increased release of cortisol which promotes eating and abdominal fat deposition. Moreover, the stress-associated release of dopamine may make a person more prone to engage in reward-seeking behaviors, such as eating comfort foods, even when the person feels guilty about doing so (Tomiyama 2019). Stress can also undermine the cognitive processes associated with a person's ability to self-regulate their eating and choosing to be physically active. It can even affect sleep quality in that short sleep duration is associated with an increased BMI (Patel and Hu 2008). In other words, the stresses associated with being perceived as "fat" can make it even more challenging to engage in the behaviors needed to be healthy!

Part of this stigmatization is as simple as the words used to describe a person's weight (Meadows and Danielsdóttir 2016). "Obesity" is commonly used but, because the American Medical Association declared obesity a disease in 2013, this term has medical connotations. And, as will be discussed in the next section of this book, a heavy person can certainly be healthy. "Person with obesity" arose due to the use of "person with (disability)" terminology among disability advocates. But heavy people are not disabled. "Heavy" or "overweight" or "higher weight" are typically considered to be the most acceptable, or the least offensive, terms to most people with a high BMI. "Fat" has historically been viewed as the most offensive term to use, especially among heavy people. However, members of the fat acceptance movement increasingly prefer this term. It is hoped that this term will help normalize the perception of weight, in the same way that "short" is simply a description of one's height, rather than a pejorative term loaded with other meanings. "Fat" may also be viewed as a term of empowerment and self-respect, in the same way that historically negative terms to describe one's sexual orientation have been embraced by members of the LGBTQ+ communities (Meadows and Danielsdóttir 2016). On the other hand, "fat" has yet to gain widespread acceptance among the broader community of heavy people and, for most people, is still a very negative term.

As can be seen by the number of different terms used in this chapter, it is not at all clear which term is the most acceptable. ("Obese" or "obesity" are used the most in this chapter because the focus in this chapter is primarily on the negative health aspects of too much body fat.) The important point here is that, when working with a client who wants to lose weight, be very mindful of how and what you say. One technique is to listen carefully to how the client describes their body and mirror that terminology. For example, if a client says they are "heavy," then use that term when discussing their weight.

Is it all bad?

As described here, there are a number of health risks associated with having too much body fat. However, simply saying "a BMI ≥ 30 kg/m² is a health risk" is too simplistic. There are several mitigating factors that can markedly reduce, if not eliminate, this risk. First, as mentioned previously, a number of studies suggest that mild obesity is not strongly associated with an increased risk of premature death. Up to a BMI of 30 or perhaps even 35, the risk is not markedly different from people in the normal weight category (Flegal et al. 2005; Flegal et al. 2013). Second, where the excess body fat is located may affect the overall risk associated with obesity. Several studies suggest that high levels of visceral fat are more worrisome than high levels of fat carried elsewhere (Bastien et al. 2014; Després 2012). Someone who is obese and apple-shaped, meaning they have a significant quantity of visceral fat, may have a greater risk for cardiovascular diseases than someone who is equally obese but pear-shaped, or carrying their fat more on their hips (Figure 8.1). This risk extends to normal weight people, too, in that people with a normal BMI but central obesity have a higher risk of dying than people who were "just" overweight or obese (Sahkyan et al. 2015).

Third, for many years, the effects that physical fitness has in offsetting the negative health effects of obesity have been largely overlooked. Only recently has the "fit but fat" concept been appreciated. Recent evidence strongly suggests that individuals who are fit but have a high BMI do not have a markedly higher risk of dying than individuals who are fit but normal weight (Barry et al. 2014; Figure 8.2). Moreover, fit-fat individuals have a lower risk of dying than unfit-normal weight peers (Ortega et al. 2016). Parenthetically, this may be because, for the same BMI, fitter people tend to have less body fat (Janssen et al. 2004). Unfortunately, relatively few obese individuals are actually fit—only about 9–20 percent of obese Americans can be considered as fit (Duncan 2010; Ortega et al. 2016).

Moreover, the protective benefits of being "fit but fat" apply most to obese individuals who are metabolically healthy, meaning they do not have any other substantive modifiable risk factors for CVD (Ortega et al. 2013). In heavy people, the positive effects of being fit cannot fully offset the negative effects of CVD risk factors. These protective benefits are markedly reduced if the client also has CVD risk factors. Recognize, too, that not all relevant research supports the "fit but fat" finding.

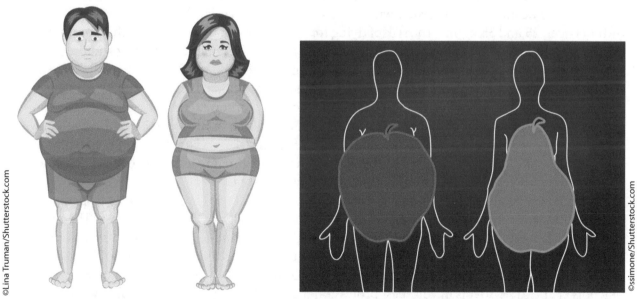

Figure 8.1 Differences in Fat Distribution or "the Apple vs. the Pear."

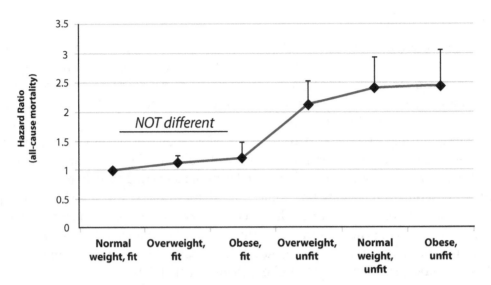

Figure 8.2   Comparison of the Risk of Dying in 92,986 Subjects across 10 Studies Where Fitness Was Measured. Data from Barry et al. 2014.

A study of 1.3 million men found that the fit, obese men had a lower risk of death than the unfit, obese men. Here, all the obese men were at higher risk of dying than the more normal weight men, regardless of how fit they were (Högström et al. 2015). Recognize that this study did not account for most CVD risk factors and there were marked differences in how fitness was measured between this study and those that found fitness benefits. Substantial evidence is beginning to emerge in support of the "fit but fat" concept, but it has yet to be universally accepted.

These controversies notwithstanding, there are a number of take-home messages. First, having an excessive amount of body fat is unhealthy. It can have a negative effect on a person's life span, or their quantity of life. It can have a negative effect on how well they are able to live their life, or their quality of life. These can result in financial and non-financial costs, both to the individual and to the public. Because obesity is at epidemic levels in the United States, these costs are substantial. Second, more and more research supports the concept of fit-and-fat. Being physically fit mitigates many, but not all, of the health risks associated with a high BMI. This is certainly the case for people with a BMI between 25 and 35 kg/m². The risk of dying for fit-and-fat people is less than that for unfit-and-normal weight people. Not enough research has been performed to either support or refute the concept of fit-but-fat in people with a higher BMI. Third, in people who are fit-but-fat *and* have no other risk factors for CVD, there does not appear to be substantive health risks associated with their high BMI. "Fatness" is not a health risk in people who meet these criteria. Fourth, defining what constitutes an "excessive amount of body fat" is more complicated than "a BMI ≥ 30 kg/m²." A person with a BMI ≥ 35 kg/m² almost certainly has an increased health risk compared to someone with a BMI < 25. Yet the risks for people with a BMI between 25 and 35 kg/m² are less clear-cut. As described in this paragraph, it very likely depends on the individual's lifestyle.

Fortunately, as a health/fitness professional, you are in an ideal position to help people with an unhealthy amount of body fat. Moreover, you will never lack for potential clients. The research supports the notion that emphasizing lifestyle changes that reduce CVD risk factors and increase physical fitness will, for all intents and purposes, neutralize the major health risks of having a BMI between 25 and 35 kg/m². Over 80 percent of people with a BMI ≥ 25 are in this range of BMI (Nichols et al. 2017). So it is in your best professional interests to become comfortable working with, and being helpful to, clients with an unhealthy amount of body fat. Methods for doing so will be discussed in the next section.

HELPING YOUR CLIENT TO LOSE WEIGHT: TREATING OBESITY

The rest of this chapter is devoted to providing you with guidance on how to help a client be successful at losing weight. The assumption is that your client has an *unhealthy* amount of body fat, which is the crux of what obesity is. Most people become unhealthily fat because of inappropriate physical activity behaviors, inappropriate eating behaviors, or both. Consequently, it is reasonable to focus on these behaviors as important components of any weight loss program. However, recall that in fit-but-fat individuals without any other CVD risk factors, their "fatness" is *not* a health risk if their BMI is < 35 kg/m² or so. And recall from earlier chapters that most of the modifiable CVD risk factors are improved with appropriate physical activity and eating behaviors. In other words, when working with a heavy client, the emphasis should be on helping them be successful at adopting these behaviors. Doing so is far, far more important to their overall health than is losing a few pounds.

Furthermore, eating healthy and being physically active are foundational factors underlying how weight loss is maintained. Consider the participants in the National Weight Control Registry (www. nwcr.ws). To join, a person must have lost at least thirty pounds and kept it off for at least one year. Not surprisingly, almost all the participants modified their eating and exercise behaviors to lose weight—but how they did so was quite variable. On the other hand, the successful weight-loss-maintainers, meaning those who lost at least 10 percent of their body weight and kept it off for at least ten years, consistently did the following: They engaged in high levels of physical activity (~1 hr/day), ate a low calorie and low fat diet, had high levels of restraint (being consistent in eating across weekdays and weekends), low levels of disinhibition (practiced self-control when eating), and also weighed themselves several times a week. The weight non-maintainers did not follow these guidelines as well (Thomas et al. 2014). The non-maintainers generally were mindful about their eating habits. However, the biggest long-term difference between weight maintainers and non-maintainers was the ~30 percent greater amount of daily physical activity performed by the maintainers (Ostendorf et al. 2019). The point here is that the lifestyle behaviors that are critical to reducing anyone's risk for CVD, and most other chronic diseases, happen to be the same ones important to losing weight. So even if your client does *not* lose any weight at all, they will be much healthier if they eat appropriately and are physically active.

There are a multitude of factors underlying why a person gains too much weight; this multitude of factors is also why losing weight can be so difficult. Some of these factors are societal but they may influence individual choices in subtle ways (Table 8.3). Socio-economic factors, such as not having ready access to high quality foods due to no neighborhood grocery stores, and environmental factors, such as not having ready access to safe exercise venues, can play a role. A person may like to eat fried foods because they grew up in a society where fried foods were viewed as "comfort foods." They may be too tired to exercise when they get home from work because they have an hour-long commute in congested traffic. They may not view a high BMI as worrisome because of their cultural or racial/ethnic background. Or if they do try to lose weight, they may not have much social support because their friends do not understand, or value, the health risks associated with being obese (Caprio et al. 2008).

Other, intrinsic, individual factors can also play a role. A commonly cited one is having a genetic predisposition to obesity (Bouchard 2007). Statistically, children of two obese parents have an 80 percent likelihood of becoming obese compared to a 15 percent likelihood if both parents are normal weight. However, children of obese parents are not "doomed" to become obese—it means that they are more likely to become obese if their lifestyle is obesogenic. On the other hand, genetics also play a role in how successful a weight loss program may be (Bouchard and Tremblay 1997); some clients will be more biologically "resistant" to weight loss than other clients. A second factor is the client's metabolism; in general, men have a slightly higher resting metabolic rate (RMR) than

TABLE 8.3 A Social-Ecological Framework for Eating and Activity Decisions	
Component (examples)	**Definition**
Social and Cultural Norms and Values (preferences for certain foods, what is viewed as an acceptable weight or body shape, or desirable activities)	Rules that govern thoughts, beliefs, and behaviors; shared assumptions of appropriate behaviors, based on the values of a society
Sectors (access to healthy foods or parks, time allotted for PE in schools, what is promoted as "beautiful" in the media)	Systems (such as governments, health care), organizations (e.g., public health, community) and businesses and industries (retail, media, entertainment)
Settings (at home, schools, worksites, child care, restaurants)	Where choices may be made, at home or away. Settings can influence individual choices and social norms and values.
Individual Factors (age, sex, socioeconomic status, race/ethnicity, knowledge and skills, psychosocial factors, food choices, genetics)	Factors that are unique to the person and which can affect healthy choices. Individual choices are affected by Social and Cultural Norms and Values, Sectors, and Settings.
Adapted from the 2015–2020 Dietary Guidelines for Americans (USDHHS 2015).	

women. RMR typically becomes lower as people age and it tends to be lower in overweight and obese than in normal weight adults (McMurray et al. 2014). This is important since, for most people, their RMR comprises 60–75 percent of their daily energy expenditure. A third factor is that, over the past fifty years, there have been substantial declines in the number of people engaged in physically demanding occupations. Since the workday makes up a large portion of most people's waking hours, this relatively low work-related energy expenditure may have contributed markedly to the obesity epidemic (Church et al. 2011). Again, while a multitude of factors can exacerbate the challenges of attempting to achieve a desired body weight, they do so by making it difficult to achieve the desired balance between caloric intake and caloric expenditure. *This balance is the key to successful weight loss* (Bond et al. 2009).

Consequently, when working with a client who wants to lose weight, you will likely help them modify their physical activity habits and, perhaps, modify their dietary practices. Doing both is more effective than doing either (Clark 2015). Most experts recommend that a client lose no more than one to two pounds per week. Consequently, the thinking is typically that, since a pound of fat is about 3,500 kcals of energy, then losing a pound per week requires a negative caloric balance of 500 calories per day (3,500 kcals/7 days per week = 500 calories per day). While that is mathematically correct, the weight loss outcome for a client can be dramatically different than what is expected (Bouchard and Tremblay 1997). In other words, a negative caloric balance of 500 calories per day will not elicit a weight loss of one pound each week in every client.

Therefore, it is critically important that you work with your client to focus on the behavior changes associated with becoming more physically active and eating a more appropriate diet rather than the outcome of weight loss. Here's why this shift in thinking is important: losing weight is challenging for most people in the long-term. Furthermore, there is substantial variability in how much weight will be lost when different people follow similar weight loss programs. The important point here is that some clients will have relatively modest, or little, success in losing weight even if they do "everything right" by modifying their eating and exercise behaviors appropriately.

Regardless of the underlying mechanisms, clients who are unsuccessful at losing weight will likely become frustrated—and understandably so! If they do not see success in their weight loss efforts (i.e., the number on their scale), they may be more likely to quit the behavior changes. Recall that CVD is the leading cause of death in the obese population. Recall also how critically important lifestyle changes are to reducing the risk for CVD and, other than not using tobacco, regular physical activity and healthy eating practices are the most important. Again, considerable evidence suggests that obese subjects who are "fit but fat" and <u>do not have</u> other CVD risk factors do not have a markedly increased risk of dying from CVD compared to normal weight subjects. Consequently, even if your client is unsuccessful at losing weight, they will become markedly healthier and have a lower risk for dying by having become more physically active and eating healthier. Therefore, keep the focus on the latter and not the former.

THE "P" AND "L" OF CRIPL: HELPING YOUR CLIENT LOSE WEIGHT WITH LIFESTYLE CHANGES

Before You Begin

Talk to your client to determine *why* they are motivated to lose weight. Why is being thinner their goal? Is it because they want to be healthier? Reduce their risk for diabetes or hypertension? Have more energy when they get home from work? Be able to go on a weekend bike ride or a hike? Have more mobility so "getting around" is easier? Talk to your client to ascertain if (1) it is the weight loss that will enable them to achieve their goals or (2) it is the methods by which they lose weight, meaning being more active and eating healthy, that will enable them to achieve these goals.

For many clients, their motivation to lose weight is tangentially related to their body weight; their long-term goal may be more about being healthier even if their focus is on weight loss. In this case, the very positive news you can give your client is that they can accomplish their goals without having to focus on weight loss at all. For many health/fitness professionals and their clients, this notion is somewhat radical—the client does *not* need to "normalize" their weight in order to be healthy. However, as described in previous sections of this chapter, this concept is increasingly supported by high quality research. Moreover, it is gaining popular support with the Health at Every Size paradigm (for more information, do an online search for "health at every size," currently at https://haescommunity.com/). The tenets of the HAES movement are in Table 8.4.

TABLE 8.4
Components of the Health at Every Size Paradigm
Respect   ► Celebrates body diversity   ► Honors differences in size, age, race, ethnicity, gender, dis/ability, sexual orientation, religion, class, and other human attributes
Critical Awareness   ► Challenges scientific and cultural assumptions   ► Values body knowledge and people's lived experiences
Compassionate Self-Care   ► Finding the joy in moving one's body and being physically active   ► Eating in a flexible and attuned manner that values pleasure and honors internal cues of hunger, satiety, and appetite, while respecting the social conditions that frame eating options
From https://haescommunity.com/pledge/

Many clients will find that changing their focus from "having to diet and work out to lose weight" to "choosing to eat healthier and being more active" to be a much more positive experience for them. The latter is *achievable* for anyone—they just have to do it. On the other hand, the *former* may not occur—even if your client is doing all that they should, the number on their scale may not change. As alluded to earlier, for reasons outside the client's control, such as their genetics, they may not be successful at losing weight even when they are diligent in eating healthy and being active.

Nevertheless, for some clients, weight loss *is* their goal. They may understand the concepts of "fit and fat" and "healthy at every size." But they may also have grown weary of being stigmatized about their weight, want to reduce the pain from knee osteoarthritis (Messier et al. 2018), or have another health condition that may improve with weight loss *per se* (Table 8.2; Garvey et al. 2016). If weight loss is truly your client's goal, then recognize that assisting them in their efforts requires a team approach. One member of this team is the client's primary health care provider (PCP). Because obesity is often associated with other comorbidities, such as hypertension, diabetes and sleep apnea, it is important that the PCP be aware of these weight loss efforts. Consequently, it is important that your client get approval and input from their PCP before beginning. Fortunately, PCPs are also strongly encouraged to emphasize lifestyle changes as part of working with obese patients in their weight loss efforts (Garvey et al. 2016; Jensen et al. 2014; Kushner 2003).

A second member of the team should be a registered dietitian nutritionist (RDN). In much the same way that you will have the training needed to become expert at developing exercise programs for clients, an RDN has the requisite training and expertise needed to make an in-depth nutrition assessment, diagnosis, and treatment plan for making dietary changes. When it comes to helping a client modify their eating behaviors, the skill set of an RDN surpasses yours. To go into professional practice, RDNs earn an appropriate bachelor's degree, complete a 1,200-hour dietetic internship, pass a national examination, and in most states are also licensed. For perspective, none of these types of experiences are required to work in a health/fitness facility; anyone can call himself a "health/fitness professional" regardless of their actual qualifications. As a health/fitness professional, you can ethically provide general nonmedical nutrition information to a client; however, you are committing malpractice if you give specific dietary advice to a client. It is analogous to practicing medicine without a license. Consequently, it is important that you have an RDN to work with. You can find RDNs in your geographic area with an internet search using the term "find an RDN" (currently at http://www.eatright.org/find-an-expert). You are encouraged to interview several RDNs to identify the ones that have similar professional philosophies as you.

Once your team has been assembled and your client has been given approval by their PCP, you can begin more overtly working with them.

Working with Your Client

Recall that you are striving to help your client change their behaviors. The recommendations made to PCPs for doing so are good guidelines to follow (Kushner 2003). Here, the first step is to assess your client's readiness to make the behavior change of becoming more physically active, or eating healthier, or both. This step is important to do so you do not waste your time working with a client who is not ready. This also ensures that the client does not become frustrated with their inevitable failure to lose weight.

The fact that your client is talking to you about losing weight suggests they are ready; however, "talk is cheap." Therefore, probe for this level of readiness in more detail. One simple method is to ask the client two questions, "On a scale from 0 to 10, with 0 being not important and 10 being very important, how important is it for you to lose weight at this time?" followed by asking,

"Also, on a scale from 0 to 10, with 0 being not confident and 10 being very confident, how confident are you that you can lose weight at this time?" (Kushner 2003). If their responses are on the low side, say a 4 or 5, you can follow up by asking them what it would take to move these scores up to 8 or more. Clients that have a goal that is important to them and have high self-efficacy are well-situated to be diligent in their efforts to achieve their goal.

You can also follow up by asking questions related to the following characteristics of clients who are ready to make behavior changes (Kushner 2003):

- ► Intention to change, or do they have a strong desire to change.
  - ► You could begin by asking, "Tell me more about how interested you are in losing weight."
- ► Obstacles to change, or do they have a minimum of barriers to success.
  - ► "Is now a good time to begin? Do you have anything in your life now that may get in the way?"
- ► Skills and self-confidence, or do they think they know what to do and can be successful at it.
  - ► "Describe your level of confidence about how successful you will be in increasing your physical activity and changing your diet."
- ► Positive feelings about the change, or do they believe these changes will ultimately benefit them.
  - ► "You said this was important to you. Do you think this is worth the effort?"
- ► Self-image and social norms, or do they think that these changes are consistent with their self-image and the norms of their peers.
  - ► "Can you picture yourself losing weight? What will (your significant others) think about your being more active and eating healthier?"
- ► Encouragement and support, or do they have enough social support from people who are important to them.
  - ► "Do you have anyone who will help you in these efforts? Who can be a cheerleader for you?"

Again, asking all these questions is simply to ensure that your client is ready to make the desired behavior changes. If they are not ready, then you can provide them with information about the health risks associated with obesity or, if they need some encouragement to become ready, then talk to them about what they think needs to happen in order for their answers to change.

If it appears that your client is ready to make the desired behavior changes, then the next step is to develop a plan for doing so. Again, the desired behavior changes will focus on becoming more physically active, eating healthier, or both. Each will be covered separately here. Recognize that when a client begins a weight loss program, then changes to their eating behaviors are more critical than are changes to activity behaviors. However, over time, the emphasis may shift toward more of an emphasis on their activity. Recall that, in people who successfully lose weight and keep it off for a number of years, they remain conscientious about their eating behaviors. However, so do many people who lose weight but do not maintain this loss. The difference between these two groups is that the maintainers continue to be much more physically active (Ostendorf et al. 2019; Thomas et al. 2014).

Becoming More Physically Active

When working with a client to become more physically active, the steps and processes to follow were introduced in Chapter 3 and reviewed in detail in Chapter 4. Recall that a four-step approach was used (Figure 8.3). This approach does not change if your client's motivation for becoming more active is to lose weight rather than improving cardiorespiratory fitness: you work with your client such that they begin at the step that is most appropriate for them. However, the major difference between the figure provided here and that provided in Chapter 4 is the addition of a fifth step. In Chapter 4, it was suggested that the goal for a client focused on improving their cardiorespiratory fitness was to expend at least 1,000 kcal/week in exercise specifically (Step 3), rather than the more general "physical activity" of Step 2. If they were interested in doing so, they could spend more time at higher exercise intensities to increase their VO_2max (Step 4). However, if the client is striving to lose weight, then the goal should be focused more on caloric expenditure (Step 5).

How much higher should this caloric expenditure be? It is ultimately up to the client and dependent upon which of the five steps they are on. However, once they've achieved Step 3 and are expending 1,000 kcal/week with exercise, then a recommended goal is 1,500 kcals/week with exercise. For perspective, in a group of over 3,500 subjects who lost an average of seventy pounds and kept it off

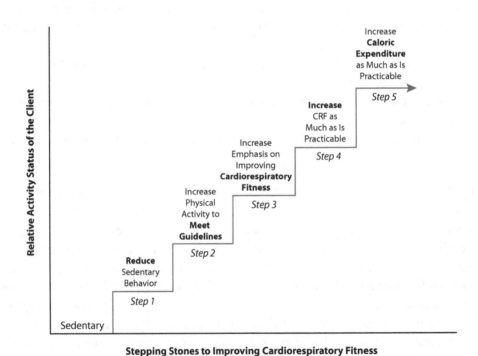

Figure 8.3 Approach to Increasing Physical Activity When Working with a Client Who Wants to Lose Weight

* 75 minutes of vigorous intensity exercise, or 150 minutes of moderate intensity exercise, or some combination of the two

for an average of five years, the caloric expenditure from exercise was about 1,500 kcals expended in almost three hours per week of exercise (Catenacci et al. 2008). However, they typically burned an average of over 2,600 kcals/week with their total physical activity (Catenacci et al. 2008; Thomas et al. 2014). This amount included both purposeful exercise and physical activity. In other words, the successful weight-losers not only exercised at least an average of 1,500 kcals/week but also moved frequently throughout the day. Their daily workout was not the only physical activity they did. This observation is important since some research suggests that overweight people who start an activity program may compensate by moving less during the remainder of their day (Drenowatz 2015; Schutz et al. 2014) and, regardless of body size, for people who have reduced their caloric intake to also reduce their physical activity (Drenowatz 2015).

Operationally, how does the cardiorespiratory exercise prescription differ if the focus is on burning calories rather than improving cardiorespiratory fitness? Again, this decision is ultimately left up to the client. However, if the client is currently at Step 4 of Figure 8.3 and is ready to move to Step 5, then the following changes are recommended:

Frequency:	Increase the frequency range from three to five days per week to three to six days per week.
Intensity:	The methods of calculating exercise intensity (i.e., Heart Rate Reserve, VO_2R RPE, ACI) are the same. The goal minimum intensity is now 50 percent rather than 40 percent and the client is encouraged to exercise at as high an intensity as they can comfortably tolerate.
Time:	The goal is to achieve an exercise volume equivalent to 1,500 calories/week rather than 1,000 calories/week. The *time* needed to achieve this goal depends on the *frequency* and *intensity* of the exercise bouts.
Type:	As before, any physical activity that is rhythmic, continuous, and involves large muscle groups will suffice. However, because of concerns about overuse injuries and excessive fatigue, the client should be encouraged to train using a variety of exercise modalities.

The notion behind increasing the frequency, intensity, and time is simply to burn more calories. How the client chooses to accomplish this is up to them. Again, this exercise program should not be the only physical activity the client performs. They should make an effort to be active throughout the day.

While physical activity is an important part of any weight loss program, a substantial body of evidence suggests that for most people, physical activity alone will not be sufficient to lose weight (Jakicic et al. 2011). Changes in eating behaviors are absolutely critical. Consequently, the following section will describe these.

Eating Healthier

As mentioned earlier, if you are working with a client who has a substantial weight loss goal, it is best professional practice to team with a Registered Dietitian Nutritionist (RDN) to help your client be successful. You should be the "go-to expert" in the area of exercise and physical activity and the RDN should be the "go-to expert" in the area of diet and nutrition. If your client has any dietary, metabolic, or medical concerns such as diabetes or Crohn's disease, then it is critically important that an RDN become part of the team. Moreover, if the client aspires to lose a substantial amount of weight (e.g., has a BMI >30 or 35 kg/m² and wants to achieve a "normal" BMI), then it is also important to include an RDN to help guide them in how to eat healthy while reducing their caloric intake.

However, in most health/fitness facilities and with many clients, it is almost inevitable that you will be asked for nutritional advice. Never forget that you do not have the expertise of an RDN and, in these kinds of conversations, you should limit your response to general nonmedical nutrition information. In other words, limit your advice to the recommendations provided by the U.S. Department of Agriculture in the most recent *Dietary Guidelines for Americans* (USDHHS and USDA 2015). The purpose of these guidelines is to "make recommen-

dations about the components of a healthy and nutritionally adequate diet to help promote health and prevent chronic disease for current and future generations" and, as such, are "a critical tool for professionals to help Americans make healthy choices in their daily lives to help prevent chronic disease and enjoy a healthy diet" (USDHHS and USDA 2015). In essence, the guidelines make recommendations that nearly everyone should follow to eat healthier. Just as this textbook is oriented toward working with apparently healthy adults and not clinical populations, the guidelines are not intended for people with special dietary needs or for treating any disease. Fortunately, this focus has resulted in guidelines that are written with obesity prevention in mind. These guidelines are summarized here but you are encouraged to read the entire *Dietary Guidelines* for a fuller understanding. The guidelines are revised every five years and the next edition should be published in 2020.

The *Dietary Guidelines for Americans* consists of five basic recommendations:

1. *Follow a healthy eating pattern across the lifespan.* It is important that each client chooses a healthy eating pattern at an appropriate calorie level. "Pattern" refers to the totality of what the client eats over time—not one particular meal or one particular day. The goal is that, by following a healthy eating pattern, the client will be better able to achieve and maintain a healthy body weight, have an adequate nutrient intake, and reduce the risk of developing chronic diseases. The remaining four guidelines help explain what a healthy eating pattern consists of. Nutritional needs should be met primarily with foods, rather than dietary supplements.

2. *Focus on variety, nutrient density, and amount.* This component of a healthy eating pattern helps the client meet nutrient needs while staying within desirable calorie limits. Nutrient dense foods contain essential vitamins, minerals, dietary fiber, and other substances that have positive health effects; they meet the fourth guideline, below.

3. *Limit calories from added sugars and saturated fats and reduce sodium intake.* Have a healthy eating pattern that is low in added sugars, saturated fats, and sodium by cutting back on foods and beverages higher in these components. For example, skim milk is preferred over whole milk, raw whole fruit over canned fruit in sweetened syrup, and diet soda over sugar-sweetened soda. For many people, this also necessitates being mindful of what their snacks consist of (e.g., grapes over cookies) or cooking methods (e.g., broiling over frying).

4. *Shift to healthier food and beverage choices.* The client should choose nutrient-dense foods and beverages across and within all food groups in place of less healthy choices. Examples are whole-grain cereal (e.g., Cheerios) over refined cereals (e.g., Rice Krispies) or a leaner meat over a fattier meat choice (e.g., skinless chicken over prime rib).

5. *Support healthy eating patterns for all.* As part of your interacting with each of your clients, remember that you have a role in helping <u>all</u> your clients adopt healthy eating patterns. There is no "one" way to eat healthy; a client's eating pattern should fit their personal preferences.

For many clients, part of the challenge in embracing these guidelines is simply knowing what to eat. In general, a healthy eating pattern includes eating <u>more</u> of the following (USDHHS and USDA 2015):

▶ Vegetables, including a variety of vegetables from all five subgroups—dark green, red and orange, legumes (beans and peas), starchy, and other.

▶ Fruits, including whole fruits and 100% fruit juices.

▶ Grains, with at least half being whole grains.

▶ Dairy products, with an emphasis on fat-free or low-fat dairy products.

▶ Protein foods, with an emphasis on a variety of protein foods in nutrient-dense foods.

▶ Oils, with choices that include a high percentage of monounsaturated and polyunsaturated fats and are liquid at room temperature. Oils that are solid or semi-solid at room temperature, even if derived from vegetables, contain high amounts of saturated fats and are not recommended. Oils are not a food group but are an important part of a diet since they are a major source of essential fatty acids and Vitamin E.

When working with a client who is trying to reduce their caloric intake and also eat healthier, a major focus may be on what they should *not* be eating rather than on what they *should* be eating. In the United States, the foods typically consumed from the aforementioned food groups are not nutrient dense. For example, whole milk is drunk rather than skim milk, soft drinks rather than water, and butter is used rather than olive or canola oil. Often, both the foods and the beverages consumed contain high amounts of extra calories in the forms of added sugars or added fats. Consequently, any conversation about a healthy eating pattern should also include a discussion on eating <u>less</u> of the following:

▶ Less than 10 percent of calories per day from saturated fats. Some saturated fats are needed by the human body but the body makes more than needed. Saturated fats are, therefore, not needed in one's diet; consequently, replace them with unsaturated fats. In addition, eat as little *trans* fats and dietary cholesterol as possible. Total dietary fats should comprise 20–35 percent of total calories.

▶ Less than 10 percent of calories per day from added sugars. The key component here is <u>added</u> sugars such as syrups and other sweeteners like corn syrup, raw sugar, or sucrose. Naturally occurring sugars, such as in fruits or milk, are not added sugars.

▶ Less than 2,300 milligrams (mg) per day of sodium and if at risk for hypertension, less than 1,500 mg per day is recommended.

▶ No more than one drink per day for women and two drinks per day for men, if the client drinks alcohol and is legally allowed to. Here, a "drink" is defined as 0.6 fluid ounces of pure alcohol, or about one 12 oz beer, 5 oz of wine, or 1.5 oz of 80 proof liquor.

When expressed as a percent of daily caloric intake, the daily macronutrient goals for following these healthy eating pattern guidelines are 10–35 percent protein, 45–65 percent carbohydrates (<10 percent from added sugars), 20–35 percent fats (<10 percent from saturated fats) in adult men and women (USDHHS and USDA 2015). While these percentages may not be part of a conversation you have with a client, it is helpful to know them in case they come up in a conversation with an RDN.

An important part of meeting these guidelines is that the client eats according to their food preferences. In other words, they are not following a particular "diet" but have a healthy eating pattern that fits their lifestyle. This pattern can take many forms—the client has complete flexibility to eat what they enjoy eating—as long as it results in a healthy pattern. Examples of three different patterns, all of which are consistent with the *Dietary Guidelines,* are shown in Table 8.5.

Implementing a Healthy Eating Pattern

When talking to your client about the various food groups that should be eaten daily as part of creating a healthy eating pattern, three questions frequently arise:

1. What foods go into a particular food group?
2. How big is a portion for these food groups?
3. What adjustments should be made if the client is trying to lose weight?

Each of these will be considered here.

What foods go into a particular food group?

Your client should move toward having a healthy eating pattern by eating a variety of nutrient-dense foods in the appropriate amounts. Thus, it is critical that your client know what the different food groups are. The *Dietary Guidelines for Americans* (USDHHS and USDA 2015) goes into considerable detail in describing the foods that are part of a particular food group. These *Guideline* descriptions are provided here. Examples from each food group are also provided. Recognize that these are just examples and the lists are not all-inclusive.

- Vegetables
  - Dark-green vegetables: All fresh, frozen, and canned dark green leafy vegetables and broccoli, cooked or raw. Examples are broccoli, spinach, romaine, kale, as well as collard, turnip, and mustard greens.
  - Red and orange vegetables: All fresh, frozen, and canned red and orange vegetables or juice, cooked or raw. Examples are tomatoes, tomato juice, red peppers, carrots, sweet potatoes, winter squash, and pumpkin.
  - Legumes (beans and peas): All cooked from dry or canned beans and peas. Examples are kidney beans, white beans, black beans, lentils, chickpeas, pinto beans, split peas, and edamame (green soybeans). This group does not include green beans or green peas.
  - Starchy vegetables: All fresh, frozen, and canned starchy vegetables. Examples are white potatoes, corn, green peas, green lima beans, plantains, and cassava.
  - Other vegetables: All other fresh, frozen, and canned vegetables, cooked or raw. Examples are iceberg lettuce, green beans, onions, cucumbers, cabbage, celery, zucchini, mushrooms, and green peppers.

- Fruits
  - All fresh, frozen, canned, and dried fruits and fruit juices. Examples are oranges and orange juice, apples and apple juice, bananas, grapes, melons, berries, and raisins.
  - At least half, and preferably more, of fruits should be whole fruits rather than fruit juices.
  - Dried fruits are acceptable but, like fruit juices, can contribute excess calories because of their caloric density.

- Grains
  - Whole grains: All whole-grain products and whole grains used as ingredients. Examples are whole-wheat bread, whole-grain cereals and crackers, oatmeal, quinoa, popcorn, and brown rice.

TABLE 8.5
Examples of Daily Servings of Food for Different Healthy Eating Patterns
at 1,800 Calories per Day

Food Groups *	U.S. Style	Mediterranean Style		Healthy Vegetarian
Vegetables	**2.5 c-eq**	**2.5 c-eq**		**2.5 c-eq**
Dark-green (c-eq/wk)	1.5	1.5		1.5
Red & orange (c-eq/wk)	5.5	5.5		5.5
Legumes (beans & peas) (c-eq/wk)	1.5	1.5		1.5
Starchy vegetables (c-eq/wk)	5	5		5
Other vegetables (c-eq/wk)	4	4		4
Fruits	**1.5 c-eq**	**2 c-eq**		**1.5 c-eq**
Grains	**6 oz-eq**	**6 oz-eq**		**6.5 oz-eq**
Whole grains (oz-eq/day)	3	3		3.5
Refined grains (oz-eq/day)	3	3		3
Dairy	**3 c-eq**	**2 c-eq**		**3 c-eq**
Protein Foods	**5 oz-eq**	**6 oz-eq**		**3 oz-eq**
Seafood (oz-eq/wk)	8	15	Eggs (oz-eq/wk)	3
Meats, poultry, eggs (oz-eq/wk)	23	23	Legumes ** (oz-eq/wk)	6
Nuts seeds, soy products (oz-eq/wk)	4	4	Soy products (oz-eq/wk)	6
			Nuts and seeds (oz-eq/wk)	6
Oils	**24 g**	**24 g**		**24 g**
Limit on Calories for Other Uses [calories (% of calories)]	**170 (9%)**	**160 (9%)**		**190 (11%)**

* Food group servings are daily amounts except the Vegetable and Protein Foods are per week; c-eq/wk = cup-equivalents per week; oz-eq/day = ounce-equivalents per day.

**Legumes can be considered either a vegetable or a protein food. In the Healthy Vegetarian healthy eating pattern, about half of total legumes are shown as vegetables, in cup-eq, and half as protein foods, in oz-eq.

Data are from *Dietary Guidelines for Americans* (USDHHS and USDA 2015).

- ▶ Refined grains: All refined-grain products and refined grains used as ingredients. Examples are white breads, refined grain cereals and crackers, pasta, and white rice. Refined grain choices should be enriched.
  - ▶ Limit eating refined grains and products made with refined grains, especially those high in saturated fats, added sugars, or added sodium (e.g., cookies, cakes, snack foods).
- ▶ Dairy
  - ▶ All milk, including lactose-free and lactose-reduced products and fortified soy beverages (soy milk), yogurt, frozen yogurt, dairy desserts, and cheeses.
  - ▶ Most choices should be fat-free or low-fat.
  - ▶ Cream, sour cream, and cream cheese are not included due to their low calcium content.
  - ▶ Other "milks" (e.g., almond, rice, coconut milks) are not included because their nutritional content is not similar to dairy or fortified soy milks.
- ▶ Protein Foods
  - ▶ They can be from both animal and plant sources.
  - ▶ All seafood, meats, poultry, eggs, soy products, nuts, and seeds.
  - ▶ Meats and poultry should be lean or low-fat, and nuts should be unsalted.
  - ▶ Legumes (beans and peas) can be considered part of this group as well as the vegetables group, but should be counted in one group only.

How big is a portion for these food groups?

Eating the appropriate amounts from each of the food groups is another important goal of having a healthy eating pattern. Many people inadvertently eat too many calories because they do not know what an appropriate food portion is. In other words, in a client's mind, eating either a Big Mac or a hamburger at lunch may mean the same thing—they had a burger for lunch. This "portion distortion" can add up. For example, a Big Mac has a serving size of 7.5 ounces, is 540 total calories and 250 of these calories come from fat, while a "regular" hamburger is only 3.5 ounces, 250 total calories and 70 fat calories (https://www.mcdonalds.com/us/en-us/about-our-food/nutrition-calculator.html). *Obviously, these two burgers differ considerably in their contribution to a healthy eating pattern!*

©stormcab/Shutterstock.com

Food group amounts in the *Dietary Guidelines* are usually expressed in cup (c) or ounce-equivalents (oz-eq) while oils are expressed in grams (g). In more "real world" terms, below are examples of quantity equivalents for each food group (USDHHS and USDA 2015):

- ▶ **Vegetables** and **fruits:** 1 cup-equivalent is
  - ▶ 1 cup raw or cooked vegetable or fruit
  - ▶ 1 cup vegetable or fruit juice
  - ▶ 2 cups leafy salad greens
  - ▶ ½ cup dried fruit or vegetable

- **Grains:** 1 ounce-equivalent is
  - ½ cup cooked rice, pasta, or cereal
  - 1 ounce dry pasta or rice
  - 1 medium (1 ounce) slice bread
  - 1 ounce of ready-to-eat cereal (about 1 cup of flaked cereal)
- **Dairy:** 1 cup-equivalent is
  - 1 cup milk, yogurt, or fortified soy milk
  - 1½ ounces natural cheese such as cheddar cheese or 2 ounces of processed cheese
- **Protein Foods:** 1 ounce-equivalent is
  - 1 ounce lean meat, poultry, or seafood
  - 1 egg, ¼ cup cooked beans, or tofu
  - 1 Tbsp peanut butter
  - ½ ounce nuts or seeds

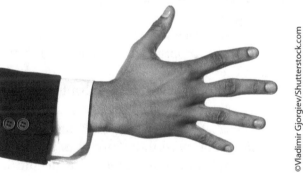

As you can see, the serving sizes can vary considerably with a food group. This is typically due to the airiness of the food, the water content, and the density of the food. For example, 2 cups of leafy salad and ½ cup of a dried fruit differ markedly in volume but both are 1 cup-equivalents. As a result, it can be challenging to recognize portion sizes when eating.

The following suggestions may be helpful: think of a half cup as being about the size of a small fist or a rounded handful; a cup is about the size of a man's fist or a small hand holding a tennis ball; 1 ounce of nuts is about one handful while 1 ounce of snack foods (like chips and pretzels) is a large handful; 1 ounce of cheese is about the size of a person's thumb while a teaspoon of fats (e.g., butter, oil) is about the size of the tip of a person's thumb. These examples are all referenced to a person's hand and, of course, hand sizes vary. This results in imperfect estimates, but using these tools to assess portion sizes will help your client increase their awareness and consideration of portions sizes when assessing their eating habits.

What adjustments should be made if the client is trying to lose weight?

This question relates to how best to modify a client's healthy eating pattern if they are trying to lose weight. Your collaboration with an RDN will be very helpful here, as they are much better qualified to address this question than you, as a health/fitness professional. However, you should understand the basic concepts so you can converse knowledgeably with this colleague and, if need be, your client.

The *Dietary Guidelines* suggest that the caloric intake of the client's healthy eating pattern be adjusted, as needed, to ensure that the client changes weight appropriately over time. A reasonable weight loss goal is to lose 1 to 1.5 pounds weekly, so reducing daily caloric intake by 500 to 750 calories each day is suggested. This reduction likely translates to a caloric intake of 1,200 to 1,500 calories per day for women and 1,500 to 1,800 calories per day for men (USDHHS and USDA 2015). Research suggests when attempting to lose weight, the caloric reduction is far more important than the composition of the diet (Atallah et al. 2014; Sacks et al. 2009). Moreover, for many people, "dieting" or intentionally reducing caloric intake is a very negative experience. For these reasons, continue to focus on teaching your client about developing a desired healthy eating pattern as described here.

However, when discussing the number of servings from the various food groups, adjust the number to reflect the desired caloric intake (Table 8.6; USDHHS and USDA 2015). If your client is best served by ingesting 1,600 or 2,000 calories per day, then you use these relevant serving sizes as the framework for discussing a desired healthy eating pattern. In other words, you help your client focus on developing a healthy eating pattern with the emphasis on what to <u>eat</u> rather then on what <u>not</u> to eat. However, by placing the pattern into the context of a desired caloric intake, you are almost "invisibly" helping your client adjust their caloric intake.

For many people who are trying to lose weight by eating more appropriately, common barriers to success are issues related to portion control (e.g., too much food) and inappropriate snacking (e.g., too much "junk food"). Becoming more aware of what constitutes correct serving sizes and being mindful of the appropriate number of servings of each food group will help resolve the former. To address the snacking concern, consider the "Limit on Calories for Other Uses" Food Group category in Tables 8.5 and 8.6. This category reflects the desired limits on non-nutritional eating, such as sweets, junk food snacks, and the like. It is acceptable to eat some of these foods, as reflected in the caloric limits for this category; however, there is a limit to these "extra calories."

When identifying how best to assist your client in adopting a healthy eating pattern, an excellent resource can be found at http://www.choosemyplate.gov/. The website has a wealth of information, including practical "how-to" tips for eating healthier and interactive learning tools. It is written specifically to complement the information provided in the *Dietary Guidelines*. Consequently, it is reasonable and appropriate for you, as a health/fitness professional, to use them to assist your client in being successful.

Finally, this section of this chapter has been devoted to assisting you in determining how to focus your eating-related conversations with a client. However, remember that you need to confine your conversations to helping your client learn how to adopt a healthy eating pattern via the *Dietary Guidelines*. You need to be careful to avoid overstepping your professional limits, such as recommending nutritional supplements or specific foods to eat. Again, it is excellent professional practice to enlist the assistance of an RDN. These professionals have the expertise to address such questions and can make significant contributions to your clients' achieving their weight loss goals.

PUTTING IT ALL TOGETHER

This chapter has been devoted to giving you the skills needed to work with a client who has a primary goal of improving his or her body composition. Common definitions of obesity were provided as well as the health concerns associated with having a high body composition. A method of helping a client improve their body composition via changing their behaviors was described. This approach emphasizes exercising more and eating healthier, and doing so as lifestyle changes. However, it is critically important to recognize that, as a health/fitness professional, the information you are qualified to provide about how to eat healthier is somewhat generalized. If the client needs more focused information or assistance, they are best served by working with a Registered Dietitian Nutritionist.

TABLE 8.6
Recommended Food Servings for Different Caloric Intakes When Following the U.S. Style Healthy Eating Pattern.

Food Groups *	Desired Caloric Intake			
	1,400	**1,600**	**1,800****	**2,000**
Vegetables	**1.5 c-eq**	**2 c-eq**	**2.5 c-eq**	**2.5 c-eq**
Dark-green (c-eq/wk)	1	1.5	1.5	1.5
Red & orange (c-eq/wk)	3	4	5.5	5.5
Legumes (beans & peas) (c-eq/wk)	0.5	1	1.5	1.5
Starchy vegetables (c-eq/wk)	3.5	4	5	5
Other vegetables (c-eq/wk)	2.5	3.5	4	4
Fruits	**1.5 c-eq**	**1.5 c-eq**	**1.5 c-eq**	**2 c-eq**
Grains	**5 oz-eq**	**5 oz-eq**	**6 oz-eq**	**6 oz-eq**
Whole grains (oz-eq/day)	2.5	3	3	3
Refined grains (oz-eq/day)	2.5	2	3	3
Dairy	**2.5 c-eq**	**3 c-eq**	**3 c-eq**	**3 c-eq**
Protein Foods	**4 oz-eq**	**5 oz-eq**	**5 oz-eq**	**5.5 oz-eq**
Seafood (oz-eq/wk)	6	8	8	8
Meats, poultry, eggs (oz-eq/wk)	19	23	23	26
Nuts, seeds, soy products (oz-eq/wk)	3	4	4	5
Oils	**17 g**	**22 g**	**24 g**	**27 g**
Limit on Calories for Other Uses [calories (% of calories)]	**110 (8%)**	**130 (8%)**	**170 (9%)**	**270 (14%)**

*Servings are daily amounts except the vegetable and protein foods which are per week;

** Pattern is same as U.S. Style from Table 8.5.

c-eq/wk = cup-equivalents per week; oz-eq/day = ounce-equivalents per day.

Data are from *Dietary Guidelines for Americans* (USDHHS and USDA 2015).

REFERENCES

Atallah, R., K. B. Filion, S. M. Wakil, J. Genest, L. Joseph, P. Poirier, S. Rinfret, E. L. Schiffrin, and M. J. Eisenberg. 2014. "Long-Term Effects of 4 Popular Diets on Weight Loss and Cardiovascular Risk Factors—A Systemic Review of Randomized Controlled Trials." *Circ Cardiovasc Qual Outcomes* 7: 815–27.

Aune, D. A. Sen, M. Prasd, T. Norat, I. Janszky, S. Tonstad, P. Romundstad, and L. J. Vatten. 2016. "BMI and All Cause Mortality: Systematic Review and Non-Linear Dose-Response Meta-Analysis of 230 Cohort Studies with 3.74 Million Deaths among 30.3 Million Participants." *BMJ* 353: i2156. http://dx.doi.org/10.1136/bmj.i2156

Barry, V. W., M. Baruth, M. W. Beets, J. L. Durstine, J. Liu, and S. N. Blair. 2014. "Fitness vs. Fatness on All-Cause Mortality: A Meta-Analysis." *Progress in Cardiovascular Diseases* 56: 382–90.

Bastien, M., P. Poirier, I. Lemiux, and J.-P. Després. 2014. "Overview of Epidemiology and Contribution of Obesity to Cardiovascular Disease." *Progress in Cardiovascular Diseases* 56: 369–81.

Beydoun, M. A., A. Lhotsky, Y. Wang, G. Dal Forno, Y. An, E. J. Metter, L. Ferrucci, R. O'Brien, and A. B. Zonderman. 2008. "Association of Adiposity Status and Changes in Early to Mid-Adulthood with Incidence of Alzheimer's Disease." *Am J Epidemiol.* 168: 1179–89.

Bond, D. S., S. Phelan, T. M. Leahey, J. O. Hill, and R. R. Wing. 2009. "Weight Loss Maintenance in Successful Weight Losers: Surgical versus Non-Surgical Methods." *Int J Obes (Lond).* 33: 173–80.

Bouchard, C. 2007. "The Biological Predisposition to Obesity: Beyond the Thrifty Genotype Scenario." *Int J Obesity* 31: 1337–39.

Bouchard, C., and A. Tremblay. 1997. "Genetic Influences on the Response of Body Fat and Fat Distribution to Positive and Negative Energy Balances in Human Identical Twins. *J Nutr.* 127: 943S–947S.

Bray, G. A., C. Bouchard, and W. P. T. James. 1998. *Handbook of Obesity.* New York: Marcel Dekker.

Brewis, A. A., A. Wutich, A. Faletta-Cowden, and I. Rodriguez-Soto. 2011. "Body Norms and Fat Stigma in Global Perspective." *Curr Anthr.* 52: 269–76.

Caprio, S., S. R. Daniels, A. Drewnowski, F. R. Kaufman, L. A. Palinkas, A. L. Rosenbloom, and J. B. Schwimmer. 2008. "Influence of Race, Ethnicity, and Culture on Childhood Obesity: Implications for Prevention and Treatment. A Consensus Statement of Shaping America's Health and the Obesity Society." *Diabetes Care* 31: 2211–21.

Catenacci, V. A., L. G. Ogden, J. Sthut, S. Phelan, R. R. Wing, J. O. Hill, H. R. Wyatt. 2008. "Physical Activity Patterns in the National Weight Control Registry." *Obesity (Silver Spring)* 16: 153–61.

Church, T. S., D. M. Thomas, C. Tudor-Locke, P. T. Katzmarzyk, C. P. Earnest, et al. 2011. "Trends over 5 Decades in U.S. Occupation-Related Physical Activity and Their Associations with Obesity." *PLoS ONE* 6: e19657.

Clark, J. E. 2015. "Diet, Exercise or Diet with Exercise: Comparing the Effectiveness of Treatment Options for Weight-Loss and Changes in Fitness for Adults (18–65 Years Old) Who Are Overfat, or Obese; Systematic Review and Meta-Analysis." *Journal of Diabetes & Metabolic Disorders* 14: 31.

Cohen, S. S., Y. Park, L. B. Signorello, A. V. Patel, D. A. Boggs, L. N. Kolonel et al. 2014. "A Pooled Analysis of Body Mass Index and Mortality among African Americans." *PLoS ONE*. 9: e111980. doi:10.1371/journal.pone.0111980.

De Gonzalez, A. B., P. Hartge, J. R. Cerhan, A. J. Flint, L. Hannan, R. J. BacInnis, S. C. Moore, et al. 2010. "Body-Mass Index and Mortality among 1.46 Million White Adults." *N Engl J Med*. 363: 2211–19.

Després, J.-P. 2012. "Body Fat Distribution and Risk of Cardiovascular Disease: An Update." *Circulation* 126: 1301–13.

Drenowatz, C. 2015. "Reciprocal Compensation Changes in Dietary Intake and Energy Expenditure within the Concept of Energy Balance." *Adv Nutr*. 6: 592–99.

Duncan, G. E. 2010. The "Fit but Fat" Concept Revisited: Population-Based Estimates Using NHANES." *International Journal of Behavioral Nutrition and Physical Activity* 7: 47.

Fallah-Fini, S. A. Adam, L. J. Cheskin, S. M. Bartsch, and B. Y. Lee. 2017. "The Additional Costs and Health Effects of a Patient Having Overweight or Obesity: A Computational Model. *Obesity* 25: 1809–15.

Finkelstein, E. A, D. S. Brown, L. A. Wrage, B. T. Allaire, and T. J. Hoerger. 2010. "Individual and Aggregate Years-of-Life-Lost Associated with Overweight and Obesity." *Obesity* 18: 333–39.

Finkelstein, E. A., J. G. Trogdon, J. W. Cohen, and W. Dietz. 2009. "Annual Medical Spending Attributable to Obesity: Payer- and Service-Specific Estimates." *Health Aff (Millwood)* 28: w822–31.

Flegal, K. M., and B. I. Graubard. 2009. "Estimates of Excess Deaths Associated with Body Mass Index and Other Anthropometric Variables." *Am J Clin Nutr*. 89: 1213–19.

Flegal, K. M., B. I. Graubard, D. F. Williamson, and M. H. Gail. 2005. "Excess Deaths Associated with Underweight, Overweight, and Obesity." *JAMA* 293: 1861–67.

Flegal, K. M., B. K. Kit, H. Orpana, and B. I. Graubard. 2013. "Association of All-Cause Mortality with Overweight and Obesity Using Standard Body Mass Index Categories: A Systematic Review and Meta-Analysis." *JAMA* 309: 71–82.

Fontaine, K. R., and I. Barofsky. 2001. "Obesity and Health-Related Quality of Life." *Obes Rev*. 2: 173–82.

Garvey, W. T., J. I. Mechanick, E. M. Brett, A. J. Garber, D. L. Hurley, A. M. Jastreboff, et al. 2016. "American Association of Clinical Endocrinologists and American College of Endocrinology Comprehensive Clinical Practice Guidelines for Medical Care of Patients with Obesity." *Endocr Pract*. 22 Suppl 3: 1–203.

Hales C. M., M. D. Carroll, C. D. Fryar, and C. L. Ogden. 2017. "Prevalence of Obesity among Adults and Youth: United States, 2015–2016." NCHS data brief, no 288. Hyattsville: National Center for Health Statistics.

Hales, C. M., C. D. Fryal, M. D. Carroll, D. S. Freedman, and C. L. Ogden. 2018. "Trends in Obesity and Severe Obesity Prevalence in US Youth and Adults by Sex and Age, 2007–2008 to 2015–2016." *JAMA* 319: 1723–25.

Högström, G., A. Nordström, and P. Nordström. 2015. "Aerobic Fitness in Late Adolescence and the Risk of Early Death: A Prospective Cohort Study of 1.3 Million Swedish Men." *Int J Epidemiol*. doi:10.1093/ije/dyv321.

Jakicic, J. M., A. D. Otto, W. Lang, L. Semler, C. Winters, K. Polzien, and K. I. Mohr. 2011. "The Effect of Physical Activity on 18-Month Weight Change in Overweight Adults." *Obesity* 19: 100–09.

Janssen, I., P. T. Katzmarzyk, R. Ross, A. S. Leon, J. S. Skinner, D. C. Rao, J. H. Wilmore, T. Rankinen, and C. Bouchard. 2004. "Fitness Alters the Associations of BMI and Waist Circumference with Total and Abdominal Fat." *Obes Res.* 12525–537.

Jensen, M. D., D. H. Ryan, C. M. Apovian, J. D. Ard, A. G. Comuzzie, K. A. Donato, F. B. Hu, et al. 2014. "2013 AHA/ACC/TOS Guideline for the Management of Overweight and Obesity in Adults: A Report of the American College of Cardiology/American Heart Association Task Force on Practice Guidelines and The Obesity Society." *J Am Coll Cardiol.* 63: 2985–3023.

Kim, S., C. G. Parks, L. A. DeRoo, H. Chen, J. A. Taylor, R. M. Cawthon, and D. P. Sandler. 2009. "Obesity and Weight Gain in Adulthood and Telomere Length." *Cancer Epidemiol Biomarkers Prev.* 18: 816–20.

Kolotkin, R. L., and J. R. Andersen. 2017. "A Systematic Review of Reviews: Exploring the Relationship between Obesity, Weight Loss and Health-Related Quality of Life." *Clinical Obesity* 7: 273–89.

Kushner, R. F. 2003. *Roadmaps for Clinical Practice: Case Studies in Disease Prevention and Health Promotion—Assessment and Management of Adult Obesity: A Primer for Physicians.* Chicago: American Medical Association.

Lamelas P., J-D. Schwalm, I. Quazi, S. Mehta, P. J. Devereaux, S. Jolly, and S. Yusuf. 2017. "Effect of Body Mass Index on Clinical Events After Acute Coronary Syndromes." *Am J Cardiol.* 120: 1453–59.

Lundborg, P., P. Nystedt, and D.-O. Rooth. 2014. "Body Size, Skills, and Income: Evidence from 150,000 Teenage Siblings." *Demography* 51: 1573–96.

McGee, D. L. and the Diverse Populations Collaboration. 2005. "Body Mass Index and Mortality: A Meta-Analysis Based on Person-Level Data from Twenty-Six Observational Studies." *Ann Epidemiol.* 15: 87–97.

McMurray, R. G., J. Soares, C. J. Caspersen, and T. McCurdy. 2014. "Examining Variations of Resting Metabolic Rate of Adults: A Public Health Perspective." *Med Sci Sports Exerc.* 46: 1352–58.

Munro, L. 2017. "Everyday Indignities: Using the Microaggressions Framework to Understand Weight Stigma." *Journal of Law, Medicine & Ethics* 46: 502–09.

Ogden, C. L., M. D. Carroll, B. K. Kit, and K. M. Flegal. 2014. "Prevalence of Childhood and Adult Obesity in the United States, 2011–2012." *JAMA* 311: 806–14.

Ogden, C. L., M. M. Lamb, M. D. Carroll, and K. M. Flegal. 2010. *Obesity and Socioeconomic Status in Adults: United States 1988–1994 and 2005–2008.* NCHS data brief no 50. Hyattsville: National Center for Health Statistics.

Ortega, F. B., D.-C. Lee, P. T. Katzmarzyk, J. R. Ruiz, X. Sui, T. S. Church, and S. N. Blair. 2013. "The Intriguing Metabolically Healthy but Obese Phenotype: Cardiovascular Prognosis and Role of Fitness." *Eur Heart J.* 34: 389–97.

Pan, A., I. Kawachi, N. Luo, J. E. Manson, W. C. Willett, F. B. Hu, and O. I. Okereke. 2014. "Changes in Body Weight and Health-Related Quality of Life: 2 Cohorts of US Women." *Am J Epidemiol* 180: 254–62.

Pasco, J. A., G. C. Nicholson, S. L. Brennan, and M. A. Kotowicz. 2012. "Prevalence of Obesity and the Relationship between the Body Mass Index and Body Fat: Cross-Sectional, Population-Based Data. *PLoS ONE* 7: e29580.

Patel S. R., and F. B. Hu. 2008. "Short Sleep Duration and Weight Gain: A Systematic Review." *Obesity* 16: 643–53.

Phelan, S. M., D. J. Burgess, M. W. Yeazel, W. L. Hellerstedt, J. M. Griffin, and M. van Ryn. 2015. "Impact of Weight Bias and Stigma on Quality of Care and Outcomes for Patients with Obesity." *Obesity Rev.* 16: 319–26.

Preston, S. H., and A. Stokes. 2011. "Contribution of Obesity to International Differences in Life Expectancy." *Am J Public Health.* 101: 2137–43.

Prospective Studies Collaboration. 2009. "Body-Mass Index and Cause-Specific Mortality in 900,000 Adults: Collaborative Analyses of 57 Prospective Studies. *Lancet.* 373: 1083–96.

Puhl, R. M., and C. A. Heuer. 2009. "The Stigma of Obesity: A Review and Update." *Obesity* 17: 941–64.

Romero-Corral, A., V. K. Somers, J. Sierra-Johnson, R. J. Thomas, K. R. Bailey, M. L. Collazo-Clavell, T. G. Allison, J. Korinek, J. A. Batsis, and F. Lopez-Jimenez. 2008. "Accuracy of Body Mass Index to Diagnose Obesity in the US Adult Population." *Int J Obes (Lond).* 32: 959–66.

Rubin, R. 2019. "Addressing Medicine's Bias against Patients Who Are Overweight." *JAMA* Feb 20. doi:10.1001/jama.2019.0048.

Sacks, F. M., G. A. Bray, V. J. Caarey, S. R. Smith, D. H. Ryan, S. D. Anton, and K. McManus, et al. 2009. "Comparison of Weight-Loss Diets with Different Compositions of Fat, Protein, and Carbohydrates." *N Engl J Med.* 360: 859–73.

Sahakyan, K. R., V. K. Somers, J. P. Rodriguez-Escudero, D. O. Hodge, R. E. Carter, O. Sochor, et al. 2015. "Normal-Weight Central Obesity: Implications for Total and Cardiovascular Mortality." *Ann Intern Med.* 163: 827–35.

Saydah, S., K. McKeever Bullard, Y. Cheng, M. K. Ali, E. W. Gregg, L. Geiss, and G. Imperatore. 2014. "Trends in Cardiovascular Disease Risk Factors by Obesity Level in Adults in the United States, NHANES 1999–2010." *Obesity* 22: 1888–95.

Schutz, Y., D. M. Nguyen, N. M. Byrne, and A. P. Hills. 2014. "Effectiveness of Three Different Walking Prescription Durations on Total Physical Activity in Normal- and Overweight Women." *Obes Facts* 7: 264–73.

Slagter, S. N., J. V. van Vliet-Ostaptchouk, A. P. van Beek, J. C. Keers, H. L. Lutgers, M. M. van der Klauw, and B. H. R. Wolffenbuttel. 2015. "Health-Related Quality of Life in Relation to Obesity Grade, Type 2 Diabetes, Metabolic Syndrome and Inflammation." *PLoS One* 10: e0140599.

Sung, H., R. L. Siegel, P. S. Rosenberg, and A. Jemal. 2019. "Emerging Cancer Trends among Young Adults in the USA: Analysis of a Population-Based Cancer Registry." *Lancet Public Health* 4: e137–e147.

Thomas, J. G., D. S. Bond, S. Phelan, J. O. Hill, and R. R. Wing 2014. "Weight-Loss Maintenance for 10 Years in the National Weight Control Registry." *Am J Prev Med.* 46: 17–23.

Tomiyama, A. J. 2019. "Stress and Obesity." *Ann Rev Psych.* 70: 703–18.

U.S. Department of Health and Human Services. 2013. "Managing Overweight and Obesity in Adults Systematic Evidence Review From the Obesity Expert Panel." http://www.nhlbi.nih.gov/health-pro/guidelines/in-develop/obesity-evidence-review.

U.S. Department of Health and Human Services (USHHS) and U.S. Department of Agriculture (USDA). 2015. *2015–2020 Dietary Guidelines for Americans.* 8th ed. http://health.gov/dietaryguidelines/2015/guidelines/.

Yi, S-W., H. Ohrr, S-A. Shing, and J-J. Yi. 2015. "Sex-Age-Specific Association of Body Mass Index with All-Cause Mortality among 12.8 Million Korean Adults: A Prospective Cohort Study." *Int J Epidemiol* 44: 1696–1705.